M000232688

The Power
of Your Angels

"Isabelle von Fallois' new book *The Power of Your Angels* (a 28-day-programme to change your life and create miracles together with the angels) is uplifting and helps readers create deep lasting bonds with angels. A positive read and a real gem of a book. Isabelle's work is bringing love, light and peace to the planet. I highly recommend it!"

Gary Quinn, bestselling author of *The Yes Frequency* and *May the Angels Be With You*

"If you are willing to dig deep and surrender with the help of the angels, Isabelle's 28-Day-Program *The Power of Your Angels* will help you to find the hidden treasures in your pain and past, to rise above your limits and to co-create miracles together with the angels."

Colette Baron-Reid, bestselling author of *The Map and Weight Loss for People Who Feel Too Much*

"Isabelle von Fallois' loving light radiates through all that she says, writes, does and is. An angel in human form, she is the most perfect channel to help us find within the pure love and power that helps us connect with our divine truth. Her first English book *The Power of Your Angels* brings us beyond anything that has ever been revealed about the angelic realm, with the grace and magic that is so uniquely hers. I cannot recommend her work enough. She is a true blessing on this planet."

Michelle Karén, M.A., D.F. Astrol. S., Astrologer to the Stars at the 78th Academy Awards, bestselling author of *Astrology for Enlightenment*

"Only in recent times have we felt alone and isolated, in need of guidance from a higher power. Countless people are struggling to find a spiritual program to turn their lives around. Isabelle von Fallois' inspirational new book provides a 28-day tool-box for changing one's life. A soul journey tapping into not only personal experiences, but the power of nature and the angels. For those seeking signposts on a spiritual pathway, there is no better map than Isabelle's book."

Glennyce Eckersley, Broadcaster and author of the bestselling book *An Angel At My Shoulder*

"Isabelle von Fallois' new book, *The Power of Your Angels* is a 28-day-programme that really works! It will help you create lasting and deep connections with your angels. This book radiates a vibration of joy and blessings that will sink deep into the hidden crevices of your soul. I highly recommend it!"

Denise Linn, bestselling author of *Sacred Space*

"Isabelle has done it again. This exquisite Angel Teacher has brought us another work of great beauty. Yet on this occasion her book *The Power of Your Angels*, designed to lovingly urge us into profound communion with the Angelic Communion, also provides us with a work manual, with which to prepare our own spiritual countenance. To become less fixed by the minutiae of life, and to discover the gravity of our existence. This means that, as in the words of St. Augustine: "Every visible thing in this world has an Angelic power placed over it" in order for us to feel the true weight and purpose of our existence. Surely when we fully embody our SOUL we will feel, see and hear the true meaning for why the Angels are overshadowing of our lives. Bravo Isabelle!"

Stewart Pearce, Angel Medium, Sound Healer, Master of Voice and bestselling author of *The Angels of Atlantis and Angel Heart Sigils*

The Power of Your Angels

28 Days to Finding Your Path and Realizing Your Life's Dreams

Isabelle von Fallois

FINDHORN PRESS

Findhorn Press
One Park Street
Rochester, Vermont 05767
www.findhornpress.com

Findhorn Press is a division of Inner Traditions International

Copyright © 2011, 2014 by Isabelle von Fallois

ISBN 978-1-84409-629-9

All rights reserved. No part of this book may be reproduced or utilized in any
form or by any means, electronic or mechanical, including photocopying,
recording, or by any information storage and retrieval system, without
permission in writing from the publisher.

Cataloging-in-Publication Data for this title is available from the British Library

Printed and bound in the United States

Translation by Sabine Weeke
Edited by Jacqui Lewis
Cover and interior illustrations by Isabell Weise
Cover design and layout by Guter Punkt and Thierry Bogliolo
Text design and layout by Geoff Green Book Design, Cambridge CB24 4GL

I dedicate this book to all people,
who would like to transform and change their lives
in accord with the angels,
in order to contribute to creating
a world in love and peace.
May this vision unfold
in divine timing.

CONTENTS

FOREWORD

I first met Isabelle at the Angel Kongress in Hamburg and was immediately attracted to her beautiful light and the number of angels around her. I soon discovered that she is warm, genuine and friendly. She is also a Master, who has undergone an initiation through illness, which she describes in her book, and has emerged triumphantly. The angels now accompany her everywhere. They look after her and are ready waiting when she sends them to help others and the world.

Angels are the most wonderful and powerful beings of light, many of whom are assigned to help, protect and watch over you during your life. You all have guardian angels, who hold your divine blueprint and try to help you on your path, making sure you meet the right people or are at the right place for something to happen. What I so much love about angels is that they see your inner beauty all the time, so they look at you with eyes of total love and joy whatever you do.

Angels will enable you to change or transform any area of your life if you are willing and ready. When you put the effort in, the assistance they can give you is incredible, from pulling out pain to helping you to see things from a higher more loving perspective, to giving you the courage to step out on a new path, to enable you to have fulfilling relationships. They also work through you to assist others. They have to wait for you to ask but when you send them to others you become a bridge of light and they will cluster round you, waiting for instructions. People will sense and feel the angel light round you.

There are many different kinds of angels in the heavenly realms, who work on various rays and frequencies so that they can more easily perform certain duties. For example, Archangel Michael generally works on a deep blue ray, offering protection, strength and courage. He can use other rays too. Archangel Raphael almost always utilizes the emerald ray of healing and abundance, though when he is bringing enlightenment he takes the frequency to a crystal clear light. I feel very close to Archangel Metatron who is often seen as a glorious golden orange colour but can appear on any colour vibration. He is overseeing the entire ascension of our planet and everyone on it.

I have never heard of or worked with some of the angels Isabelle talks about but I could feel their light as I read about them and brought them close to me. We are living at a time when millions of new angels are flocking into this universe and to this planet to help us all rise in frequency in preparation for the new Golden Age ahead. There has never been such an opportunity for spiritual growth in the entire history of this planet. We are moving towards a time of contentment and personal satisfaction, when everyone will be on their right soul mission. In the civilization that we are birthing people will enjoy good relationships, feel loved and have a good sense of self-worth and confidence. We will be using our gifts and talents to enrich our lives and those of others. Everyone will do what is for the highest good of all. Can you imagine such a time of honesty, integrity and oneness? In order to bring this new world into being we have to clear out the old habits and beliefs and replace them with pure, constructive, helpful ones. As many have discovered this is challenging but with the help of the angels it becomes not just possible but joyful.

Isabelle von Fallois has written no ordinary angel book. If you are ready for a deeply transformative soul journey it may be one of the most important and life-affirming books you have ever read and worked with! There is a power and inspiration in Isabelle's words and the angels that work with her that will sustain you through the twenty-eight-day change. I really felt deeply moved by the inspirational stories she shares in each chapter. They all seemed to touch me with that 'aha' feeling as I felt their truth. And I thoroughly enjoyed the fresh ideas, meditations, visualizations and activities to keep your interest and good intentions alive.

As you read and work with this book not only will your life and relationships transform. You will become a beacon of light, one of those who will help the world ascend into the glorious future that is envisioned by the angels for this planet.

Diana Cooper

PREFACE

We shall find peace.
We shall hear the angels.
And we shall see the sky sparkling with diamonds.
                                                    Anton Chekhov

During the last few years I have repeatedly encountered people telling me that they would love to change their lives and have already tried quite a few things but that it has never really worked. I, on the other hand, have achieved nearly all the changes that I have wished for, with the help of the angels: They helped to save my life that, over the course of four years, was repeatedly hanging by a silken thread as I battled life-threatening leukaemia. And to this day they continue to support me in realizing and living my dreams.

As nearly every time I've felt touched by something, and looking to receive a profound answer, I eventually turned to the angels and meditated with them on this topic: why so many people do not succeed in fulfilling their life's dreams.

We humans – the angels told me – usually start something new full of enthusiasm; however, often we are not able to sustain this – instead, long-standing beliefs and belief patterns that we all carry around with us for years affect us much more strongly than we would like and than we are even aware of: they sabotage us in such a subtle way that we often do not even notice when our subconscious mind has once again switched to autopilot. I think nearly every one of us is familiar with these mechanisms. Let's take the following example: we have resolved to nourish ourselves more consciously and to lose weight. For this reason we have filled our cupboards and fridge with high-quality food. We start the day with fitness training and enjoy the marvellous feeling that this generates in our body.

Within a short period of time, though, something like the following usually happens: we get a cold or injure ourselves and therefore cannot stick to our planned fitness programme; we are invited to a celebratory event and are unable to say no when alcohol or a scrumptious dessert is placed in front of us, even though at home we had strongly resolved to stick to our guns and not give in – and we may not stop at one glass of beer or one *mousse au chocolat*, not to mention all the other dishes that go straight to the hips, undiluted and undigested.

The reason for this kind of "relapse" can be found in the synapses, which carry connections between the nerve cells in our brain. Throughout our life to date the synapses have been activated in the same way so often that we always (re)act to a given situation in the same way. In order to change these ingrained reactions and to create new connections to help us achieve our desired goals, it is necessary to work continuously over a period of twenty-eight days towards a "new" programming. This number is because studies have shown that it takes between twenty-one and twenty-eight days to break an old pattern and program a new, positive one. Then new neural pathways will emerge in the brain and thus different, life-promoting belief systems.

While I was meditating with the angels on Maui, Hawaii, they warmly suggested creating together with them a twenty-eight-day programme in order to help people reach their goals. I loved the idea instantly, since I myself had already experienced wonderful effects and fantastic changes with such programmes.

As an example, ten years ago I worked with Julia Cameron's book *The Artist's Way*: a three-month programme (!) with daily tasks. At that time I was still extremely weakened by the many chemotherapy treatments I had received for my leukaemia. My greatest wish as a pianist, however, was to finally be able to play a piano recital again. I also knew though that I was likely to sabotage myself in this: because before my long period of illness, before a performance I was used to playing the piano every day for between four and eight hours; but now, due to my weakened body, I was just about able to rehearse for one or one and a half hours per day.

Obviously, my mind teemed with bleak prophecies: "You are never going to make it if you don't rehearse any more!"; "Who do you think you are?"; "There is no way you will master all these pieces by heart!"; "You will make a fool of yourself and will never again be invited to play a concert!"; "The whole audience will walk out of the concert!".

The Artist's Way came along right on cue. Every day, following its programme, I had to consciously confront my belief systems and work on myself in order to effectively change them.

I finished the twelve-week programme about a week before my first recital after recovering from leukaemia; and promptly experienced the proof that it really had worked. Three days before the concert I was once again bed-bound with a high fever (which had been a common occurrence for more than eighteen months), and was unable to continue rehearsing. Under normal circumstances this would have been the end of the concert – as I had been absolutely convinced that without the intense preparation of the last days before the event I would just not be able to perform the rather virtuoso pieces reasonably well. But this time, because I had thoroughly got rid of my old belief patterns and in addition placed great trust in the angelic powers, the concert turned into an exhilarating success and was rewarded with a standing ovation from the whole audience.

I also achieved phenomenal results with the five-week programme "Living from Vision" by Ilona Selke, Dr. Rod Newton and Don Paris, as you can read in my second book *Die Engel so nah* (*The Angels So Close*). At that time, I was already intensely connected to the angels; during the five weeks they were always by my side. Even back then, I had the feeling that it would be wonderful to create something similar with angels, and lo and behold this was exactly what the angels on Maui asked me to do – to write for my next book a twenty-eight-day programme working with the angels .

A few days later, my husband Hubert and I rose very early in order to drive along the ocean to an old, closed-down lighthouse, in the vicinity of which whales could often be seen in the mornings. Neither of us had ever seen a whale in the wild before, and the night before we had prepared ourselves for the encounter by meditating with the help of various water goddesses, the merangels, and the energy of dolphins. Nevertheless, I could never have guessed what a powerful experience I was in for. Leaning against the lighthouse, I was drinking from my cup of hot tea that we had bought from Starbucks on the way and enjoying a breathtaking dawn landscape when suddenly my whole body started vibrating inside in an utterly new way for me. Then I saw, not too far from me, the huge tail of a whale and heard the distinctive sounds it was making. Gradually, more and more whales came into view in the water!

Suddenly I felt an extremely powerful crystalline energy flooding my whole body; it opened my solar plexus and crown chakras in a way I had never experienced before. This was followed by a feeling of complete oneness with All-That-Is, a state of absolute happiness and crystalline clarity that lasted for hours.

When around lunchtime we finally reached our bathing beach, I was still deeply filled with the experience and felt a profound connection to the whales. I was on the beach daydreaming when I suddenly became aware again of this amazing power in my solar plexus and the vibration in my crown chakra. I sat up instantly: I sensed that the whales were calling me. And sure enough, in the distance I recognized two whale tails rising out of the water. Never before had there been whales sighted on this beach. I plunged into the ocean at once, knowing that something significant was going to happen. As soon as I started swimming, the messages from the whales started flowing through me. They transmitted the whole structure of this book as well as a large part of the material for the second module of my ANGEL LIFE COACH® training.

When I returned to the beach I immediately reached for pen and paper – which, following the recommendation of the angels, I always carried with me – and wrote down everything the whales had told me. And in front of my eyes emerged the breakdown of the twenty-eight chapters of this book, including the according angels and quite a bit more. I would have loved to start writing there and then, but the holidays were already coming to an end.

Now half a year has passed, during which I had to travel extensively, and exclusively to give people a better understanding of the angels, and no time was left for writing. But I know that during these six months I was given some important experiences that are essential for this book.

Now I am on an island again and I am connected with the energies of the sea, the water goddesses, merangels, dolphins, whales, seagulls, and angels. I am very much looking forward to finally being able to put this twenty-eight-day programme on paper.

With all my heart I greet the transforming energies of the ocean. May the angels support you so that you can take the time to dedicate yourself to these twenty-eight days with full resolve, focus, and commitment: they will change your life to the bone!

In love and deep solidarity

Isabelle von Fallois
Ibiza, August 1, 2010

PS: The remaining parts of the book I also largely wrote in "ocean locations". So this book is full of the energy of the sea, which helps you to transform everything that no longer serves you with grace and lightness – that allows you to stay "in the flow", so to speak – and to create the life of your dreams.

✦ Introduction ✦

HOW TO BEST WORK
WITH THIS BOOK

Angels hover around us wherever we go.
Angels surround us wherever we turn.

Friedrich Rückert

However this book has come into your hands, your soul has proclaimed that it is time for you to commit, with the help of the angels, to an even deeper connection with yourself and your authentic self. Only if you know yourself in your deepest, innermost being are you able to heal and become the highest expression of yourself.

Returning to your true self will not always be easy since, on this journey, you will be confronted again and again with your fears and weaknesses. But only if you face the truth courageously will you transform yourself, follow your own path and realize the dreams of your life.

To be able to use this book in the best possible way, the angels ask you to consciously read and take in this introduction.

Of course, there are different ways in which you can use this programme brilliantly well for yourself. The really important thing is that you find the right way for yourself, seriously commit to working on yourself, and start and persevere with the programme.

Should it be easier for you to see such a commitment through together with a friend, then find someone who is as enthusiastic about the angels as you are and who would like to effectively change his or her life. Begin at the same time and consult each other regularly (in person, via phone or Skype) with regard to which activities you have accomplished and your experiences. This way you can support each other to persevere even if (when!) old, uncomfortable themes surface.

If you are more of a lone wolf you can of course also work through the book by yourself. I tend to do it this way; all the programmes of this kind I have followed have been done alone. In this case though, you should have someone by your side (partner, friend and/or coach[1]), who can listen and support you if you feel like talking about the experiences or emotions you go through on your journey of transformation.

Each chapter has more or less the same structure and consists of:

- quotes;
- channelings (angel messages, at the beginning of the chapters);
- true stories from my husband, friends, ANGEL LIFE COACH®es, clients and so on, and me[2];
- reflections;
- activities;
- soul affirmations;
- soul journeys.

You can also extend the Angel Programme to more than twenty-eight days. It is important though that you work on it with discipline, continuously and without breaks, so that you attain the best possible results for yourself. If you know right away that you have little time for yourself and will need more than twenty-eight days, the angels recommend working every day on at least the soul affirmations and the soul journey of the chapter you are engaged in at the time. Only move on to the next chapter once you have performed all the "Activities for today".

Again: please work with the Angel Programme on a daily basis so that you develop strong new synapses to help you to manifest the life of your dreams.

If you have completed the programme once already and a topic pulls you in to it particularly strongly, so that you feel you would like to work on it more deeply, you can use the book as a kind of encyclopaedia. In this case, work from the appropriate chapter for as long as it feels right for you. Furthermore, you can employ the book as an oracle by opening it to any random page and then considering what this chapter is about. As the law of attraction always works, it is no "coincidence" which page you have opened. Engage with it; it definitely has something to tell you.

Last but not least: you can repeat the Angel Programme at any time when you would like to concentrate on looking more deeply at yourself and would like to manifest new goals. I have done the course "Living from Vision" twice – both times with excellent results.

ᘉ *Preparations for your journey of transformation* ᘉ

⟲Choose a period of twenty-eight days in which you will find it easy to create at least one hour of time each day for yourself and for the Angel Programme.

⟲ Find yourself a beautiful diary that you like to write in; also paper, Post-it notes, and different-coloured pens. It is very important that you answer all the questions in writing.

⟲ Buy some seeds, soil, and a fitting flowerpot – you will need it on day 6.

⟲ Maybe you would like to have one or the other "angel crystal" for your work with this book. It might be best to leaf through the pages to start with and skim the activities to see which crystal could be important to you. The crystals correspond to the energy of each particular angel. Sometimes they improve access to the light beings of the angels, as crystals are at home in the three-dimensional world and tangible.

I will briefly explain the crystal ritual here:

• Find yourself one specimen each of the named crystal(s) that particularly attract(s) you. Should you find yourself with several, take the first one into your receiving hand (the hand that you do *not* use for writing), close your eyes, and sense into them; or hold them to your third eye, close your psychic eyes, and note the vibration that you receive. Test every single crystal. Afterwards you will know which crystal belongs to you and which one does not.

• Cleanse the chosen specimen for at least twenty seconds under cold running water with the intention of purifying it of all old energies.

• Then call the corresponding angel and ask them to from now on have the crystal charged with the energy of this angel only. You will note how the energy of the crystal will increase.

After charging you can take the crystal into your receiving hand, close your eyes, and let the special energy affect you.

⟳ Before you start each daily programme, create a sacred space for yourself: make sure you will not be disturbed while working with the tools of the book. Switch off your mobile, your phone, your computer, your TV etc., so that you will not be distracted. Surround yourself with things like beautiful music, candlelight, or a pleasant fragrance (perhaps an aroma lamp, incense, aura spray) as well as with the specific "crystal of the day" (if you have one) or another crystal, in order to prepare and raise the vibration in the room for your sacred work on yourself.

⟳ Every morning before getting up call the Archangels Haniel and Michael to you. Ask Haniel to protect your soul essence with her silver light and Michael to surround you with his golden light, so that you are protected on all levels. You can repeat this at any time when you feel that your protective cover is weakened.

⟳ Please always read the chapter of the day in the mornings, even if you do not start with the tasks right away. Beginning the day like this is recommended and very important, so that you connect with the desired energy throughout the day.

If you do not have the book with you during the day, make a note of that day's soul affirmations so that you can speak them again and again over the following hours.

⟳ Speak the soul affirmations several times (at least three times) per day and afterwards always inhale and exhale deeply at least three times, so that you really internalize them.

In order to anchor them more profoundly in your whole system you can, while speaking, rap the palm of one hand with the fist of your other hand two or three times alternating hands, and as quickly as possible for best effect.

⟳ Before starting a soul journey find yourself a quiet space. Should you feel like listening to the soul journey twice a day, this is fine, but the angels recommend that you should definitely do it before going to sleep.

All soul journeys begin in the same way in order to facilitate you relaxing more easily as you get into the pattern of doing them. After the twenty-eight days, you will thus also have learned to move with the help of only one breath into the Theta state (the very deep brain state of relaxation and meditation). In this way, you can later achieve phenomenal results even with short meditations.

Introduction

Maybe you wonder why I have written Theta instead of Alpha, as I have been instructing for a long time. The angels asked me to change this in May 2011. The vibration frequency of the world and its people has risen further, and the Theta frequency has suddenly become much easier to reach for many people, as through techniques like ThetaHealing® and ThetaFloating it has been anchored more and more in the morphogenetic field.

⌒⊘ You can read the soul journeys and let them affect you. Even more effective, though, is to listen to the recordings (you can download from www.fallois.momanda.com) or to record the meditations yourself. This programme has very consciously been created by the angels in the yin and yang mode in order to achieve an inner balance. This means that it consists of active and passive aspects. Particularly important for deep inner healing are the yin parts, the so-called soul journeys. Only in the yin mode can healing on the inner planes happen. Thus the angels highly recommend that you listen to the soul journeys; only then are you in yin mode.

This is also the reason why the angels have named the meditations "soul journeys": they have a great effect on the soul level.

As I have been privileged to experience in countless cases, smaller or bigger miracles happen often during these meditations channelled by the angels – as short as they may be. (An example is the story of Peggy on day 3.) Thus the soul journeys are of particular importance during the daily programme, and the angels ask you to experience them consciously, not while asleep, so that their full effect can unfold on all levels.

⌒⊘ In chapters 3, 4, 6, and 18 a special breathing technique is used. This form of breathing helps to activate the parasympathetic nervous system instead of the sympathetic nervous system, which controls stress, anger, fury, frustration, and panic.

As long as the sympathetic nervous system retains the upper hand the heart works more, and cortisone and adrenaline are being pumped into the system – this is when people find themselves in the so-called "fight or flight mode", where they are no longer in a position to think clearly but behave like scared, stressed children, and furthermore damage their health.

The breathing technique works like this (have your limbs uncrossed):

• Breathe in deeply through the nose without raising the shoulders and without tensing any muscles; as you do so, count to 4 (the number of the angels).

- Breathe out slowly and with a "(H)aaaaah" sound through your mouth.
  - In addition, some of the activities suggest tapping certain acupuncture points: they correspond with the respective emotions that are being worked on in this context. The numbers that are assigned to the acupuncture points can be found in Roy Martina's flow chart *Emotional Balance* and in my flow chart *Emotionale Balance mit Engeln (Emotional Balance with Angels)*.
  - Please remember to ask Archangel Michael at least every evening to cut all energetic cords that are attached to you and do not consist of light and love, so that you may sleep better.

Following this it is also helpful to ask Archangel Raphael to wrap you in his emerald-green healing energy, so that healing can happen.

Finally, repeat the morning ritual with Haniel and Michael, so that you will also be protected on all levels in your sleep.

Contract with Yourself

It so often happens that people resolve to do something but do not manage to put it into practice long-term. For this reason, the angels have asked me jointly with them to draft a contract for you, so that you seriously commit to working through the whole twenty-eight-day programme. This does not, of course, mean that you have to have managed the whole programme in four weeks; you can also take longer, as discussed earlier, if you would like to internalize one chapter more intensively.

It would be very helpful, however, if you did not completely miss a day, as the new synapses that form in your brain through this intense process will not be as powerful if there are breaks. This again would make it more difficult for you to persevere with the programme.

Contract

I, _____, am aware that with the help of the angels I engage in a very intense encounter with my past, my present, and my future as well as with myself.

I, _____, am also aware that this intense examination of myself and my themes will trigger emotions within myself, which I will face in order to move into my power as well as walk my own path and realize the dreams of my life.

I, _____, hereby commit to follow the twenty-eight-day programme in all its parts without breaks at my own speed.

I, _____, commit to look after myself well throughout the course of the pro-gramme, to eat wholesome food, sleep enough, move regularly, pamper myself, and look for the support and help that I need.

Place, date

Signature

↬ *Notes* ↫

Angels are androgynous beings and have no gender, though their energies differ; some angels clearly radiate a masculine energy, for example Archangel Michael, while others, like Shushienae, the angel of purity, appear markedly feminine. Therefore I use the masculine and feminine personal pronouns for different angels, in order to remind us of the quality of their energy.

As it is cumbersome to always write or read the masculine and the feminine form of a noun I have mostly decided to use the male form. I do, of course, wish that all women feel addressed too.

↬ *Wishing You Well* ↫

It is my heartfelt wish that you will have a wonderful start to this journey towards your true self and towards realizing your life dreams. You can be sure that my thoughts will accompany you with love; and you might also become aware of me on other levels, as many of my "students" have done in the past.

May you always feel the blessings and the love of the angels!
Aloha!

Isabelle von Fallois

~ *Part 1* ~

Purification

Day 1

BECOMING CONSCIOUS WITH ARCHANGEL MICHAEL

I walk on clouds ...
The voices of the world disappear in their glow...
Behind me the humming of angels, before me the light...
Like in a dream, so close to freedom.

Michael Adolph

"Greetings, beloved human being. I AM Archangel Michael. If you want to live your dreams, it is very important to free yourself from all the old burdens, pain, and debris of the past. It is only when you do this that you will resonate with the wishes of your heart and become able to manifest these. So I urge you to take time away from the world to reflect on your life in silence and to recognize where you really are. It is from this recognition that you will gain much truth about yourself, your true desires, your spiritual mission, and your current surroundings. Doing this will bring you the freedom to make new decisions for your life that will bring you closer to your goal with every single day. It is a great joy for me to support you in this

with love and energy, if you so desire. Thus feel yourself surrounded by my
cloak of protection so that you can start your journey without fear."

Archangel Michael
greatest angel of protection
Aura colours: royal blue, violet, gold
Crystal: sugilite

Gary Quinn, best-selling author and angel expert to the stars of Los Angeles (City of Angels!) became conscious of his calling in the following manner:

The Visitation

When we come into this world, everyone is blessed with a gift. I knew as a child that I had special vision. For as long as I can remember, I have been able to see lights around people and discern information about them. For a while, I thought that everyone had this ability; however, it did not take long before I recognized that others were not on the same wavelength. It would take years before I could make my gift available to others – I had to wait a long time before I met Archangel Michael.

The key experience of my life took place in the cathedral of Notre Dame in Paris. Before this moment, I was exactly like hundreds of other people: I wanted to become a singer. I had given up my job, my apartment, and my car in Los Angeles for a recording deal in Paris because my dream had come true. However, the bitter reality was that the deal fell through. There I was in Paris, without a job, without an apartment, or any way to cross the Atlantic again. I was completely beside myself and walked the street in desperation, trying to find a way of staying in France.

Every day, I went to the cathedral of Note Dame to pray as I had been taught, but no answer came. Even though I prayed and listened, there was never any answer. Nevertheless, I practised this daily for three weeks: first I lit candles and then, sitting on a bench, went into deep meditation.

At the end of the third week, I received my answer. On this afternoon, I had entered the church the same way as always; however, I felt completely different on this special day. Instantaneously, I let go of all the thoughts and ideas that had blocked me. Then it happened: I sat down, closed my eyes, and went into meditation. Within five minutes, I was aware of a beam of light touching my head. I opened my eyes and was astonished to see that a swirl of violet light surrounded my head. It continued to open as if it would swallow me up. From the ceiling of the cathedral another current of violet light floated down towards me, bathed me, and danced around me; then I suddenly saw five to seven angels. They swirled around my face and one of them spoke telepathically with me.

I should trust my journey, they said, because it was part of my plan to be here. My guardian angel, Archangel Michael, made himself known to me by giving me his name. He assured me that everything would be well.

Nevertheless I was still afraid: I was almost out of money and could only stay one more week with my friends. But the energy of the angel was amazing – warm, lively, strong – it held me in a wave of stillness. Since the angels all communicated telepathically with me, no words were exchanged until Archangel Michael approached me directly and spoke to me. "I AM Archangel Michael. We are here to explain to you that we brought you here, so that you would recognize your spiritual path and to show you your life journey."

At first I was speechless, but I managed to speak telepathically with Archangel Michael. He was very close to me and I started to cry. Never before had I felt so loved, protected, and secure. Archangel Michael said lovingly: "There is no reason to be concerned. Everything that is needed is provided for you and your stay in France." His presence promised security, love, and light. Never before had I experienced such peace.

I thanked Archangel Michael, who started to ascend through the opening of the sky into the light. The violet light also started to dim.

At this moment I knew the answer. For the first time I recognized that everything would be fine. I knew that the angels had revealed themselves to me because the three weeks of praying and meditation had finally made me receptive to them. I had opened my heart and trusted that I would be cared for and guided. They gave me more than an assurance that it was right to be in France, more than a feeling that I was in the process of following the life path destined for me. They also did more than ban my fears and doubts; I knew inwardly that they prepared me for the next important step in my life. They prepared me for the work of my life, which at this point I began to understand and to embrace. The reason for my stay in France and the visits to the cathedral of Notre Dame was now clear to me. These keen and loving angels needed my help as much as they need yours, as much as they need all of our help. They wanted me to spread the news. Healing – joy – enlightenment – fulfilment – enthusiasm – meaning – love: all these deeply longed-for conditions are more easily attainable than most people know.

My message is to let everyone know that love and guidance are there for all of us, right now. You just have to invite them into your life.

If you only had a glimpse of how perfectly and strongly you are loved by the angels, you would cry with joy, and you would very quickly become convinced that you had all the resources needed – even more than you can dream of – to change your life into this wonderful adventure that you desire.

⋰⋱ *Reflection* ⋰⋱

Today, on the first day of your twenty-eight-day-long journey to your self and to the manifestation of your dreams, it is necessary to be honest with yourself about what works in your life and what does not. This consciousness will allow you to decide what you want to work on for the next four weeks in order to create your life, together with the angels, according to your dreams.

Remember to first create a sacred space as described in the introduction, before you answer the following questions in written form.

Call Archangel Michael to your side for as long as you engage in today's work on yourself and ask him to surround you with his golden light, so that you will be completely protected and at the same time united with the frequency of love. Breathe deeply in and out to absorb the light into yourself, and relax. The more relaxed you are, the easier it will be to face the unmasked truth, which will help you to be free. A long time ago Jesus Christ said: "Then you will know the truth and the truth will set you free." (John 8, 32)

Now give the following questions a ranking from 0–10, where 10 is the worst imaginable state and 0 the most wonderful state that you consider possible. Do this spontaneously without reflecting too long on each question.

- How is your health?
- How fit do you feel?
- How much do you exercise?
- How fulfilled are you in your profession?
- How happy are you in your relationship, or without?
- How close are you to your family?
- How do you rank the quality of your friendships?
- How satisfied are you with the time that you can spend alone (is it too much or too little)?
- How disciplined are you on your spiritual path (meditation, prayer, affirmations and so on)?

After you have answered all the questions with an appropriate number, get a general idea of where you are. Which subjects make you feel very comfortable and satisfied, and which subjects demand change urgently? Consider this when you decide which goals you want to achieve with this twenty-eight-day programme.

ᑒ *Soul Memory* ᑒ

The angels say that when we humans incarnate in this world, we take along the dreams of our soul that we would like to fulfil in this life. These dreams are consistent with our life purpose. But quite a few people lose sight of them over time, due to being told by society that they are mere fantasies.

Only few people manage to follow their "burning desire", as Dr. Wayne W. Dyer calls it so beautifully in many of his books and talks (though this expression originates from the author Napoleon Hill). Often we admire these people with our whole heart: their eyes radiate an indescribable bright-ness, because they are deeply fulfilled with their lives. It feels good to spend time in their presence since they radiate such a positive energy that it feels catching.

When we dare to live this so-called burning desire, an immense power lives within it, which can even have life-saving qualities: as I experienced for myself ten years ago while I had life-threatening leukaemia.

I had gone to the doctor a few times over some months as I was feeling increasingly weaker with no explanation. One morning, I collapsed and fainted during my jogging exercise. The examinations and tests of all kinds, though, did not come up with any clear diagnosis – until I was finally sub-jected to a rather painful bone marrow puncture in Großhadern hospital in Munich.

The same night, close to midnight, a doctor unknown to me opened the door to my hospital room and said without further ado: "This is a life-threat-ening situation – you hover between life and death. At the worst you will be dead in three days – at the most, three weeks. The diagnosis is acute leukaemia." Unrelenting words that plunged me into deep shock!

Within the same week, I had also lost my partner, my house, and my place to study in California. I had hit rock bottom and did not know how I would ever recover from this blow. As I did not want to remain at the hospital under these circumstances, I left to clear my head. I knew this was my only chance of surviving.

When I finally returned to Großhadern hospital, two and a half weeks later, the doctors were more than encouraged to see that I was still alive. Having listened to my stories, they were aware that music was my "burning desire" and that the piano would help me to mobilize all my strength to keep living. For this reason, they allowed my family, friends, and parents of my piano students to deliver an electrical stage piano including headphones to the hospital, although this would usually be unimaginable in a sterile, single hospital room.

And so I sat at the piano and played as much as I could, even with chemotherapy infusions running into my arm. When I could not play, it helped me to instead visualize that I could travel again and give concerts. And this is exactly what happened!

ᴄᴏ *Activities for today* ᴄᴏ

Create a sacred space for yourself as described in the introduction. Call Archangel Michael to your side and ask him to surround you with his powerful light; then take a deep breath in and out.

Now it is time to gain clarity (if you are not clear about it yet) on your "burning desire", your gift, and to write it down.

- As a child or teenager, what did you dream of for your future? Imagine yourself back to your childhood and you will know it. In most people's cases, this is exactly that burning desire that exhilarates our soul.
- Should you not remember, ask yourself: what is it that you are absolutely determined to create before you leave this world? And you will find your special gifts.

ᴄᴏ *Soul Affirmation* ᴄᴏ

First ask Archangel Michael to enfold you in his purple-royal blue-golden light. Then take a deep breath in and out, before you speak (ideally aloud):

The longing of my soul is a sign of my life purpose. I deserve to realize my inner and outer dreams effortlessly, with joy and grace, and I will achieve this.

ᴄᴏ *Soul Journey* ᴄᴏ

Have pen and paper ready before you begin. You might want to take some notes during or directly after your journey.

With your eyes open take a deep breath in, and then slowly exhale while you close your eyes in slow motion and order your brain to automatically move into the Theta state. Breathe deeply in and out, and relax. Let your thoughts pass by like leaves gliding along a river, and turn inwards. Enjoy feeling your breath and move further and further into a state of deep relaxation.

In front of you appears a beautiful golden bridge that invites you to cross over. As soon as you step on it you notice how your frequency starts to increase.

Day 1

As you reach the end of the bridge you recognize a paradise garden in front of you, in which Archangel Michael is already awaiting you. He embraces you with his enormous wings and wraps you in his golden light. You feel wonderfully safe and secure.

Then he takes you by the hand and both of you rise up into the sky. You move higher and higher until you reach a celestially beautiful, ethereal temple. Michael accompanies you inside, and the beauty that welcomes you there stuns you. When you are surrounded by the most brilliant light you have ever seen, Michael asks you to seat yourself on the crystalline throne in the middle of the hall. As soon as you sit down, Archangel Michael connects you to your higher self. Enjoy the feeling of becoming one with it.

Then the voice of Archangel Michael rings in your ear:

"Move into your heart and realize from the place of your higher self what you would like to change in the coming weeks. Identify an inner and an outer goal that you would like to work on over the following twenty-eight days. Do not be surprised, beloved being, if what you will hear will not necessarily correspond with the greatest wish of your heart. Your higher self might choose something else since it is connected to your soul and has an overview of your life from a higher perspective. Thus it knows exactly what to work on in order to change your life for the better, so that it lasts. Trust your higher self and me: I will be by your side throughout the whole process."

If you like, write down those two goals – the inner and the outer one – now.

Then visualize your life with a view to having reached both your goals and observe how you feel about this; notice what this means for your whole life. Enjoy the feeling and decide now to realize these two goals with discipline and focus, supported by the angels.

Feel the power of Archangel Michael by your side; he will give you the strength to follow your goals effortlessly, with grace and joy. Know that you will make it!

Michael enfolds you in a dark-blue coat that protects and warms you on your way to your goals, so that worldly things begin to mean less and less to you. He takes you by the hand again and accompanies you out of the heavenly temple.

Together you rise up into the air and fly back to earth. Very gently you land on your feet in the paradise garden. You enjoy feeling Mother Earth underneath you and connect with the roots beneath your feet. Stretch your limbs, open your eyes, and return fully into your body and into the here and now.

If you have not yet written down both your goals, the inner one and the outer one, then please do so now: the power of the written word is much greater than that of a thought.

Day 2

STRENGTHEN YOUR CONNECTION TO YOUR GUARDIAN ANGELS

*Sometimes the guardian angels of our life fly so high
That we cannot see them any longer,
But they never lose track of us.*

Jean Paul Richter

"Greetings, beloved human being. We are your two guardian angels who have accompanied you from the beginning of time. We are very honoured and joyful to surround you on your life journey. But please include us more in your life, so that we can support you even better, in beautiful as much as in difficult times. You are familiar with the law of free will: due to this, we are only allowed to help you if you ask us or if you find yourself in a life-threatening situation before your time is up.

Please talk to us about your suffering and your joy at any time, so that we can support you, just like best friends do, as this is just what we are – and so much more. That would be our greatest delight, and it would map out a much lighter life for you. Accept our help and enjoy your life more and more."

Day 2

Guardian angels
they watch over you from the beginning until the end of your life
Aura colour: white
Crystal: angelite

 *Reflection*

Even people who do not generally believe in angels have occasionally let out the sentence: "Your guardian angels must have been looking out for you there!" For example, when someone emerges miraculously unscathed from a severe accident. In fact, every person, whether they believe in angels and/or God or not, is accompanied by two guardian angels from the beginning to the end of their life. One of them usually radiates a more masculine, the other one a more feminine energy – this of course does not mean that angels have a gender, but their energies nevertheless often feel quite distinct. The more feminine guardian angel has the task to be by your side and support you, to open your heart, to listen to you, and to comfort you when necessary; while the more masculine angel protects you and also occasionally pushes you so that you do not lose your way, since he has to make sure that you fulfil your life plan. Contrary to the assumption that our burning desire to communicate with the angels is much greater than their wish to be in direct contact with us, they say:

We angels love you with all our hearts and wish even more ardently than you to make contact with you.

Also remember that nothing is too trivial for the angels. They would like to support you in all aspects of your life.

 *Activities for today*

Create an Angel Box

You will place those wishes that you would like to manifest in your angel box. It can be a ready-made box or a shoe box that you paint and stick pictures of angels on. You can often find beautiful boxes in stationery departments, some even already decorated with angels.

Place the completed angel box in an appropriate place (e.g. on your altar if you have one). Whenever you want to manifest something (the most powerful time for this is at the new moon), write it on a piece of paper with the addition "…– this or better than this", since many a time, not even in our

---

Short story about guardian angels

The son of family friends of ours had time and again been unlucky in matters of love and women, so that he had nearly stopped believing in a fulfilling relationship. At one point he told my mother about his dilemma, and she responded full of faith: "You know what I will be doing every evening now? I will pray and ask your guardian angels to contact the guardian angels of the woman of your dreams. Then your guardian angels will arrange for you two to run into each other at the right time." Whereupon he laughed: "Ach well, it cannot do any harm. Thank you!"

And so my mother started to pray, every evening, for the meeting of those two.

It did not take long before he met a woman, pretty as well as wonderful. From the first moment on he knew that he had finally found the right one – although it took a bit longer to convince her of this! After a while, however, the two of them found each other; they are a match made in heaven and are now happily married.

---

wildest dreams can we imagine the most extraordinary manifestations. Then place the piece of paper in the box and let go of the wish, as if it was a balloon! Only if you are not attached to it will you not sabotage yourself with doubts and fears, so that your wish can come true.

ᘓ Write a letter to your guardian angels

Remember to first create a sacred space for yourself as described in the introduction.

This time you write the letter not into your diary but on to loose sheets of paper, so that you can subsequently place them in your angel box. You can be as creative as you like and use nice stationery as well as colourful pens or crayons. The angels love colour!

Now write to your two guardian angels that you would like to become more familiar with them and tell them about your goals, which you would like to realize within the next twenty-eight days with their help and the support of the other angels. Describe also where in particular you need their support, so that you do not sabotage yourself. You can be certain that the two will do everything to make the time of transformation as pleasant as possible for you. Tell them everything that is important to you.

Should you also wish for the partner of your dreams, as described in the guardian angel story earlier on, you can ask your own guardian angels to make contact with the guardian angels of your future loved one and to help you two to be in the same place at the same time and meet (please do not specify the place, though – exactly how something happens should always be left for the angels to arrange). Naturally, you can add in anything that you wish for in this context.

If you are already in a relationship, you can ask your guardian angels to contact the guardian angels of your partner and tell him or her everything that is important to you. Interestingly enough, people sometimes find that it is then no longer necessary to clarify certain things on a personal level, since this has long happened with the help of the guardian angels on another plane.

This, of course, goes also for all other kinds of relationships – those with family, friends and colleagues, for example.

Finish your letter with a heartfelt thank you and a farewell. You can be certain that your two guardian angels will help you. When you have finished writing, place your letter in your wonderful angel box.

Soul Affirmation

First ask your guardian angels to enfold you in their white light. Then take a deep breath in and out, before you say (ideally aloud):

At every turn I am surrounded by my guardian angels, who watch over me, protect me, and help me achieve my life purpose. I am always loved and completely accepted as I am. I am never alone.

Soul Journey

Have pen and paper ready before you begin. You might want to take some notes during or directly after your journey.

With your eyes open take a deep breath in, and then slowly exhale while you close your eyes in slow motion and order your brain to automatically move into the Theta state. Breathe deeply in and out, and relax.

Let your thoughts go by like birds flying past. Observe only, do not grasp at anything while you relax more and more deeply. Enjoy feeling the flow of your breath that fills you with life energy, and relax even further. Move more and more into a state of deep relaxation.

You find yourself on a narrow path in the woods that leads you higher and higher up a mountain. Joyful birdsong accompanies you, and you feel clearer and lighter the higher you climb.

Suddenly you hear a small mountain brook splashing nearby, and you joyfully embark upon discovering it. You step into a wonderful clearing that shines resplendently in the clarity of the morning sun, and you see the small brook. With pleasure you settle down at its bank and make yourself comfortable in the lush grass. The morning sun warms you and allows you to relax even more deeply.

Then you hear a rustling sound. You turn round and recognize a transcendentally beautiful, delicate angel with quite feminine features who speaks to you in a gracious voice:

"Greetings, beloved soul. I am one of your guardian angels. My task is to stand by you, to open your heart, to gently embrace you with my wings, to comfort and to carry you when your life places great challenges in front of you, and to relieve you of sadness and pain, so that you can become increasingly more joyful and gracefully dance through your life."

You feel how she lovingly enfolds you in her wings and very quietly whispers her name into your ear. Enjoy the feeling of being carried and of being loved.

Then another angel appears by your side. He radiates great strength and magnificence, and he feels strangely familiar to you. He too speaks to you, in a beautiful, sonorous voice:

"Beloved soul, I greet you. I also am your guardian angel, and I know that you recognize me since whenever you have run into peril or have been in danger I have protected you. This is my task. I am also the one who keeps gently urging you on, so that you follow your path and fulfil the (life) purpose with which you have started out in this life."

He too surrounds you with his wings and you feel completely safe and protected. At that point you hear the sound of a familiar name close by your ear. Maybe you become fully aware of it in that moment. It is the name of your guardian angel.

Continue to enjoy this sweet gathering on the banks of the exquisitely splashing mountain brook for a while before you embark upon your return journey down the mountain.

Arriving at the foot of the mountain you feel wonderfully nourished by this encounter with your two guardian angels, and you rejoice at feeling a stronger bond with them than ever before. Now connect your feet consciously with the earth, stretch your body, open your eyes, and enjoy knowing that your guardian angels are always by your side, also in the here and now.

Day 3

RECONCILE YOUR PAST WITH THE HELP OF ARCHANGEL JEREMIEL

Live such that when you stumble,
An angel's hand may guide you to the goal,
That vanished before you.

Hafiz

"*Greetings, beloved soul. I AM Archangel Jeremiel. It is time to reconcile your past, since only through this will you once again become the pure vessel that you were when starting out on this globe. As long as you carry and foster all the wounds, traumas, and disappointments that you and others have inflicted upon yourself, your frequency does not correspond to your dreams and you will not be able to achieve them. Therefore, I warmly recommend that you dedicate yourself with my help to your past, so that it may lose its power over you for good. Through recognizing the gifts in your soul lessons and accepting them gratefully you will start to shine again with a pure heart and a clear spirit. This is the path that may lead you to the stars.*"

Archangel Jeremiel
the angel who helps you to overcome difficulties
and to let go of attachments to the past
Aura colour: violet
Crystal: amethyst

⟨∞⟩ *Reflection* ⟨∞⟩

There is something fascinating about our past. Everyone, I think, knows the scenario in which we always attract the same type of person (and I don't just mean romantic partner), even though we have vowed to ourselves to not ever again be taken in by someone like that. In a similar way, other situations seem to repeat themselves in cyclic fashion throughout our lives.

The reason for this lies in the fact that while we may well wish for a different type of person or situation we have not yet come to terms with the past, so we are like a canvas painted in layers; even when we create a new painting there are many layers underneath, which affect and sabotage us. All these "paintings" together form the resonance that we radiate to the outside world, and according to the law of resonance it is impossible to attract something entirely new as long as we are still a colour blend of the old. That is why it is so important to clear the past and leave our life as a victim behind us for good in order to become an empty canvas, so bright and pure that everything becomes possible for us.

I myself was a prime example for repeating patterns...

For years, I had always – in various ways – attracted one of the following types of men: men who were not available; men who were not faithful; and men who were afraid of my power. It was as if I was jinxed.

When I then, on top of that, completely physically collapsed (I had a hunch that it could be leukaemia, though this was only confirmed after the bone marrow biopsy as I was suffering from a rare form that is not easy to recognize), and my partner dismissively ran out on me, I was utterly devastated and resolved (I thought) irrevocably to break with men once and for all.

But what followed was absurd. In the oncology department of Großhadern hospital I was more or less the only woman without a partner by her side, and I felt so alone and desolate that I longed for nothing more than a new man in my life. Even though I really had other concerns – since I was fighting just to survive, after all! – a major part of my thoughts centred around this topic.

When, on top of this, I went bald, lost my eyelashes and eyebrows, and due to the hormones I had to take in order not to bleed to death, looked puffed up, I was close to lapsing into a deep depression. I was absolutely certain that I would never ever find a man again, ugly as I was. For a short while, I downright wallowed in my existence as victim.

Whenever I was allowed home in between the chemotherapy sessions, even for a short while, I was searching for someone. Each time, this ended more than disappointingly.

Somehow I realized that this way was the sure road to ruin again, as far as men were concerned, and I began to seriously deal with my past. I discovered various unacceptable behavioural patterns in myself that I started to change step by step; and above all, I recognized that I first had to find love within myself and become whole before I could radiate the frequency to attract the partner of my dreams.

Eventually I did learn this, was content with myself, and no longer needed anyone to feel complete. And suddenly the men came running towards me; I could choose who to hang out with. Among all these men, I finally found the one who walks through thick and thin with me – truly no picnic, given my story! And I am deeply grateful for this.

Peggy, one of my translators (and now also ANGEL LIFE COACH®) experienced the following wondrous events:

The erect spine

The angels have a real sense of humour! Almost without you noticing, something happens which you had never thought possible, and you think that what has become possible could just not be... but I have been disabused of that notion.

I had one thing as my painful companion for years: recurring problems with my back. Just the very thought of my back was permanently connected with the idea of pain, which naturally had me on edge all the time. All medical diagnoses had confirmed the apparent fact that my back showed a distinct curvature of the spine, which just could not be corrected.

I had tried so many things, and what was the result of it all?! Numerous X-rays, treatments and recommendations over time had left me even more frustrated.

"Man proposes – God disposes!" This is exactly what I was recently given to experience, live in action, so to speak. As a matter of fact, I learned closely and through the effects on my own body what is truly possible, and I am still profoundly touched by it. It all happened on a seminar weekend where quite a few things would change for me.

"The Power of the Angels" – this was the topic of the seminar Isabelle and Gary Quinn offered in Velden, Worthersee, in Austria. It was only their second joint workshop but it seemed as if they had been working together from time immemorial. This

---

special weekend, the heavenly powers were extremely present and made themselves visible to the human eye through numerous orb photographs.

The wonderful combination of various interactive elements, exercises, and guided meditations brought us increasingly into contact with what is truly possible, even if it previously seemed to be completely impossible. Thinking back to this weekend, an incredible gratitude fills me, because I was blessed to experience this tremendous amount of activity happening, both seen and unseen. I could only guess the forms all this would take but, on the Sunday morning, I was totally baffled. Doing my morning routine and those rituals that I often perform quite unconsciously, I realized that suddenly something felt completely different, something that I could not really grasp at all. Since I was young, the lower part of my spine had always protruded as a distinct "knob", no matter how erect I stood. This very area now seemed to suddenly have "unfurled". Whether I wanted to believe it or not, something had happened in my back – and actually in a physical and thus quite visible way!

When I then – still completely baffled – pondered how this could have happened at all, I remembered that on the previous day Isabelle had channelled a meditation in which Archangel Jeremiel dissolved past traumatic experiences in our spines. Then she worked for a few minutes on straightening my spine. I cannot remember too much about this; the effects, though, I felt all the more.

When I visited my mother a few days after this profound experience, she looked at me and said with surprise: "How weird, you've grown?"

Thinking about this confirmation from outside makes me smile with all my heart about the boundless miraculous work of the angels.

The most remarkable thing in all this is that since that weekend my back seems to be continuing to work, in an almost magical way. My spine seems to effectively "unfurl" further and further, and I feel day by day how it is becoming more and more flexible again.

What stays with me is the vital sense of how miracles happen in such wondrous ways, often when we no longer expect them. What a gift!

⟡ *Activities for today* ⟡

Inventory

Remember to first create a sacred space for yourself, as described in the introduction.

Call Archangel Jeremiel to your side and ask him to accompany you throughout the whole day, surrounding you with his violet light, so that you are connected with the frequency of gentle transformation. Take a deep breath in and out in order to absorb the light, and relax.

With Archangel Jeremiel, review your past and consider your present. Recognize the events and experiences that you could not accept and with which you have wrestled or are still wrestling, and write them down on a piece of paper.

✑ *Release your past*

Now close your eyes, ask Jeremiel to surround you once more with his violet light, and take three deep breaths.

Be conscious of the fact that all experiences, without exception, have contributed to shape you exactly into this wonderful person that you are today.

Point with your right hand behind you and say: "This is only the past." Then place your left hand on your heart chakra and say: "My reality is a different one." Repeat this procedure three times, and afterwards take another three deep breaths while you breathe in through your nose, counting to four, and then slowly breathe out through your mouth with an "Aaaaah" sound.

At all costs, pay attention to your precise choice of words! If you said: "That is my past", you would continue to "hold" it. We, however, want to leave it behind us with this simple, but infinitely often tried and tested, very powerful, affirmation.

✑ *Recognize your soul lessons*

Now have your diary to hand (not loose sheets of paper) and consider: what do the soul lessons and hidden gifts in the events and experiences that you have described above look like? What have you learned from them? Write down your insights.

When you are done, send the following intention out into the universe (best done in an enthusiastic voice!):

From now on, whenever anything unpleasant happens in my life I ask myself immediately: "What soul lesson do I have to learn in this and which gift is hidden therein for me?"

As long as you are sending this out and also acting accordingly, you will no longer end up with the attitude of a victim and on a downward spiral. Instead you will remain the director of your life and consequently shape your storyline in line with your insights.

Now write the above intention on one or more Post-it notes and place them at strategically important locations, e.g. at your computer, since as is well-known we do not receive exclusively loving emails!

ᐧ ᔕ *Soul Affirmation* ᐧ ᔕ

First ask Archangel Jeremiel to enfold you in his violet light. Then take a deep breath in and out, before you say (ideally aloud):

I gratefully accept my past since it has made me into the person that I am today. In doing so I release the anchor that has kept me back and connect myself with the insights that I have gained in the course of time. From now on I am the director of my life.

ᔕ *Soul Journey* ᔕ

Before you start this soul journey take another quick look at all you have written down while taking stock earlier on. This is what you want to let go of during your journey.

With your eyes open take a deep breath in, and then slowly exhale while you close your eyes in slow motion and order your brain to automatically move into the Theta state. Breathe deeply in and out, and relax.

Let your thoughts go by like birds flying past. Just let them go and enjoy feeling the flow of your breath. With each breath you take you move more and more deeply into a state of relaxation.

You find yourself in a starry night on the shore of a magical lake that glistens wondrously in the light of the stars. Simply observing the sparkling water causes your body to start to oscillate and change its vibrations.

Then, out of nowhere, a boat steered by an angel appears by the water's edge. It is Archangel Jeremiel. He greets you with a loving smile, and extending his hands to you he invites you to join him in the boat. You enjoy gliding through the night in the boat with Jeremiel.

When you finally reach the other shore, Jeremiel again extends his hand and helps you onto safe ground. A path lined with candles leads you from the lake directly to a perfect dream of a palace, which shimmers in the starlight as if dusted with diamonds. Jeremiel escorts you inside and guides you into an enormous hall, at the end of which you see a large mirror. Jeremiel motions you towards the mirror, and you step closer.

As soon as you approach the mirror, the pictures of your past that you would like to leave behind appear in it. Then Archangel Jeremiel steps behind you and envelops you in his gentle violet light of transformation, and you notice how your heart starts to feel more at ease.

Suddenly you hear Jeremiel's voice very clearly and distinctly:

"Now send, together with me, the golden-silver-violet fire of transformation, grace and unconditional love into these pictures, and they will transform and very gently disappear."

You both lift your arms and send out the powerful light towards the mirror; and in front of your eyes your past instantly transforms into light and love.

You feel countless burdens drop away from you. Grace permeates you, now that the shadows of the past have lost their grip on you.

All at once, the pictures in the mirror disappear and Jeremiel says:

"Beloved being, now you are ready to take responsibility for your life and to choose what you would like to create for the future, since you are the director of your life."

Full of gratitude, you turn to Jeremiel and embrace him while a profound feeling of happiness flows through you.

Then it is time to leave the palace again. Together you set out, returning along the candle-lined path.

Eventually you reach the moored boat, and with you aboard it again glides smoothly through the shimmering waters back to the shore from whence you came. With Jeremiel's help you find firm ground underneath your feet again, and you thank him with all your heart.

Feel Mother Earth underneath you, stretch your limbs in order to fully come back into your body and into the here and now, and open your eyes.

You should now burn the paper on which you have written the result of taking stock earlier on.

Day 4

TAKE CARE OF THE TEMPLE OF YOUR SOUL WITH ARCHANGEL RAPHAEL

What is impossible to all humanity
May be achieved by the might and power of the angels.

Joseph Glanvil

"Greetings, beloved human being. I AM Archangel Raphael. It is important to me to remind you that your body is the temple of your soul, since in the course of events on earth this tends to keep being forgotten. Often you really only become aware of your body when it suddenly does not function perfectly by itself. I ask you though to treat your body from now on as that temple that it truly is. Listen daily to its voice, that whispers or sometimes even calls out to you what it needs, and act accordingly. Remember that a powerful body is predestined to be surrounded by a powerful aura. So strive for that!

In particular in these times of light-body development, it is of greater importance than ever before, since the oscillations that affect your body can sometimes be immense when new light frequencies pervade your being and accelerate your *evolution on all levels. Do not be surprised if there are cycles when all you want to do is rest. Just allow yourself to give in to this need, and your body will subsequently thank you with more power. To this effect, I surround you with love and enjoy accompanying you with all my heart on this, your earth journey."*

Archangel Raphael
angel of healing and travel
Aura colour: emerald-green
Crystal: emerald, malachite

My friend and assistant Dani experienced the following:

With Raphael on the spinning bike

During one of my spinning classes Archangel Raphael came through to me. He alerted me to the importance, for the body and the whole system, of honouring our food by being in a state full of gratitude and love when preparing as well as consuming it.

"How often do you sit with your friends, eating in a great restaurant, and during the meal you speak about the fact that you have not eaten for the whole day, so that you can now eat a several-course menu without putting on weight? You discuss how many calories the individual dishes have and declare that you absolutely need to do an extra round of sports the next day in order to digest everything. You also talk about all the diets that are on the market.

This behaviour can lead to the body reacting negatively to the – in actual fact fantastic – food, through things like toxic reactions, burping, nausea, or diarrhoea. This also happens if you speak negatively about other people or discuss unpleasant situations during the meal. You thus transform the positive energy that you are taking in through the food into negative energy, which can among other things lead to gaining weight.

I ask you, from now on, to put your mobile to the side during meals and speak about positive topics; also about how wonderfully your food nourishes you and increases your energy. Should you really need to watch the TV or listen to the radio, avoid negative news or programmes, so that you do not absorb this information into your system along with the food. When you follow this, you will immediately feel that your energy increases and you have more energy available."

I was horrified when I realized what I had been doing to myself. During meals with other people I now began to direct the conversation towards nice things in order to do all of us some additional good. As well as the fact that the food agrees with me considerably better, these shared moments with my friends have become much more joyful, animated, and lighter. A very pleasant side effect.

I received another message from Archangel Raphael and Angel Roufina, one of the angels of self-love, while on my spinning bike:

"Physical fitness is very important for the body sense of every person. This is not only about endorphins but also contributes to you liking to be touched. If you do not like being touched or hugged, or freeze, hold your breath, and pull in your belly when someone does it to you, it means that you are not happy with your body. Fitness, on the other hand, promotes your awareness of your body and your self-confidence as much as your self-love. Besides this, you will receive better grounding and clarity in spirit. Fit people stand erect and are more content with their bodies and their lives even when they maybe carry a few pounds too many. With a healthy and regular amount of fitness you radiate more sovereignty and stability, and feel sexy too."

I can only say that the two angels are absolutely right!

⟶ Reflection ⟵

You have already reached day 4 of the twenty-eight-day programme. It might be new and may also feel exhausting for you to invest that much time in yourself every day, but this is necessary in order to effect a sustainable change in your life.

As Archangel Raphael says, it is very important to care for your body every day, particularly during these twenty-eight days of transformation, since the programme affects you more deeply than you might think.

Remember to first create a sacred space for yourself before you answer the following questions in writing.

Call Archangel Raphael to your side and ask him to accompany you throughout the whole day, surrounding you with his emerald-green light, so that you are connected with the frequency of healing. Take a deep breath in and out in order to absorb the light, and relax.

- How many hours per night do you sleep on average? Is that sufficient?
- Do you sleep well? Is your sleep deep?
- If not, why?

⟶ Activities for relaxing sleep ⟵

What can you do in order to change this? Ask Raphael to help you with your answer. Maybe you need to listen to beautiful, relaxing music before you go to sleep, take a warm bath, or meditate. Whatever the answers, put them into practice today and stick to them from now on.

⚬⚭ *Reflection* ⚬⚭

- How healthy is your diet?
- Where do you go shopping? Predominantly in supermarket chains or in shops with organic food?
- Do you eat at regular or irregular intervals?
- Do you eat standing up, or do you really take time and space in order to eat?
- Do you feel rather unpleasantly full and tired after your meal, or do you feel full, light, and full of zest for action?
- Are you slim, too skinny, or too big?
- Do you have a daily intake of coffee, sugar, alcohol, and meat? If so, begin to slowly reduce this consumption with the help of Archangel Raphael. What food can you take in instead?
- Are there times when you fast or detoxify your body?

⚬⚭ *Activities for a healthy diet* ⚬⚭

Now go to your fridge and your cupboards, and decide which of the foods stored there really nourish your body as the temple of your soul. Dispose of everything that contradicts this.

Then write, together with Raphael, a shopping list made up of food that best nourishes your body. Go shopping as soon as possible.

Also note how you would like to change your habits and act accordingly, today.

Maybe it is time to learn about new forms of nutrition. A book that has much inspired me is *Skinny Bitch*, by Rory Freedman and Kim Barnouin. The title put me off at first, but after I had come across it a few times and, during a very long stay at a London airport, it had eventually even fallen off the shelf in front of me, I knew that I had to read it.

Another cookbook that crossed my path several times while working on this book was Alicia Silverstone's *The Kind Diet: A Simple Guide to Feeling Great, Losing Weight, and Saving the Planet*. That book particularly inspires me.

You will find a few more suggestions in the bibliography at the end of this book.

∽ *Reflection* ∽

- How much exercise do you get?
- Do you do any sports? If so, what kind?
- Or do you do yoga, t'ai chi, qigong or the like?

∽ *Activities for a fit body* ∽

↪If you do not already do this, plan and fix your fitness dates, your trial session in the yoga studio etc. as wholeheartedly as all your other dates; and it's best to start today, so that you also actually realize them.

↪Get moving today in some way or other in order to get your body going (minimum: 15 minutes) – even if it is "only" at home and you put on your favourite songs and dance your heart out! The angels call this "chakra shaking", by the way, since it rocks the chakras and relieves them of ballast in a wonderful way.

∽ *Reflection* ∽

- Do you care for your body?
- Do you use lotions or oils on a regular basis?
- Do you have a massage? Or visit a spa?
- Do you pamper your body in another way?

∽ *Activities for the benefit of your soul's temple* ∽

↪If you do not have one already, buy a scented body lotion or a captivatingly fragrant body oil, and use it on a regular basis.

↪Take a bath with scented oils.

↪Book yourself in for a massage, for example a lomi lomi nui massage that brings you into flow; a wellness day at a spa or a weekend in a beautiful wellness hotel.

↪Or create other opportunities to care for your body and to honour it as the temple of your soul.

⤳ *Reflection* ⤳

- How often do you allow yourself time to be still and just be by yourself? Often enough for you?
- Do you make these times your priority or are you always the last one you look after?
- Do you grant yourself times out when you can just enjoy life?
- Or are you a workaholic and cannot slow down at all?

⤳ *Activities for more stillness in your life* ⤳

⤳Meditate regularly, ideally at least once a day, since when done on a regular basis meditation relaxes the fidgety mind as well as regenerating the body. For this, select the form of meditation that suits you best: silent meditation, transcendental meditation, primordial sound meditation, candle meditation, guided meditation journey, dancing meditation, walking meditation, trance meditation... Or, if you love variety, integrate various forms of meditation into your life.

⤳Plan regular time for yourself and note these slots in your diary or your mobile agenda just like any other date. Use this time to do something that you enjoy.

⤳Create mobile-, computer-, and TV-free hours, days, and/or weeks for yourself.

⤳Plan holiday time for yourself, either with others or alone, just as you like.

⤳ *Conclusion* ⤳

Talk to your body every day and ask it what it needs. Your body is alive and does not like to be treated in a habit-driven way. This means, for example, that it probably does not always like to get the same breakfast or complete the same yoga practice. Every body has its own cycles: there are times when your body is more or less panting to exert itself, and other times when the very same exercise programme could be toxic for your body. Sometimes it suffers heavy food well, on other days this makes it sick.

Thus, in these sensitive times of light-body activation, please listen to your body's messages and act accordingly! No one knows your body better than you, and it will thank you with energy, vitality, and health.

You can also always ask Archangel Raphael for advice if you are not sure:

he knows exactly what is good for you. Raphael is happy to show you food that supports you and your body in a special way.

Just ask him for a clear answer and you will receive it in the form of words, thoughts, images, emotions, or signs.

⟶ *Soul Affirmation* ⟵

First ask Archangel Raphael to enfold you in his emerald-green healing energy. Then take a deep breath in and out, before you say (ideally aloud):

I am looking after myself well and take care to get enough sleep, to nourish myself with healthy food, to meditate regularly, and to exercise daily. The fitter I am the easier I find it to increase my vibration and have a strong powerful aura.

⟶ *Soul Journey* ⟵

Have pen and paper ready before you begin. You might want to take some notes during or directly after your journey.

With your eyes open take a deep breath in, and then slowly exhale while you close your eyes in slow motion and order your brain to automatically move into the Theta state. Breathe deeply in and out, and relax.

Let your thoughts go by like leaves gliding along a river, and turn inwards. With each breath you take you move further into a state of deep relaxation.

Feel, sense, see, or imagine how you are being enveloped in healing, emerald-green golden light and enjoy feeling how this powerful light permeates your whole being and reconnects you with your divine blueprint. It is a wonderful sensation.

You find yourself on a winding path that leads up a hill. Suddenly the path in front of you forks and you do not know which direction to choose. At that moment a raven appears above you and telepathically conveys to you the message to follow it. Trustingly, you accompany it. Before long a sparkling crystalline pyramid looms in front of you. You look gratefully at the raven, who seems to nod at you approvingly. Marvelling, you walk around the pyramid until you discover its entrance, which is lined with truly beautiful white flowers.

You have only just entered the pyramid when Archangel Raphael comes towards you and welcomes you with open arms. He leads you to a magnificent water basin, at the bottom of which you see sacred geometric forms and huge emeralds that make the water shimmer a beautiful green colour. In addition, an enticing fragrance wafts from the water basin up to your nose.

Raphael asks you to take off your clothes and immerse yourself in the healing water. As soon as you are ready and slide into the basin you feel how all your stress falls away from you, and you dive into a dimension of relaxation far from this world. You feel brighter and lighter, and you enjoy the wonderful feeling of absolute timelessness.

Finally it is time to lift yourself out of the basin again. Raphael gives you a silken bathrobe, shimmering in all colours of the rainbow. As soon as you put it on next to your skin you feel that your body, and all the chakras and layers of your aura, are being gently balanced by its rainbow colours. You feel marvellous.

Then Raphael guides you to a crystalline bed, which is decorated with emeralds of all shapes. You lie down and realize that the bed is placed right underneath the pyramid's cusp, through which opening pleasantly warming sunlight shines on your solar plexus.

Now Raphael's warm-hearted voice sounds next to you:

"Beloved being, while I am sending my emerald-green healing energy into every single one of your cells and connecting you with your divine blueprint – the perfect form of your body, your DNS, your cells, your whole being – the sunlight will simultaneously unite you with your true life force. While this happens I ask you to smoothly take seven deep breaths in and out."

As you breathe deeply seven times as requested, right away you feel your energy level increasing. At the same time you are being permeated by the purest, untainted love and know on a deep soul level that you are infinitely loved just the way you are. A profound feeling of happiness flows through you.

You feel entirely energized when Raphael finally helps you down from the bed. Gratefully you fling your arms round his neck. He gently strokes your back and assures you that you can return to this place as often as you would like to. Then he accompanies you back to the entrance where the raven is already awaiting you. With a heart full of gratitude you take leave of Archangel Raphael, and together with the raven you start on your journey home.

Once you have arrived, take a deep breath in order to anchor your experiences in your whole being; then stretch your body and very gently arrive back in the here and now. When you are ready, open your eyes.

·⟶ Day 5 ⟵·

FACE YOUR SHADOWS WITH ANGEL LAVINIA

When you are born with wings you should do
anything to use them for flying.

Florence Nightingale

"Greetings, beloved soul. I am Lavinia, the angel who helps you to transform your shadows in love. In these times of change and increase in vibration it may sometimes seem very strange to you that there is nevertheless so much darkness in the world, and ever more is being revealed. Even in you, although you are striving for the light, time and again shadows appear that you have long believed overcome. The reason for this is that the increases in vibration happen in spiral movements and pervade your light body more deeply than a few years ago. Every earth increase in frequency also effects an increase in frequency within yourself, and at the same time brings hitherto unresolved aspects of yourself to light. The higher the intensity of the light, the less even the smallest blind spots can be covered. Thus I ask you, beloved soul, not to judge yourself when you are once again faced with *one of these shadows, but to transform it with help from me, my transparent green healing energy, and my platinum-coloured beam. Through learning to accept and love your shadows they will turn into the greatest helpers you can imagine on your path towards wholeness. Now be enfolded in love by my wings."*

Angel Lavinia
the angel who helps us to accept and love our shadows
Aura colour: transparent green
Beam: platinum-coloured
Crystal: danburite

Since I have not mentioned the angel Lavinia so far I would like to tell you at this point how she stepped into my life.

ᥫᥬ First meeting with Angel Lavinia ᥫᥬ

Exactly a year ago I was sitting on a plane with my husband, on my way to enjoy a week's holiday at the Bay of Angels in Nice, France. I could hardly wait to finally get to the sea and to have a rest; after all, I was coming out of a very intense year, packed with work: as well as my practice work I had written a book, had channelled and recorded more than twenty meditations, and on top of all that had travelled a lot in order to facilitate workshops and speak at international conventions. For more than six months I had not slept more than two to four hours a night, which did not show as the angels kept flooding me with energy, but which made my body feel very exhausted.

So I was really enjoying being able to read in peace on the plane, when suddenly, between me and the seat in front, appeared a graceful angel with a beautiful oval face, wavy light brown hair, a silvery-green sparkling dress, and a transparent green aura. I had never seen this angel before. Astonished, I looked at her, and before I could ask anything I heard a wonderfully melodious voice:

"I am Lavinia, the angel of shadows. Greetings to you. I am very happy to help you during the coming week to work on your shadows and transform them."
I could not believe my ears; I had seriously determined not to work during these holidays. But once again the angels had different plans for me. I knew that it was completely pointless to rebel. Thus I surrendered to the inevitable.

I had hardly arrived at the water and started on my first swim when Lavinia appeared, floating above the water, saying with determination:
"Now please think of the person who presently irritates you the most."
I did not have to think long here.

Within seconds one of my friends showed up in my mind's eye.

"OK, and now look at which of his behaviour patterns have hurt you most, was her next instruction.

Not much thinking to do there either. Immediately the slights from him came to the surface. Lavinia, though, did not give me any time to feel hurt and vulnerable, and lick my wounds, but held the mirror up to me:

"When have you hurt people in exactly the same way? This might date back somewhat but if you are really honest with yourself you will know that you have behaved in this same way before."

I knew she was right, I was already starting to see the friend with different eyes. Unhurriedly, I then looked back to the scenarios where I had behaved quite similarly while Lavinia worked on me and on these topics with her transparent green healing energy and her platinum-coloured beam, which penetrates the deepest corners of our being. I sensed how I felt increasingly lighter and freer, and how I could accept these shadows of mine in love.

When I left the water some time later I felt perfectly at peace with these behaviour patterns, which this friend, but also I myself, had shown, and my heart was filled with a wonderful pure frequency of love. I was incredibly grateful to Lavinia!

In the next days, she continued to work intensively with me on further shadows within myself, and the results were just unbelievable. No sooner had I arrived home again when the said friend behaved as if turned by 180 degrees; and other things changed in an extremely amazing way, even though I had "merely" worked on myself and my shadows. Then Gandhi's wonderful words came to mind: "Be the change you wish to see in the world." How right he was with this. Lavinia has continued to be one of my constant companions; she supports me with my work on the shadows of my clients as well as participants in my ANGEL LIFE COACH® trainings and shadow workshops, with unique results.

My friend Gido, who works as a coach and also as an actor and singer, spent an intense, extremely healing time with Angel Lavinia:

On the couch with Lavinia

It is not that long ago that I had to go through a very tough phase in my life. During this time, Lavinia, an angel I had never much worked with before, helped me in only a few days to transform my most difficult shadows into light. It was only then that I truly realized all that is possible and how much lighter and more beautiful life can be if we only allow it. What had happened though?

My relationship that I had very happily been living in for five years threatened to break apart. Completely out of nowhere and without any obvious warning, I suddenly faced the prospect of being single again, without the person who meant more to me than anything else.

One morning, while I sat meditating, I once again slipped into the kind of self-pity which, I think, everyone in this situation knows well, and I asked insistently: "Why me? Why did this have to happen? I have not deserved this…" etc., until suddenly another question crept in, which went: "What can I learn from it, how can I grow through this?" At once the whole energy around me changed, and I felt like taking the reins to my own life again. I felt Angel Lavinia next to me, and she informed me that I had finally reached the point of daring to step into self-empowerment. I sat up and heard, or rather felt, her say:

"You cannot change any situation, any person in the outer world, but only ever heal the things within yourself. With your last question you have given me the opportunity to help you now and do just this. Look closely at your feelings, your fears and hurts, and then ask me to jointly with you transform these shadows into acceptance."

I knew right away what she meant. During the past years I had been made aware of some of my patterns – like the fear of aging, of being alone, or of the fact that I ascribe more importance to other people than to myself – and yet I had so far successfully managed to push all these shadows aside. Now there was no longer any escape route, and I was faced with only two possibilities: to either hold someone else responsible for my misfortune or to take responsibility for this myself. It was clear to me that the pain I felt was not the pain of being abandoned but the lack of trust that I was OK as a person.

Thus I got on to the couch with Lavinia, still grumbling a bit, and spent several hours every day for two weeks looking closely at myself in order to move, with Lavinia's help, into self-love. Many patterns I was enabled to break through brought new ones to the fore, but step by step it became lighter, and I knew that I was absolutely fine, with or without my shadows. Many of these old themes evaporated within minutes, while others needed a bit longer, and that was fine too.

It might appear somewhat unmanly to admit that I spent about two weeks just crying on the couch, but the strength and new confidence that I drew from these processes spoke for themselves and gave me a hitherto unknown trust in the world; because I was at peace with myself, no matter what happened. It was thrilling to hear the remarkably frequent comments of people around me about how healthy and happy I looked, and their surprise when I told them about the challenges I was currently experiencing.

Meanwhile I have learned to regularly look at my topics with Lavinia and to ask her for help. You really do not need to tackle everything in one go.

ᐸ᠍ᑈ *Reflection* ᐸ᠍ᑈ

I could actually fill several chapters, or even a whole book, on the theme of "shadows" alone. Please really take time over this chapter – it is key to purifying your frequency! That is why it is also longer than any of the other chapters. Now dedicate yourself in particular to the shadow that could perhaps be connected to one of your goals.

Recognize that we all carry everything within us: the most radiating light and the most gloomy darkness, the most wonderful behaviours and the most prohibitive thoughts, which are put into practice often, even if we mostly refuse to believe this.

How often do we judge other people for their behaviour and believe that we are distinctly different? The truth is that we nearly always judge or smile at exactly that which in others mirrors our most adeptly hidden shadow. I can tell you a thing or two about that myself:

I just could not believe how I could no longer recognize some women once they were settled in a relationship, and how they changed from independent, strong women to distressing shadows of themselves. I would never fall into that trap – I was so sure of that! I was, after all, a most autonomous woman, went my own path of becoming a concert pianist with iron discipline, travelled the world by myself, and allowed no man to get in the way of my plans – and then everything changed!

I met a man who I was not even head over heels in love with and who absolutely did not fulfil my expectations. To be honest, I knew from the first moment that he was not at all suited to me, but fate had different plans (as I know now after having looked into our past lives). In any case, he made such an effort in the most beautiful ways: brought me the most gorgeous flowers I had ever received; wrote me tender poems in which he described me as "angel"; lavished attention on me without being intrusive; was always there when I needed anything – all things that I had never before experienced.

Eventually, my piano lecturer warmly suggested I move to a house in the countryside, so that I could practise piano without disturbing anyone, since at that time I was having severe trouble with a tenant in the house I lived in who felt annoyed by my music.

Well, and who wanted to move with me out of beautiful Munich city into a village in the countryside? That was the only place where I could afford a detached house for practising piano in, and only if I moved with another person. Said man, of course, and no one else. So I thought: "Why not? Let's try it out." And the catastrophe began.

At our first encounter I had had quite a strange feeling, which had seriously warned me off this man; but after he had shown his best behaviour I had cast all doubt to the wind.

It became more and more clear that he had serious problems. We were in a never-ending maelstrom of feelings. I would have loved to leave this relationship behind as swiftly as possible, but there was the house that I could not afford by myself, and besides, I had promised that I would walk through thick and thin with him. While I was not married to him, I still wanted to honour my promises – honour them too much.

To cut a long story short, I became co-dependent, lost myself completely, and became a shadow of my former self, which eventually led to my life-threatening illness. I lost the house, the partner, my place for studying in California – and nearly my life! If this was not an extremely well hidden shadow, then what was it?! But through unconditionally facing this shadow I became a person who today speaks with the angels and is allowed to positively transform the lives of many people.

Thanks to Angel Lavinia, these days I usually look into the "mirror" right away if something bothers me about another person, and I gratefully recognize similar traits in myself. It is much easier to confront, accept, and love these shadows with her help.

The angels and particularly Lavinia warmly recommend you do the same as soon as something annoys you. In this way you will lose much less time and energy, since your thoughts will not circle around the behaviour of others for hours, days, or even weeks. Rather, use this time wisely to realize your dreams.

You too can work in this way, with Lavinia, on the shadows mirrored to you by others. The activities below will show you how.

As the great C. G. Jung, the founder of analytical psychology, said so wisely: it is not about being perfect but about becoming whole.

You do not necessarily have to get rid of all your shadows but you need to learn to recognize them, to work with them, and to be at peace with yourself, with as well as without your shadow behaviour; since as long as we are human beings on earth, and no enlightened ones or ascended masters, we will have shadows.

Interestingly, we often see only our so-called negative sides as shadows, but do not acknowledge that those characteristics that we admire so much in other people are also shadows of ourselves. These "light shadows", as best-selling author and shadow expert Debbie Ford affectionately calls them, are parts of your unlived potential and strive towards reaching the surface. Often though, it is more comfortable to adore someone else than to get on with it yourself, and muster the courage and discipline to bring this potential into the world. But more on this later on in the soul journey.

On day 4 of our programme you examined your sleeping, eating, and fitness habits. Today though it is essential to go one step deeper and uncover your shadow habits and behaviours, as these are the ones that sabotage you on the way to your dreams.

If you do not manage to deal with all the reflections on your shadow behaviour in one day, take more time to work through this chapter.

Remember to first create a sacred space for yourself, before you answer the following questions in writing.

Call Angel Lavinia to your side and ask her to accompany you throughout the entire day and to surround you with her transparent green light, so that you are connected to the frequency of healing. Take a deep breath in and out in order to absorb the light, and relax.

- What kind of food fits into your so-called "shadow food" category (e.g. cream cake, a whole bar of chocolate)?
- Are there any triggers that turn you into a "shadow eater"? Which times of day are particularly critical for this shadow behaviour?
- What shadow feelings do you have when you have once again stuffed yourself with this shadow food?

⤳ *Activities for conscious and healthy eating* ⤳

If you like you can have Lavinia surround you once more with her transparent green light in order to renew it. Now ask her to send her transformative platinum-coloured beam into your need for this food, and into your shadow feelings, and then take seven deep breaths. Count to four while breathing in through the nose and then very slowly breathe out through the mouth with an "Aaaah" sound.

Now say, while you tap or massage acupuncture point no. 5 underneath your mouth:

I love and accept myself wholeheartedly with my shadow behaviour with regard to certain foods (you can name them).

Take a deep breath in and out and then speak, while you again tap or massage the point underneath your mouth:

I love and accept myself wholeheartedly without my shadow behaviour with regard to food.

And again, breathe deeply in and out.

Subsequently ban those shadow foods from your home during the twenty-eight-day programme. This does not mean that you should throw everything away; you can give it to a friend to store for you for the duration of the programme.

Now reflect, together with Lavinia, on what you can do instead of the "shadow eating", and write your ideas down. Afterwards, create an intention that you send out into the universe and say (ideally in an enthusiastic voice, coming out of the resonance of your heart). For example:

I send out the intention to from now on dance to my favourite song when anything bothers me.

Then transform this intention into an affirmation, write it on several Post-its and stick them to your fridge and your storage cupboards.

From now on I dance to my favourite song when anything bothers me.

 *Reflection*

If you do not answer the next questions immediately after working on your shadow foods, call Angel Lavinia to your side again and ask her to enfold you in her transparent green light, so that you are connected to the frequency of healing. Take a deep breath in and out in order to absorb the light, and relax.

- What is your shadow behaviour with regard to physical fitness? Do you maybe get up too late in the mornings or prefer to get stuck on your couch in front of the TV in the evenings? Or what else comes to mind for you?
- What shadow feelings do you experience when you once again sabotage your fitness programme?

Answer the questions in writing.

Activities for a healthy exercise regime

You can at any time ask Lavinia again to surround you with her transparent green light in order to renew it. Ask her now to send her transformative platinum-coloured beam into your sabotage behaviour with regard to your fitness regime, and into your shadow feelings, and take seven deep breaths. Count to four while breathing in through the nose and then very slowly breathe out through the mouth with an "Aaaah" sound.

Now say, while you tap or massage acupuncture point no. 5 underneath your mouth:

I love and accept myself wholeheartedly with my shadow behaviour regarding my fitness (you can describe it in more detail if you like).

Take a deep breath in and out and then speak, while you again tap or massage the point underneath your mouth:

I love and accept myself wholeheartedly without my shadow behaviour with regard to my fitness.

And again, breathe deeply in and out.

Now reflect, together with Lavinia, on what you would like to change and write it down. Afterwards create an intention that you send out into the universe and say (ideally in an enthusiastic voice, coming out of the resonance of your heart), for example:

I send out the intention to from now on get up at 5:45 a.m. every day in order to practise half an hour of yoga.

Then transform this intention into an affirmation, write it on a Post-it and, in this case, stick it to your alarm clock and/or place it on your bedside table:

From now on I get up at 5:45 a.m. every day in order to practise half an hour of yoga.

Reflection

If you do not answer the next questions directly after working on the previous section, call Angel Lavinia to your side and ask her to surround you with her transparent green light, so that you are connected to the frequency of healing. Breathe deeply in and out in order to absorb the light, and relax.

- What is your shadow behaviour with regard to money?
- Are you in debt? Do you spend more money than you have available?
- Do you buy things out of frustration or indulge in retail therapy when something in your life does not go smoothly?
- Do you always need to have the most fashionable thing on the market (clothes, car, technical appliances etc.), in order to feel good?
- Do you pay your taxes on time?
- Do you work for cash in hand?
- Do you complain about organic food being expensive but at the same time spend a lot of money in restaurants?
- How much do you tip in a restaurant or in a hotel?
- Are you stingy (with others or yourself)?
- What are your shadow feelings like when looking at this topic?

Answer the questions in writing.

ᴄ❦ *Activities for healthy money handling* ᴄ❦

Remember, you can always ask Lavinia again to surround you with her transparent green light in order to renew it. Ask her now to send her transformative platinum-coloured beam into your sabotage behaviour with regard to money, and into your shadow feelings, and take seven deep breaths. Count to four while breathing in through the nose, and then very slowly breathe out through the mouth with an "Aaaah" sound.

Now say, while you tap or massage acupuncture point no. 5 underneath your mouth:

I love and accept myself wholeheartedly with my shadow behaviour regarding money (you can, of course, describe it in more detail if you like).

Take a deep breath in and out and then speak, while you again tap or massage the point underneath your mouth:

I love and accept myself wholeheartedly without my shadow behaviour with regard to money.

And again, breathe deeply in and out.

Now reflect together with Lavinia on what you would like to change, and write it down. Afterwards create an intention that you send out into the universe and say (ideally in an enthusiastic voice, coming out of the resonance of your heart), for example:

I send out the intention to from now on be generous with my fellow human beings and with myself, since I am a magnet for limitless abundance.

Then transform this intention into an affirmation, write it on a note, and place it in your purse:

From now on I am generous with my fellow human beings and with myself, since I am a magnet for limitless abundance.

Also remember to delete the adjective "expensive" from your vocabulary: If you label goods or services as expensive, other people will find your services expensive too and will not be prepared to pay for them.

Naturally, you can still decide to not spend money on something. There is a huge difference between judging/evaluating and being discerning. When you think or say: "This is too expensive for me!", you instantly do not feel very good because you affirm with this sentence that you lack the financial means. If, however, you use the wording "I would not like to spend any money on that", your frequency does not decrease: you do not judge, but take a decision for yourself.

Bless your invoices and the people whose services you have to pay for. Stick a Post-it with the following affirmation on the folder or filing tray where you keep invoices to be paid:

I love to pay my invoices promptly.

And remember: if you would like to receive more money – in particular when your resources are scarce – it is important, within your means, to wholeheartedly give money to other people who have less than you. This is not about quantity but purely about giving. Thus money keeps flowing.

Never expect to receive anything back from the same people. The more you give without expectation, the more comes back to you, in different ways.

 *Reflection*

If you do not answer the next questions directly after working on the previous section, call Angel Lavinia to your side and ask her to surround you with her transparent green light, so that you are connected to the frequency of healing. Breathe deeply in and out in order to absorb the light, and relax.

- What is your shadow behaviour with regard to relationships?
- Are you selfish and think predominantly about your own needs?
- Or do you do everything expected of you just to make sure that you are loved?
- Do you offer yourself up completely once you are in a relationship, and become easily co-dependent on the other person? Do you always attempt to please your partner, and thereby suppress your own desires?

- Are you sometimes disloyal or unfaithful?
- Do you often keep silent in order to prevent an argument? Do you hide behind your partner?
- What else can you think of?
- What are your shadow feelings when you find yourself displaying relationship shadow behaviour?

Answer the questions in writing.

ᴄ᷉ᴥ᷁ *Activities for healthy relationship behaviour* ᴄ᷉ᴥ᷁

You can always ask Lavinia again to surround you with her transparent green light in order to renew it. Ask her now to send her transformative platinum-coloured beam into your sabotage behaviour with regard to relationships, and into your shadow feelings, and take seven deep breaths. Count to four while breathing in through the nose, and then very slowly breathe out through the mouth with an "Aaaah" sound.

Now say, while you tap or massage acupuncture point no. 5 underneath your mouth:

I love and accept myself wholeheartedly with my shadow behaviour regarding relationships (you can describe it in more detail if you like).

Take a deep breath in and out and then speak, while you again tap or massage the point underneath your mouth:

I love and accept myself wholeheartedly without my shadow behaviour with regard to relationships.

And again, breathe deeply in and out.

Now reflect together with Lavinia what you would like to change and write it down. Afterwards create an intention that you send out into the universe and say (ideally in an enthusiastic voice, coming out of the resonance of your heart), for example:

I send out the intention to from now on lovingly express my truth instead of keeping silent.

Then transform this intention into an affirmation, write it on a Post-it and stick it in a place that you look at regularly, for example on the bathroom mirror or by the phone. If you live with a partner and it is not beneficial that he or she reads the intention, then think about keeping it somewhere else, please.

From now on I lovingly express my truth instead of keeping silent.

Naturally there are more topics that we could examine in a similar way, but then this chapter would get out of hand! Should you have another shadow topic that you would urgently like to work on, you can do it in the same way.

Be aware: should you find yourself – even you have dealt with this chapter – in one of your realized shadow behaviours, there is no reason to be alarmed. Just move with Angel Lavinia through the above activity steps that led to the behaviour.

ᔕᕇ᷍ᕊ *Soul Affirmation* ᔕᕇ᷍ᕊ

First ask Angel Lavinia to enfold you in her transparent green healing energy. Then take a deep breath in and out, before you say (ideally aloud):

From now on I confront my shadows with grace and ease because I know that this way I can be more and more in my power and live my potential. Through loving my shadows they fall behind me and allow me to become whole.

ᔕᕇ᷍ᕊ *Soul Journey* ᔕᕇ᷍ᕊ

Have pen and paper ready before you begin. You might want to take some notes during or directly after your journey.

With your eyes open take a deep breath in, and then slowly exhale while you close your eyes in slow motion and order your brain to automatically move into the Theta state. Breathe deeply in and out, and relax.

Let your thoughts go by like birds flying past. Just let them go and enjoy the sensation of your breath. With each breath you take you move more deeply into a state of relaxation.

See, sense, or imagine how you are being enfolded in the most luminous golden light that you have ever seen. It protects you on all levels and simultaneously connects you with the frequency of love. Enjoy the sensation of feeling the powerful light permeating your whole being and reconnecting you with your divine blueprint.

You find yourself at the foot of a crystalline mountain that shimmers in all colours of the rainbow. You are looking up that mountain, wondering how to reach the summit, when a stunningly graceful angel, immersed in transparent green light, appears by your side. It is Lavinia. She gazes deeply into your eyes and you know that she looks right down to the bottom of your soul. However, you feel completely safe and trust her with all your heart.

She takes you by the hand and rises up into the air with you. The cool breeze is caressing your skin and you feel heavenly when you finally arrive at the summit of the crystalline mountain. An enormous building looms in front of you; it is surrounded by numerous flights of stairs that lead to patios of the most unusual, but breathtakingly beautiful, designs. Lavinia asks you to choose one of the patios and start walking up towards it. Full of joyful expectancy, you climb the stairs by yourself, though without any idea as to what might be waiting for you at the top. As soon as you reach the top step of the staircase you see a wonderful person who, in your everyday life, you have been greatly admiring for some time. He or she steps towards you and greets you with warmth. The two of you start talking with ease, and you realize even more clearly what it is that you value so much about this person.

After a while he/she says goodbye and Lavinia appears in his/her place. She leads you to a marvellous viewing platform and asks you to lie down on a crystalline bed. Once you are settled comfortably she sits to the left of you and speaks in a graceful voice:

"Beloved soul, now turn inside and recognize that all these wonderful attributes are also present within yourself and only wait to be accepted and lived by you. Take your time to look deeply."

You look inside and are surprised at how true Lavinia's words are.

When you finally look at Lavinia again, she holds up a mirror, in which you view yourself living all these attributes.

Enjoy the feeling of being fully connected to your potential and take three deep breaths in order to anchor this in your consciousness.

Now it is up to you to return to the three-dimensional level in order to embody this feeling more and more. You get up from the bed and enjoy the heavenly view one last time before you and Lavinia descend the steps together. You look around once more and, holding Lavinia's hand, take off into the air. Smoothly you glide in spirals back to earth where Lavinia embraces you with her wings and whispers into your ear:

"Have courage! Every day you'll achieve living your potential more fully; every day there is in you more of the light that you have promised to become before your incarnation. I accompany you in deep joy!"

An intense feeling of happiness flows through you since you know that you have moved a big step closer towards your dream of living your potential.

Now connect with Mother Earth beneath you, stretch your limbs in order to fully arrive back in your body and in the here and now, and open your eyes.

Now write down what you have realized. Naturally, you can do this journey as often as you like and meet a different person each time.

LEARN PATIENCE WITH THE SUPPORT OF ARCHANGEL JOPHIEL

*The angels are of ineffable beauty,
and love radiates from their countenance,
their speech, and all details of their life.*

Emanuel Swedenborg

"Greetings, beloved being. I AM Archangel Jophiel. I am delighted to speak to you since your evolution on planet earth is very close to my heart. In these times of change and transformation the ready temptation is to push your spiritual development forward at high speed. Even when it is of enormous importance to increase your vibrational frequency in order to be able to cope with the changes the transformation will bring about, it is truly of even greater importance to be at peace with yourself and not fall prey to stress. This means you need to be patient with yourself and lovingly shut up your inner 'slave driver'. Grant yourself the time to regularly enjoy the beauty of nature: it will show you in a wondrous way that there is no need to force. Every seed that has been sown needs time to develop so

that the plant radiates in full blossom; the same goes for you. While you gaze at nature, contemplate it, and become one with it, internalize the knowledge that all happens in good time, and you will also feel this in your heart. You will learn to be patient with yourself and your path.

Believe me, beloved soul, this will simplify your life enormously and help you to live more and more in the flow, in the Now. There will no longer be any reason to torture your mind with thinking about what you might need to do; with patience, peace will enter your being. If this is what you wish I will do everything in my power to support you hereby in unconditional love."

Archangel Jophiel
angel of beauty, patience, creativity
Aura colour: dark pink, magenta
Crystal: pink tourmaline

Joey, son of Roy Martina and among other things an ANGEL LIFE COACH®, experienced the following with Archangel Jophiel:

Surprising turn

As far as I remember it was spring when I could finally travel home again from Europe to see my mother, my brother, my friends, and my dog. I was booked on a flight from Amsterdam to West Palm Beach (Florida), and everything seemed to go according to plan. Since I was a special member of the airline, KLM, I was one of the first ones to board the plane. I was booked in to the middle seat in row 20. After all special members had boarded, all the other passengers came on board; first quite a big man who sat to my left and told me that he came from India. I had nothing against the man but he spread such an intense body odour that I felt anything but comfortable.

At this point, even before all the passengers had boarded, the captain announced a delay of fifteen minutes.

Then a second man, who was even bigger than the first one, so that he had to have two seats, sat down next to me. For some reason this man leaned towards me instead of using the extra seat. Again I felt the urgent desire to do something but I had no idea what.

Suddenly I heard a subtle voice, almost as if someone were whispering behind me: "Just wait."

Before I had time to question the message further, the captain announced that, due to problems, our departure would be delayed further – by one hour. More and more passengers started to grumble.

At this point, the smell of the man to my left and being wedged in by the man on my right started to really get on my nerves. I noticed how many passengers were bombarding the flight attendants with questions about more space and the one spare seat in first class. Our section of the plane was pretty crowded, and the contents of the luggage compartments above the seats were spilling over. The passengers became more and more annoyed and complained more and more.

About half an hour later, I was just about to ask one of the flight attendants whether I could take that seat in first class – I was, after all, a special member – when I suddenly started coughing hard. A flight attendant walked by my seat, but due to the coughing I wasn't able to stop her.

When I had finally recovered from my coughing fit I again heard a whisper: "Just wait."

Within five minutes the very smelly man to my left was allocated a seat at the exit, and I started to feel a sense of freedom. Then another man sat down in the spare seat next to me – and he was as big as the man on my right side. Again I was completely wedged in.

At the same time the captain "delighted" us with further news, namely that we would not take off for at least another two hours, since two members of the crew were missing.

As nothing else was going to happen in the next two hours, I decided and somehow managed to go to sleep.

About five minutes before we eventually made our take-off, a flight attendant woke me up to ask: "Would you like the seat in first class?"

Naturally I said yes and made my way to the luxurious first class cabin. At the next opportunity I asked the flight attendant: "Why did you choose me for this seat?"

She replied: "Because you're the only special member who has not asked for it!"

Thinking about this, I suddenly realized that the whispering voice was no one else but "my special friend" Archangel Jophiel. With her words she made me be patient and wait. The seat in first class was the result!

Reflection

Over the past five days you have worked on yourself intensively and maybe been surprised many a time as to how many "interior nooks" there still are to be examined, even though you have already worked so much on yourself. This is normal: the deeper you go, the more you discover. Our life topics resemble an onion: as soon as we have peeled off one layer, the next one appears. We think we have dealt with a topic and here we go meeting the next layer. However, as already explained in the "Lavinia" chapter, we do not need to get rid of all of our shadows – as long as we are not ascended masters on earth we will have to go on learning soul lessons – but we are supposed to be at peace with ourselves. That is why today the aim is to spend time with yourself in peace and to continue the process in a gentle way.

✑ Activities for today ✑

✑ Go into nature

Go out into nature, call Archangel Jophiel to your side, and open up to the beauty of your surroundings. Go for a walk or sit down in a meadow or on a bench (if the weather allows), and gaze at grass, flowers, bushes, and trees. Connect yourself with their energy, feel the inherent healing power of it, and enjoy.

✑ Plant your seeds

When you return, create yourself a sacred space. Ask Jophiel to enfold you in her dark pink and magenta-coloured light, and plant the seeds that you bought before the start of the transformation journey, as a symbol of the divine schedule of your own growth. Put the flowerpot on your altar or in another place that feels meaningful to you.

✑ Let go and relax

Allow yourself to do nothing, or to do something that your soul desires.

✑ Write down all you have already accomplished

Again create a sacred space and ask Jophiel to surround you with her dark pink and magenta-coloured light. Take a deep breath in and out, and consider everything you have already accomplished; with all your human eagerness, it is natural that you will forget this often. Then write about your progress in your notebook.

✑ Activities when stressed

Take four deep breaths. Count to four while breathing in through the nose, and then very slowly breathe out through the mouth with an "Aaaah" sound.

Ask Archangel Jophiel to envelop you in her dark pink and magenta-coloured light. Say (ideally aloud) while you tap or massage acupuncture point no. 4 underneath your nose (see page 58):

I love and accept myself wholeheartedly with my stress (you can describe it in more detail if you like).

Take a deep breath in and out and then speak again, while you tap or massage the point underneath your nose:

I love and accept myself wholeheartedly with my patience, my ease, and my relaxation.

And again, breathe deeply in and out.

Soul Affirmation

First ask Archangel Jophiel to enfold you in her dark pink and magenta-coloured light. Then take a deep breath in and out, before you say (ideally aloud):

I am patient with myself because deep in my heart is the certainty that everything happens at the right time. I allow myself to pause on my path of growth in order to radiate in peace.

Soul Journey

Have pen and paper ready before you begin. You might want to take some notes during or directly after your journey.

With your eyes open take a deep breath in, and then slowly exhale while you close your eyes in slow motion and order your brain to automatically move into the Theta state. Breathe deeply in and out, and relax.

Let your thoughts go by like birds flying past. Just let them go and enjoy feeling your breath that continually connects you with the breath of God and nourishes you. With each breath you take you move further into a state of deep relaxation.

All at once, you realize that you are in a magnificent garden, like paradise. Full of awe you look around at the exotic flowers in all colours of the rainbow, whose shape, radiance, and aroma completely mesmerize you. You have never before seen anything like them.

Then a squirrel bounds gracefully up to your feet and looks at you with innocent eyes in a way that warms your heart; he radiates such love and trust. Eventually he turns and starts to run ahead. You have a sense that he wants you to follow, so you walk after him until he stops in front of a huge, ancient tree that emanates an incredible magic. You look at the tree and sense right away the power and wisdom it radiates. You lean your back on the trunk and connect with the tree, and very soon you become aware of an intense vibration within yourself; the tree does not only relieve you of old burdens but also activates old knowledge in your DNS. Breathe deeply in and out while you note how your energy level rises and you start to feel more and more powerful.

Then an angel of breathtaking beauty appears next to you. It is Archangel Jophiel. Without words she embraces you with her wings and envelops you in her magenta light. It feels as though you are inside a cocoon of unconditional love and comfort. A wonderful feeling!

Now Jophiel's gracious voice sounds at your ear:

"Beloved being, stop twisting your beautiful mind by again and again reproaching yourself for not being quick enough. This is utterly useless and does not serve you in any way, since the ways of nature are different. Just look at this magical tree in front of you. Do you think it has developed as much as that within a few months or years? Not at all. It is much the same with you, beloved soul. It takes a certain amount of time to develop into that radiant being that you would so love to become as quickly as possible. Even the best seeds need care and patience to grow into something wonderful. Do you understand now that you do not need to push yourself beyond measure? Be patient with yourself and your path, and miracles will manifest in front of you."

Immensely comforted, you look at her as she presents you with an enormous book. It is the book of your life. As you leaf through the pages you suddenly realize how much you have already accomplished in this life, and a deep feeling of gratitude starts to flow through your whole being. Joyously you embrace Jophiel, who is overjoyed because you have truly understood how important patience is for you and for your life. Thank her and your two new friends, the tree and the squirrel – who has observed everything with his loving eyes.

Now take three deep breaths in order to anchor deeply within you all you have experienced. Reconnect with the earth underneath your feet, stretch your limbs in order to feel your body, and, when you are ready, slowly open your eyes.

✦ ✦ *Day 7* ✦ ✦

HEAL YOUR INNER CHILD
WITH ARCHANGEL GABRIEL

Let the angels wake with us,
That we may laugh like children,
That we may cry like children,
Let us be all, nothing appear to be.

Clemens von Brentano

"Greetings, beloved being. I AM Archangel Gabriel. Countless people, just like you, have in their childhood been hurt by their parents, tutors, teachers, classmates, and others. Due to this some of your zest for life has vanished, since your original enthusiasm has given way to a certain amount of distrust. You show this not only towards others but also towards yourself because, more than anything else, you want to protect your inner child from further disappointments and traumas.

But only when you heal your inner child, and your divine laugh adorns your countenance again, will you be able to become the radiating being that you truly are.

Thus take time and listen to the needs of your inner child. Attempt to fulfil

72

them in such a way that it can heal with grace, lightness, and joy. I am delighted to help you with this!"

Archangel Gabriel

messenger angel, support angel for the inner child and all children
Aura colour: white, golden-white and coppery
Crystal: citrine (yellow quartz)

Florian, a friend of mine who among other things is also an ANGEL LIFE COACH®, experienced a wonderful healing of his inner child:

Gabriel by my side

After an amazing healing that I received with Isabelle's support I began to believe in angels, who before this I had considered to be just another fairytale. Thus I started working with the angels myself. When the following happened I had just turned twenty-three and had been working with angels for about six months. Every morning I drew an angel card for the day. For the third time within three days I drew the card for Archangel Gabriel; it appeared that the messages of the preceding two days had not been complete and that there was a deeper message within I needed to discover.

When I connected with Gabriel's frequency on this third day, I felt her much more strongly than before. I also saw her much more distinctly than before. Thus I knew that I had to listen even more attentively.

While I linked in more deeply, I heard her voice for the first time, loud and clear: "I would like to work with you every day for three weeks."

It was up to me whether or not I wanted this. Since I understood what she wanted to help me with, namely my conflicts from childhood onwards so that I could come to terms with my inner child, I agreed to her offer.

As a small boy I had many social fears and suppressed many of my feelings. Everyone knew me as a sweet boy but the truth was that I was afraid to say what I wanted to say, and to stand up for my convictions and wishes. Instead of directing my own life I followed other people's wishes.

Archangel Gabriel wanted to dissolve these conflicts that were in my system, so that I would not only be able to connect with my true inner strength but also express these with my voice.

From this day onwards, I began to work with Gabriel for a few minutes every morning. She guided me to my inner strength and showed me what caused my inherent power to be held back. While we continued to work she helped me to balance my energies in my body, so that this inner strength found its way to my voice. Gabriel explained to me how to express my truth, how to set boundaries in a neutral way, and how to put my inherent power into words.

All this happened through me feeling her energy, which led me to my weaknesses, limiting beliefs, and suppressed emotions. There were times when tears rose up, but by the end I always felt pure joy and happiness.

Within three weeks I was able to express so many more emotions than before. In addition, I was able to impart suppressed emotions in a neutral way to the people around me, as I was now more myself in their presence.

Due to this healing of my inner child I am now able to pursue my path even better without worrying what other people might think about me. I am also now able to express myself better, as I am no longer afraid to be judged. On top of this, I am much more congruent with my words and feelings, which is apparent in the fact that I am much more honest with the people around me.

I am very grateful for this experience since I know that it has made me into a happier and more loving person.

⁓ Activities for today and for the future ⁓

⁓ Experience the wishes of your inner child

Create a sacred space, call Archangel Gabriel to your side, and ask her to surround you with her white-golden light. Breathe deeply in and out, before you start a silent dialogue with your inner child.

Ask what needs and wishes it has and write them down.

⁓ Put your inner child's needs and wishes into practice

Whatever you have learned from your inner child, put it into action bit by bit.

My inner child reacted very enthusiastically when I bought an "energy bear" for myself. Originally, I had chosen him during my recuperation time in order to facilitate bringing my organs' energies into a smoother flow. As well as this effect, though, it is also nice to observe how my inner child loves to take this bear along on all journeys.

⁓ Do something playful

Do something that your inner child loves: for example go on a swing, play football, paint, mould something from plasticine, make pottery...

ᒐᕊ Recognize with the help of Archangel Gabriel what needs healing

Create a sacred space for this too. Call Archangel Gabriel to your side and ask her to envelop you in her white-golden light. Take a deep breath in and out, in order to fully absorb the light.

Now connect with your inner child and ask it to show you where it still feels hurt.

Write down what you are aware of. Sometimes healing starts to happen simply through getting the hurts off your chest by writing them down.

You can ask Archangel Gabriel to start the healing at this point, or do it in the next step.

ᒐᕊ Allow Archangel Gabriel to heal your inner child

Before you go to bed ask Archangel Gabriel to work with your inner child overnight, and to heal it. This is particularly effective because during sleep you are freed of your ego and thus cannot have any doubts about whether it will be successful.

If there is much to heal it might be a good idea to repeat this over several nights.

For this purpose, you can of course also use the soul journey below.

ᒐᕊ Soul Affirmation ᒐᕊ

First ask Archangel Gabriel to enfold you in her white-golden light. Then take a deep breath in and out, before you say (ideally aloud):

I listen to my inner child and recognize his/her needs. Through doing this I recognize how I may heal with grace, lightness, and joy.

ᒐᕊ Soul Journey ᒐᕊ

Have pen and paper ready before you begin. You might want to take some notes during or directly after your journey.

With your eyes open take a deep breath in, and then slowly exhale while you close your eyes in slow motion and order your brain to automatically move into the Theta state. Breathe deeply in and out, and relax. Let your thoughts go by like leaves gliding along a river and do not hold on to them. Just let them go and move into a state of even deeper relaxation. Take pleasure in feeling how your breath flows through your body and nourishes you.

With each breath you take, relax more and more deeply.

Feel, see, or imagine a luminous golden light pervading you; this instantly links you to the frequency of love. Feel how this wonderful light arrives in each single cell of your body, so that they all start to vibrate, hum, sing, and maybe even dance in the rhythm of love as they are reconnected with your divine blueprint.

A wonderful landscape appears ahead of you, giving way to a kind of enchanted forest. You gaze at it with big eyes and simply cannot get enough of the view. Suddenly you become aware of a delicate squirrel in front of your feet. He looks at you with such trusting eyes that your heart is very touched. You bend down to the animal and detect, not far from him, a bright white rabbit that observes you with the same affectionate eyes. It hops towards you and sits next to the squirrel. Bit by bit more and more animals gather around you, and now you also start to become aware of all the fairies that hover gracefully above the animals. It is an enchanted picture that has your inner child beaming with joy.

Then a radiant angel appears by your side. It is no other than Archangel Gabriel, surrounded by a bright yellow-golden aura. She gazes at you seated in between all the fairies and animals and smiles with joy.

After a while she touches your shoulder and says to you in her resonant voice:

"Beloved being, would you like to come along to a protected place, so that I can heal your inner child?"

There is nothing you would rather do! You are on your feet right away. Followed by the whole host of animals and fairies, you accompany Archangel Gabriel into the enchanted forest. Old, familiar, and beautiful memories of childhood well up in you as Gabriel leads you through the woods towards a bright golden pavilion, in front of which a dainty water fountain splashes cheerfully.

The animals assemble at the door of the pavilion, just as if they want to protect you while you receive healing from Archangel Gabriel inside. Their faithfulness touches you greatly and makes you smile.

Gabriel motions for you to enter the protected place with her. A beautiful room that makes your child's soul rejoice opens in front of you. Full of joy, you dance through the space until Gabriel asks you to lie down on a golden divan. As soon as you lie down you again hear her loving voice:

"Beloved child, I will now relieve you of the old memories and traumas of your inner child, so that your child's soul can be restored and return to being completely happy."

Just as she has promised, she very gently dissolves everything out of all your chakras and the whole of your being. You feel laughter bubbling up in-

side you until you finally laugh joyfully, as hard as you can; your inner child has been released.

Enthusiastically you jump up from the divan and fling your arms around Archangel Gabriel's neck, whereupon she tenderly pulls you towards her.

Eventually you leave the pavilion to run to your friends, the animals and the fairies that await you expectantly and begin to dance a jig around you as they see you looking so radiant. A wonderful feeling! How beautiful life is!

Then you discover a huge swing – and right away you sit on it and swing, full of enthusiasm, into your new life.

When you finally have firm ground underneath your feet again it is time to return to the here and now. Have a stretch, with all your heart, and slowly return fully into your body, the temple of your soul, by taking deep breaths in and out. Open your eyes once you are ready.

Day 8

RECOGNIZE THE SOUL LESSONS IN YOUR RELATIONSHIPS WITH THE HELP OF ANGEL MIHR

Love is a pair of wings
That God has given to the soul
In order to ascend to him.

Michelangelo Buonarotti

"Greetings, beloved soul. I AM Angel Mihr. I would very much like to acquaint you with the fact that every relationship in your life serves a higher purpose. On the soul level you have drawn every single one of your relationships to you. You might find this difficult to believe, but this is the case, whether it concerns wonderful or painful, pleasant or unpleasant relationships. Every single one of your relationships teaches you something that is indispensable for your inner growth.

It is also a fact that you have chosen all this on the higher levels before you arrived on this earth, because your highest wish is to surpass yourself by getting the lessons of the world over with. Only then will you be able to ascend, just as is your higher purpose.

When you know this in the depths of your heart, you will learn to free yourself

78

of being a victim and to recognize the gifts that are hidden in each ever-so-painful relationship or the tragic ending of each heavenly relationship. And not only this: even in the most loving relationships there is something for you to recognize and to learn.

Thus I ask you from now on to view your connections with other people with fresh eyes; every single one of these people is a teacher for you and your life – the 'good' ones as well as the 'bad' ones.

It is my biggest desire to be allowed to support you with this at every moment and in all circumstances, so that you may recognize and learn your soul lessons full of grace and ease. But I am only able to do so, beloved being, if you ask me to."

Angel Mihr
angel of relationships
Aura colour: dark green
Crystal: aventurine

Susanne, a former client of mine, came to know in one go the soul lessons from all of her difficult relationships:

With Mihr into a new life

After some positive experiences with the helpful support of the angels, I had enthusiastically agreed to organize in Germany a seminar for the American representative of a product that I sell here in Europe.

"No problem," I thought, "there are enough customers and interested people here, this is going to be a sensational success!"

The only downside was that the German manufacturer wished to cooperate with the Austrian competitor, who aggressively pushed into the market and perceived me as a threat. Austria was supposed to host a seminar too. For the sake of peace I agreed, offered my cooperation in a very friendly manner, and entrusted Raguel to not only attend to my extremely difficult private relationship with a self-righteous partner but to also arrange for harmonious cooperation with the Austrians, who more or less explicitly disapproved of collaborating with me as competitor. Well. I remained optimistic and trusting.

Then the first shock (Act 1): even though after a provisional enquiry two months before, nearly forty people had expressed interest in the seminar, now no one registered. For two weeks nothing happened. No enquiries, no orders. Had I died and not realized?

Lucky for me, Cultus Animi® Radio once again ran Isabelle's radio show Angel

---

Messages. The topic was "The Essence of Miracles". This was exactly what I needed! I wrote an email and was actually put on air. Apparently the angels had not given up on me – Isabelle worked with me and confirmed that another send-out of promotional cards to all customers in the coming week after full moon would be a very good idea. In addition, I was supposed to relax and work on being all right with any outcome, in order to remove the pressure and stress from the issue. I arranged for the cards to go out the day after full moon. I was feeling very relaxed and looking forward to many registrations.

The days went by – no registrations, no enquiries. My stress level increased. "Hello, angels! Where are you – are you on holiday? What is happening here?" I thought. Eventually, though, I understood. I was supposed to be relaxed with regard to any outcome!

I cancelled the seminar. The attempt was a flop – but really it was a success: for the first time in my life I did not feel guilty. Under the circumstances I had done the best I could. Instead of hiding in a hole I phoned the Americans and openly talked about everything that I had found dissonant and frustrating in the course of the preparations for the seminar. I did so without reproach but also without feelings of guilt or shame.

The result: closer cooperation and the promise of more support from America. A complete success! But the angels were planning more…

The second shock (Act 2): The Austrians had noticed an error in my publicity for the seminar: I had, by mistake, quoted 5 per cent too much discount for the product sale during the seminar. Rather than contacting me they wrote a long email to the manufacturer, full of financial claims, name-calling, and allegations, which found their dramatic culmination in threatening legal action. The manufacturer was not amused and contacted me instantly. After brief indignation I quickly calmed down and requested to be able to solve the conflict with the Austrians via phone in a friendly way. By now I trusted the angels so much that I was feeling increasingly more courageous.

The talk with the competitor resembled a bad theatre performance. My apology and the offer of a quick correction that I would pay for was not only met by rejection but also by the aggression and allegations beyond any common sense. I had asked for help from all of my angel friends beforehand, so I remained (mostly) calm and we managed some kind of conversation.

Then came the third shock (Act 3): when after the phone call it slowly dawned on me what I had just experienced, I had a physical collapse. Shivering, I took a hot saline bath to flush out the acute stress and did everything else necessary. I had enough know-how about the physiological sequences of trauma and shock to understand how to get through a typical three-day process. On the second day, I was lying in the sun on the balcony, staring nearly hypnotized at the dark green [aura colour of Mihr] fir trees on the other side of the road, and asking myself: "What is this for? Is there another lesson apart from the one that I am not supposed to get stuck in shock but observe it while living it?"

Suddenly it was as if I was hit by lightning: my father, my partner, the Austrian competitors. Exactly the same relationship pattern throughout my whole life. The male aggressors who make a mountain out of a molehill to their own advantage and in order to increase their power over me, the "poor" victim, who provoked the aggressors and gets knocked down for it. Guilt, depression, a sense of inferiority. Well, under such circumstances you cannot become strong, confident and successful in the long run. Or, phrased differently: the masochist has found the necessary sadists. Stalemate. Rien ne va plus. Brilliant!

I continued staring at the fir trees and suddenly knew: Mihr had done his work well. I had been so focused on the problems with my partner and the help from Raguel that I had missed the bigger picture. Luckily I had asked for general help and now Mihr, the angel of relationships, had taken over. Weeping with gratitude, I understood the drama of the decades past on a much higher level than ever before. My deep wounds from painful relationships were finally allowed to heal. I learned that I no longer need to provoke anyone into becoming aggressive so I can remain as the victim. Now I am free to experience a self-determined life and harmonious relationships!

Epilogue: On day four I felt clearer than ever before. I clarified the legal situation with regard to the typo, informed the manufacturer, and offered a simple solution to the problem. All the demands and threats by the competitors were now completely untenable and the ball was now in the manufacturer's court; they still had to speak to the Austrians.

Permeated with an entirely new strength, I was ready to keep my integrity and if need be break off all business relations if I was asked to make even the smallest concession. Over the previous weeks I had understood enough to know that I could completely surrender the decision.

A few hours later the scare was over. As in a miracle, the manufacturer had come to an entirely new strength and clarity, refused everything, and my simple solution was implemented. Our business and friendship relationship has now reached a completely new level of harmony.

Reflection

Every single one of our relationships serves our growth. We are always and everywhere teacher and pupil at the same time.

For exactly this reason it is so important to view our relationships from this angle, so we can recognize our lessons sooner. In order to also accept and learn them we need to understand that we not only have chosen these soul lessons for our growth, but also that our so-called "challengers" have made themselves available on a higher level – and indeed out of love (!) –, so that we learn what we have resolved to learn in this life.

The book *The Journey Home* by Lee Carroll and Kryon very vividly explains exactly this in the form of a parable featuring seven angelic beings.

Activities for today

Recognize the soul lessons within your relationships

Remember to first create a sacred space for yourself before you start answering the following questions in writing.

Call Angel Mihr to your side and ask him to accompany you throughout the whole day. Also ask him to envelop you in his dark green light, so that you are connected to the frequency of healing. Take a deep breath in and out in order to absorb the light, and relax.

Now think about the relationships in your life:

- Is there a relationship pattern that runs like a common thread through several relationships?
- Are there different patterns in your personal and professional life, your love life, and your family relationships? Or does the same common thread run through all your relationships?

Once you have recognized the patterns try, together with Angel Mihr, to trace the soul lessons that hide behind them. Write these down too.

Learn to trust

Ponder whether or not you find it easy to trust others. If not, then consider in which parts of your life you do not trust yourself. As long as you do not trust yourself you also mistrust other people, and the process of life. However, as you know, you create a big part of your reality with your thoughts and beliefs. That is why it is so important to learn to trust.

When you are conscious that your whole essence is light and love (and that is the truth!), there is every reason to trust yourself. This is the same for every other person too, because their essence also consists of nothing other than light and love. Of course this does not mean that you should blindly trust others, but that you should follow your intuition. I personally prefer to trust once too often rather than not meet a wonderful person because of fear.

Since by this point you are aware that you have drawn every person you know into your life at least on the soul level, you can start trusting again because everything was and is your choice, which you have made in order to grow.

Only by trusting do you create the resonance to attract wonderful, reliable people, and experience heavenly relationships in every form.
More on the topic of "trust" in day 13.

⤫ Soul Affirmation ⤬

First ask Angel Mihr to enfold you in his dark green light. Then take a deep breath in and out, before you say (ideally aloud):

I recognize the soul lessons in my relationships with grace and ease. I learn them in the same way and create for myself harmonious relationships on all levels.

⤫ Soul Journey ⤬

Have pen and paper ready before you begin. You might want to take some notes during or directly after your journey.

With your eyes open take a deep breath in, and then slowly exhale while you close your eyes in slow motion and order your brain to automatically move into the Theta state. Breathe deeply in and out, and relax. Let your thoughts go by like birds flying past. Just let them go and enjoy feeling your breath that continually connects you with the breath of God and the energy of the angels. With each breath you take you move further into a state of deep relaxation.

You find yourself in the middle of an ancient enchanted forest and are surrounded by huge fir trees that sway gently in the wind. Listen to the rustling of the treetops and feel the warm sunbeams, glimmering through the branches, on your face. Not far away you now discover a graceful doe. She looks at you with profound eyes full of love, so that your heart wells up with warmth.

Slowly you move towards the doe, who turns round as if indicating that you should follow. Expectantly you walk behind her through the magical woods, until you reach a clearing where stands a magnificent golden castle that shimmers with the colours of the sunset. As you approach the castle an exquisite angel bathed in deep dark-green colours appears on the steps to the gateway. It is Angel Mihr. He welcomes you with open arms of such unconditional love that you instantly feel yourself to be in wonderful hands. You sense how your heart opens further and further as his dark-green light starts flowing through your aura.

Then he opens the grand entrance door of the castle and you step into a breathtakingly beautiful, sacred hall, in the middle of which stands a huge round table. Mihr escorts you to a chair at the table and asks you to take a seat. He stands behind you and heals your heart with his dark-green light full of grace and lightness, so that your heart chakra shines more and more. While standing behind you he speaks to you:

"Beloved soul, now it is time to examine the relationships in your life on a deeper level."

Gradually the chairs at the table fill with various people from your life. You recognize family members, lovers and business partners, friends, and acquaintances.

And again Mihr's warm loving voice sounds behind you:

"Now look around and recognize one by one the soul lessons these people have bestowed upon you."

Remember to keep breathing deeply in and out.

Once more Mihr's voice sounds:

"When all soul lessons have revealed themselves, give heartfelt thanks to all the people at your table, since they have made themselves available to you on a higher level so that you may grow in such a way as you have resolved to do in this life."

Take the chance to thank every single person in peace.

When you have expressed your gratitude it is time to leave the sacred hall again. Together with Angel Mihr you leave the golden castle and step out into dusk, which appears absolutely beautiful to you as you now feel light of heart. Enjoy it and once more breathe deeply to anchor within what you have just experienced.

Now connect again with Mother Earth; feel the roots underneath your feet reaching down to the centre of the earth. Stretch your body and slowly open your eyes.

Now write down the soul lessons that you have recognized and perhaps already learned.

Day 9

RETRIEVE YOUR SOUL PARTS WITH ARCHANGEL MICHAEL

Pain is a holy angel;
through him men have become greater
than through all the joys in the world.

Adalbert Stifter

"Greetings, beloved being. I AM Archangel Michael. Every time in your life you
have received deep emotional wounds and the pain has been more than you could
bear, some parts of yourself have taken their leave from you. This is the reason
why you may ask yourself time and again: "Why is it that I do not feel complete?"

This does not by any means have to stay the same, though, since the power of
love and of the angels can transform everything. Your only task is to face your
hurts and to understand that it is they that have been the greatest influences on
your way, and which have allowed you to grow into the person that you are today.
Believe me, beloved being, we on the higher levels deeply honour you for that!

Now though it is down to me to help you retrieve your lost soul parts. You only
have to ask me to bring them back to you and I will joyfully hasten to do so.

Always remember, the truly great things happen in sacred simplicity, and it is the same with this one. To this effect, I now envelop you in my dark-blue coat of heavenly protection in anticipation of your requests."

Archangel Michael
greatest angel of protection
Aura colour: royal blue, violet, golden
Crystal: Sugilite

Roy Martina has provided me with this very personal story about himself, which shows beautifully how Archangel Michael arranges for soul parts to return:

Healing of the soul

Archangel Michael is my personal bodyguard and friend. I was born on 29 September, the so-called Day of Michael, and for that reason my second name is Michael. My mother has always told me that I should trust in Archangel Michael, and that I was a special child as I had the best guardian angel of all. As she repeated this so often I started to pray to Michael when I felt bad or was confronted with big challenges or traumatic experiences.

The severest challenge of my life has been my divorce from my wife, thirteen years ago. She is a woman who I still love to this day; but living with her did not work for me. She cared for our two sons while I travelled and taught all over the world. When I came home after my workshops, though, we fought with each other time and again: she wanted me to spend more time at home and tried to get me to open a practice, work five days a week, and have time for the family at the weekends. Her ideas were great and they were based on her concept of what a family should look like. My problem was that through working in a practice I had twice ended up with terrible burnout because I was getting too stressed out. For that reason I did absolutely not want to return to that kind of career. Thus we were constantly arguing – at least, on the ten days per month that I spent at home. I was not able to cope any longer. Also, I no longer had a safe space where I could share my successes and my challenges with someone else.

It got so bad that, although I would arrive home from my journeys tired and jet-lagged, after two weeks at home I would feel even more tired. In order to save myself from burning out for a third time, I asked my wife for the divorce. This was the most painful moment of my life: I felt a complete failure. The family that I felt responsible for and that I loved had destroyed my health.

Erica and I agreed that I should take a year's break and live in an apartment. Over this year I became more and more depressed and felt worse than ever before. I was completely torn between the love I felt towards my family and my attempt to save myself from a further physical collapse. I saw no solution, since both ways seemed to me to mean complete failure. Besides, Erica and I were arguing fiercely about what each of us should get in the divorce. This caused much anger, bitterness and frustration for both of us and seemed like a never-ending struggle.

One night, when I was close to falling asleep, I was suddenly visited by Archangel Michael. It was like a dream, but I knew I was not yet asleep. He told me that divorce would be the right decision at this point and that it had been part of the plan from the beginning, since it contributed to both of our soul journeys and healing.

"Don't be afraid. All will be well. With time, Erica will find someone else who loves her and wants to share his life with her, and you too will find someone who loves you and will be with you. Now, however, it is time to cut through the karmic connections that bind you two to each other. These are why you cannot let go and suffer so much."

The next moment he was holding a blue sword of flames in his hand, and I saw a vision of Erica: she stood in front of me and we were connected by thousands of wires. One was rusty and as thick as the trunk of an elephant, and linked our hearts to each other. There was no energy flowing to and fro. Michael declared that our heart connection had dried up because of the bitterness and conflict, and that by this point we were exchanging only negative energy. With a quick, subtle movement he severed this connection and all the other energetic bonds between us. Then he spoke the words:

"You have to forgive Erica and ask her for forgiveness, otherwise new negative energetic cords will manifest themselves. I shall return tomorrow and finish my work."

Then it was abruptly quiet again and I "woke up" from my dreamlike state. I began to cry and felt at the same time relieved and sad. Alone, I performed a long forgiveness ceremony for Erica, until I could again feel love for her and respect for what she desired as a mother. I also recognized her wisdom, and understood her pain: she had lost her own mother very early on and now wanted to give more to our children than she had received herself. In the ceremony I also asked Erica for forgiveness for my decision to leave her.

Then I fell into a deep sleep and dreamed that some of my soul parts started returning: I saw that my heart had some parts left behind because of the pain with regard to my mother, Erica, and my children. At this moment, I understood that these were parts of myself, and my body was instantly flooded by a new energy.

Later, just before dawn, I dreamed that Archangel Michael returned and once again severed the heart connection between Erica and me that had developed again. Afterwards, a new pulsating connection full of golden energy emerged into the space between us.

After this experience the energy between Erica and me changed, and the divorce proceedings went smoothly. We solved our conflicts peacefully and found the best solutions for our two boys, so that they would not have to suffer from our separation. We have created a strong base for staying friends until the end of our lives. Twelve years later, I can now say that we are really good friends, trust each other one hundred per cent, and care for each other.

Reflection

Every time you have been wounded on the soul level, some of your soul parts have gone missing. With traumas or in situations that remind you of them, your ego strongly makes itself felt, not because the situations are necessarily so bad but because it wants to protect you – a so-called self-protection mechanism.

However, only if you see through this can you stop condemning your ego and fighting against it. Then you will be able to accept it as it is and move more and more towards healing your duality.

Activities for today and for the future

Watch the "Ultimate Ego Show" (inspired by Colette Baron-Reid)

This visualization exercise is fantastic for demonstrating to your ego that you fully accept it. As you know, this is the best way to weaken the influence of your ego. If, on the other hand, you fight against it, it only becomes stronger.

Set out to visit a truly beautiful old theatre. Even from afar you see it shining in the exquisite brilliance of the evening sun. Eventually you reach the theatre and see a huge poster with the following inscription in golden lettering: "The Ultimate Show of My Ego."

Curious, you open the grand entrance door and arrive in the foyer, which is decorated with fragrant white lilies. Since there is no one there apart from yourself you progress into the auditorium, which is equally deserted. You look for the best seat available and are getting comfortable when the velvet curtain is raised and a very special character, your ego, appears on stage.

While watching it, remember that this is only a show and you are a neutral observer. In whatever way your ego appears, it is perfect. Don't think about it any further but just observe. This is very important!

Now your ego starts to move in adventurous ways; it wants to release everything that you have ever suppressed. Let it romp, dance, sing, scream etc., and always remember that you are merely a neutral spectator who is amusing himself with an interesting show.

After your ego has got rid of everything you move towards the stage, walk up the steps, and embrace the ego exactly as you would do with a small child. While you hold it in your arms, you say to it "I accept you exactly the way you are." And if you are able to do this, add: "And I love you just the way you are."

In this way you convey to your ego that it is not a troublemaker in your life; thus it will start to leave you when this is what you wish for.

Now it is time to rock your ego to sleep like a baby. When it has fallen asleep in your arms you can either take it off-stage to the green room, just like a great artist, and put it down there to sleep, or leave the theatre with it and place it very gently on the grass under a tree. Do whatever feels right to you.

Do this exercise whenever your ego has to release something. Afterwards you will instantly feel freer.

ᘓᘉ Send your ego out "to play"

When Doreen Virtue asked us participants in her mediumship class: "What do you do in order to get rid of your ego?", my husband, who is rather practical, answered: "I send my ego to the beach with Archangel Michael."

Doreen loved this so much that she used this image the very next day in order to relieve us of our egos.

Naturally, you can send your ego to a different place with Michael – as long as it has fun at this place. This makes it much easier for you to connect with your higher self.

ᘓᘉ Allow Archangel Michael to retrieve your soul parts

Before you go to sleep, ask Archangel Michael to bring back your lost soul parts during the night. This is particularly effective as, while you sleep, you are freed from your ego and thus cannot entertain any doubts about whether or not it works.

When there is a lot of healing to be done, it is advisable to repeat this exercise over several nights. You can of course also use the soul journey that I have channelled.

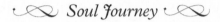 *Soul Affirmation*

First ask Archangel Michael to enfold you in his violet-royal blue-golden light. Then take a deep breath in and out, before you say (ideally aloud):

Through facing my hurts I can heal them and retrieve all my soul parts.

Soul Journey

Have pen and paper ready before you begin. You might want to take some notes during or directly after your journey.

With your eyes open take a deep breath in, and then slowly exhale while you close your eyes in slow motion and order your brain to automatically move into the Theta state. Breathe deeply in and out, and relax. Let your thoughts go by like birds flying past. Just let them go and enjoy feeling your breath that continually connects you with the breath of God and nourishes you. With each breath you take you move further into a state of deep relaxation.

Sense, see, or imagine how you are enfolded in a cocoon of bright silvery-golden light that protects you on all levels. You feel entirely safe and secure as you realize that you are in a clearing in an ancient enchanted forest in the middle of a starry night. Not far from you in the mossy grass stands a magnificent white wolf with radiant blue eyes. He looks into your eyes and you feel the deep compassion that he emanates. Somehow he feels enormously familiar to you.

Then he starts moving and tells you telepathically that he would like you to follow. Together you run through the sacred forest until you encounter another clearing, in which stands an iridescent white tower that seems to be glowing from inside.

As soon as you start up the steps leading to the entrance of the tower, your faithful companion transforms into the lustrous beautiful shape of Archangel Michael, surrounded by a golden halo. Now you know why the white wolf seemed so familiar. Archangel Michael, full of love, smiles at you, and guides you into the tower.

A grand room opens up in front of you, a room that shines in the most resplendent golden light that you have ever seen. In the middle of the room you see a crystalline couch. Michael asks you to take a seat and as you settle down you notice that the couch immediately adapts to the temperature of your body. It feels very pleasant.

Now Archangel Michael begins his healing. With his gleaming sword of love, light, and truth he severs all energetic cords still clinging to you that are not of light and love. You feel the ancient bonds of the past fall away from you, and continue feeling clearer and lighter because you are being freed of the old pain and suffering that have accumulated through the various relationships in your life.

Then Archangel Michael speaks to you in his powerful voice:

"Beloved being, I will now start on the journey of retrieving your lost soul parts. Wait for me here. It will not take too long."

And right away he raises his wings and vanishes from your sight. He flies at the speed of light through the dimensions to all those places where parts of you have stayed behind.

You hardly have time to start wondering when he will come back when he is by your side again. He places his hand lovingly on your heart chakra. At this moment you sense the parts of your soul returning. With each breath you feel yourself become more whole again. It is a truly wonderful feeling.

Finally the process is completed and Michael asks you to get up. He envelops you in his dark-blue hooded coat, so that you are entirely protected. Full of gratitude, you look into his eyes and know that you do not need to say anything since he can read it in your gaze.

Together you move out into the night again, and you take a few deep breaths in the refreshing air in order to anchor all that you have experienced. Now feel Mother Earth underneath your feet again, stretch your limbs in order to fully return to your body, the temple of your soul, and fully open your eyes.

~ Day 10 ~

LEAVE YOUR TRAUMAS AND PAST LIVES BEHIND WITH THE HELP OF ARCHANGEL RAZIEL

Throughout the string of your lives, close to and far from Earth,
Always by your head your angel holds your star.

Manfred Kyber

"Greetings, beloved soul. I AM Archangel Raziel. It is time to prepare you for the life of your dreams, though you will only succeed in this if you leave behind any traumas from this or other lifetimes. Understand that you may well be speaking wonderful affirmations, creating collages of your wishes, and much more; but your heart's desires will still come about in limited measure only, because as long as you are still affected by karmic traumas you send out ambiguous messages to the universe. That is why I ask you for permission to help you with erasing these painful memories from your energy field, your cell memory, and your DNS. This might sound like a major intervention but I assure you, beloved being, that the acts that the powers between heaven and earth are able to perform happen so fast that they appear effortless, even though to the human eye they may seem like huge undertakings.

As you know, everything truly great is in fact extremely simple. It is such a well-kept secret that many people travel to the remotest areas of the world but still do not find what they are searching for; or rather, they find the truth but don't think it is the truth, because it seems just too simple. But that is exactly how it is! Transformation can happen within seconds – when you really want it, believe it, and let it happen. You have the choice. Choose wisely."

Archangel Raziel
angel of spiritual secrets and the Akashic chronicle;
the magician among the angels
Aura colour: rainbow-coloured
Crystal: mountain crystal

∽ *A wound disappears* ∽

During my student years suddenly an open wound appeared in my throat, although I hadn't injured myself. It just would not even heal, much less disappear. Over and over again people asked me about it, to the point that I started wearing a silk scarf whenever I left the house. Neither my doctor nor my homeopath had any solutions.

At some point I gave up hope as I was pretty certain that the reason behind this wound was a trauma from a past life. At the time, though, I did not know anyone who could help me dissolve it.

Years later I got into deep contact with Archangel Raziel and did a regression with him. The images that surfaced were anything but pleasant: at the time of the Inquisition in Spain, I had been a monk who did not conform to the Church. I had lived a reclusive life in nature, was in deep contact with all animals and elementals, and had taught people in the countryside how to read and write. All in all I had been a thorn in the flesh of the institution of the Church.

Eventually they sent men with bloodhounds and horses after me; they chased me through the woods and caught me with a kind of lasso. With the lasso around my neck I was pulled along behind a horse for so long that I died, in terrible pain.

The lasso had chafed exactly on that part of my throat where, in this life, the wound had appeared. When I became conscious of that I asked Archangel Raziel straight away to completely erase the trauma from my whole system, including at cellular level. And guess what, a few hours later my throat was once again unblemished!

A further story of transformation from Peggy:

From the ocean of sadness to the ocean of love

Too often I have lost my belief in the angels and also in myself. The angels, however, have never given up on me. Again and again they have led me to the right place at exactly the right moment, so that I could experience their boundless support.

I felt torn. On the one hand, I felt that I had always been close to the angels and heavenly beings; on the other hand I simply could no longer consider this closeness a gift or present from God, but instead experienced it as some kind of curse. Why on earth did I have to be so sensitive to the heavenly beings?

Very often I had experienced that my connection to the spirit world intensified exactly when something shattering happened in my life. When my father died completely unexpectedly, once again the words just came to me:

"Your soul has gone to rest." Why though? Why? Why now, so soon?

"It is not as it seems / in our hearts we are united for ever."

How was I supposed to accept all that if it meant that I had to lose everyone I loved? Could I ever love again, was I allowed to, without also losing people and being constantly sad?

Over the years I had got used to the feeling that a dark cloud of sadness seemed virtually stuck to me. Mostly it stayed well hidden; nevertheless I also seemed to magically attract and absorb oceans of the sadness of others.

But then, suddenly, there in my life was Isabelle, who affirmed to me, full of trust: "All will be well!" In a life-changing session with her I then actually felt that certainty for myself; she had encouraged me by saying: "Everything is possible with the help of the angels!"

I truly felt embraced from all sides, since she did not sit by herself in front of me but was surrounded by endless angels. The ocean of divine love that flowed from her eyes meant that I was able to experience complete trust. She and her heavenly helpers knew exactly what was happening. This I truly felt in my heart.

I had for a while been very afraid of this kind of profound experience, but the fear suddenly changed completely and became instead trust and familiarity. Isabelle assured me that the old traumas that had controlled me for so long would now dissolve, with the help of Archangel Raziel. She told me: "All this is allowed to go now – very gently, and in just the right way for you. Archangel Raziel is standing behind you and Archangels Michael and Raphael are also by your side."

With the help of the angels and their divine grace and lightness, Isabelle accompanied me through an incredibly powerful session. Step by step, full of love and compassion, she led me through the most profound levels; levels I had previously only known as deepest darkness. Tears were running down my face and I felt just how much and for how long I had held all that back and hidden it.

"Just let it happen," I heard Isabelle say in her loving and compassionate voice, which seemed to be accompanied by an angelic choir of divine love. "I see all the images. They are now leaving your body. It is OK. Everything is allowed to find its way out."

As if an old film reel had been wound back to the point when there were not yet any traumas, all my painful and traumatic experiences dissolved from out of my back – entirely pain-free, effortless, and fast as lightning. My body felt increasingly lighter and clearer. Archangel Raziel had done such a good job.

I felt overwhelmed by divine grace. Only shortly before, a live meditation with Isabelle and Archangel Jeremiel had led to my spine becoming more straight again. Now the angels had already initiated the sequel to my "development", the completion of which sent me into transports of sheer delight. Thus the deep sobbing I was so familiar with quickly transformed into a liberated laughter, which now happily gurgled out of my solar plexus.

"Yes, that's one way of doing it," I heard Isabelle say, laughing.

A blissful gratitude started spreading in me, followed by a deep inner peace. Suddenly everything felt different. I had experienced quite a few inner transformations already but I knew that this one was much more profound than any I had experienced before.

The session with Isabelle and the angels, in particular Raziel and his effortless way of completely dissolving old traumas, has given me an entirely new attitude to life. Instead of constantly swimming in the ocean of sadness, I have been given a new life in the ocean of love – and through the gifts of loving grace, ease and divine quickening! Thank you, thank you, thank you...to all earthly and heavenly helpers!

Ruth, one of my workshop participants, experienced a wonderful healing, more or less overnight:

The Raziel miracle

As a child I had always wished to be able to fly because at home we always had fierce fights. My parents, intense Scorpio and Cancer people, argued a great deal, until my father died in 2005. My mother also told me once that she had tried to have an abortion when pregnant with me.

So I used to try to "fly", when I was ice- or roller-skating. Unfortunately my right foot always buckled, and so it never worked.

I developed water on the knee in both knees; I couldn't walk and my father had to drive me to school and carry me up the stone steps on his back. Only as I started being able to distance myself from my family did my health begin to improve.

Right after my divorce, though, I again had problems with my ankles and feet: one sprain followed another until I finally tore my ligaments, which brought me into contact with reiki and other worlds. This led me to train in a wide variety of healing practices. I loved this work of helping people and practiced for some time, eventually going self-employed.

However, my "foot stories" did not end there. Time and again I hurt myself, and eventually I broke my left foot, including the tibia, so that for weeks I could only get around in a wheelchair. After that, I was in more or less constant pain.

Once, in a workshop in Berne on communicating with angels, I received confirmation from Isabelle that Archangel Raziel had been accompanying me for a long time. Nevertheless, I was very tentative about asking him for help. Funnily enough, I also always went into a kind of trance when Raziel appeared in Isabelle's angel trance meditation and could never remember him.

Only after I had visited my mother in her retirement home on Mother's Day did I have the courage to contact Raziel before I went to sleep. I asked him to dissolve for me all blockages and traumas from this life and past lives that were connected to my feet, but to do it in a very gentle and comfortable way, because my foot had recently been operated on and I had had increased pain in it for two or three weeks.

The next morning in bed, I started stretching my body as usual and was absolutely astounded to feel the flexibility of my feet…

I can still hardly believe that I can bend my ankles without them feeling stiff. As we have a four-storey house with a lot of stairs, I have to do a lot of walking. Negotiating the stairs had previously always been painful for me, but on the day after the blockages were dissolved by Archangel Raziel I suddenly realized that I was bouncing down the steps to answer the phone; something I had not been able to do for ages!

I am still overwhelmed with gratitude and joy when I think about Raziel's miracle.

 *Reflection*

Archangel Raziel can indeed dissolve traumas and blockages from past lives within the shortest of times, sometimes in just a few minutes or even seconds. His power is without limits! There is a reason why he is called the magician among the angels. I have witnessed how, with Archangel Raziel's help, countless people have been healed within minutes.

Day 10

Activities for today and for the future

Recognize your themes

Create a sacred space for yourself and call Archangel Raziel to your side. Ask him to envelop you in rainbow-coloured light, take a deep breath in and out, and relax.

When there is a theme in your life that you have not been able to solve with any other methods, it is usually a trauma that is still connected to your experiences from past lives. I have discovered that this is the case not only for myself but also for countless clients.

With Archangel Raziel, however, this can be remedied in a miraculous way, as you have seen in Ruth's story.

If you would like to go even deeper, please look for someone who offers regressions with angels or dissolves traumas in a gentle way with Archangel Raziel.

Since February 2012, the first ANGEL LIFE COACH®es, trained and certified by me, have been working with a method that Archangel Raziel channelled through me.

Allow Archangel Raziel to dissolve your traumas

Before going to sleep, ask Archangel Raziel to dissolve particular traumas overnight in a way that is gentle and comfortable for you. This is particularly effective because while you are asleep you are freed of your ego and thus cannot block the process with doubts as to whether it works.

Please pay attention to the phrase "in a way that is gentle and comfortable for you". This is necessary because Archangel Raziel is so powerful that he otherwise might release powers with such unbelievable force that you might be unable to handle them properly. For this reason please take note: Raziel's energy must be handled carefully or it might have serious consequences.

If there is much to heal I would advise you to repeat this over several nights. Naturally, you can also use the Soul Journey that I have channelled.

Soul Affirmation

First ask Archangel Raziel to enfold you in his rainbow-coloured light. Then take a deep breath in and out, before you say (ideally aloud):

With Archangel Raziel's help my traumas and karmic blockages dissolve within the shortest possible amount of time, in a way that is gentle and comfortable for me.

༄ Soul Journey ༄

Have pen and paper ready before you begin. You might want to take some notes during or directly after your journey.

With your eyes open take a deep breath in, and then slowly exhale while you close your eyes in slow motion and order your brain to automatically move into the Theta state. Breathe deeply in and out, and relax. Let your thoughts go by like leaves gliding along a river and do not hold on to them. Just let them go and move further into a state of deep relaxation. Enjoy perceiving your breath, which nourishes your body and at the same time connects you with the higher levels.

Feel, see, or imagine yourself being wrapped in the most shimmering rainbow-coloured light that you have ever seen. It is of high, cosmic energy, and fills you with all the colours that have been missing from your energetic body because of painful experiences. Feel the gentle light stroking and caressing your aura while at the same time it heals you right down to the deep layers and connects you with your divine blueprint.

You find yourself in an enchanted garden, in which fairies and animals of all kinds reside. Breathtaking, rare plants are flowering here, providing countless beings with a celestial home.

As you look up to the sky you discover two beautiful rainbows above you whose ends meet the ground. They resemble two sacred portals and you feel an urge to step through. Thus you reach the other side of the rainbows and instantly meet a black raven whose feathers glisten in the sunlight. He looks at you with extremely wise eyes and you know that he will show you the path to deep healing.

After another look into your eyes he indicates to you to follow him. He rises into the sky and you follow him through the magical jungle stretching in front of you. The energies emanating from the various shades of green vibrate, full of joie de vivre *and vital strength. It is just as though you are being nourished on many levels while you wander through this enchanted landscape, following the raven.*

Just as you are feeling that the green thicket cannot become any more impenetrable, suddenly a clearing, filled with cosmic light, appears ahead of you. In its centre you see a crystalline pyramid that shimmers and glitters in all the colours of the rainbow. You know that this is the intended destination of your journey. At this moment the entrance of the pyramid opens and a mighty angel with wings like an eagle and the energy of a wise one steps on to the stairs in front of the big porch. It is Archangel Raziel, the magician among the angels, who knows all of God's secrets.

The raven flies towards him and sits on one of his shoulders. Raziel thanks him and approaches you. He welcomes you and embraces you with his eagle wings. You know that you are utterly safe and secure. Then Raziel takes you by the hand and leads you into the pyramid, which shines in celestial beauty and is decorated with a myriad of quartz crystals. In its centre, right under the cusp of the pyramid, you see a crystalline bed that is ornamented with crystals in all the colours of the rainbow. Here Raziel asks you to lie down. As soon as you are on the bed you perceive how your frequency rises.

Archangel Raziel stands at your head and begins to speak to you in his deep mighty voice:

"Beloved being, it is time to deliver you from the old painful traumas from this and other incarnations. Believe me, this can happen in a very gentle way within a few minutes without you having to walk through the pain once more. Are you ready?"

You have deep trust in this mighty, yet so loving angel, and nod as sign of your consent.

Thereupon Archangel Raziel begins, with the speed of light, to conduct a very profound, yet gentle ceremony in order to relieve you of traumas and karmic blockages, some of which you have been carrying around with you for many incarnations. He releases them from your whole system, so that they are also erased from the cell level and DNS. Continue taking deep breaths in order to become part of this process. Then you hear Raziel's voice close to your ear:

"You are doing great! Everything is fine."

You feel how uncountable burdens fall from you and you become clearer and lighter. Your cells start to vibrate in the frequency of joy and you feel like a new person. With each second your frequency increases more, and your aura shines in the wonderful rainbow colours; Raziel has taken care that all the colours of your soul are complete again and ready to irradiate anew.

Enjoy the delightful feeling of being an infinite being of light and love that does not know any boundaries… Not only do you radiate bliss, but also Raziel's eyes sparkle with joy over your wonderful recovery.

He lifts you off the crystalline bed and embraces you, full of deep, deep love. You know that you are always and forever loved unconditionally and that you can ask Raziel for help at any time. Gratefully you leave and, together with the raven, your faithful companion, you start your journey home through the magic jungle. As you walk through the blooming vegetation your energy level increases even further, so that you return to the here and now full of strength.

Feel Mother Earth underneath your feet and the roots that connect you with the centre of the earth. Stretch your body and open your eyes when you are ready.

·✑ *Day 11* ✑·

FORGIVE OTHERS AND YOURSELF WITH THE HELP OF ARCHANGEL ZADKIEL

*It is in rugged crises, in unbearable endurance,
and in aims which put sympathy out of the question,
that the angel is shown.*

Ralph Waldo Emerson

"Greetings, beloved soul. I AM Archangel Zadkiel. The truth is that without the ability to forgive, you will never achieve the freedom that you are longing for so much. Thus I ask you to recognize that, if you hold on to distress and pain that others have caused you, you are the one who will take him- or herself into an unconsciously chosen prison. Indeed, it is yourself who increases your suffering as every repetition of your torment in thought or word hurts you anew and stores the experience even deeper in your DNS.

Beloved soul, I know that this is really not your wish. Thus I ask you to understand that things are very definitely not the way they seem to you. The higher purpose for your life, which you yourself have chosen together with us, stipulates your wish to learn certain soul lessons during this life. Since this incarnation is *of particular importance for the entire development of the history of humanity, you are dealing in this life with the royal disciplines. One of them is learning to forgive.*

Also important is to set up true boundaries that will prevent you from further hurts. Thus I ask you to in future no longer just say: "It's OK" if someone apologizes for something they have inflicted upon you. If you do this you will draw further experiences of this kind to you, since it will be stored in your resonance field that it is fine if someone hurts you. In this way you remain in the position of a victim.

Instead, thank the person; this way you give out the message that you forgive. At the same time, the gratitude enables you to move into self-empowerment. Thus you will find it – even in the most severe cases – increasingly easier to forgive, because you will be able to recognize that certain people are being sent to you according to your wishes so that you can turn into a true master of forgiveness, as was your plan before you came to this earth. If you do wish so, I will stand by you in any situation – and you will realize the gifts in them and attain peace."

Archangel Zadkiel
angel of compassion and forgiveness
Aura colour: dark blue, violet
Crystal: lapis lazuli

✎ *Reflection* ✎

Time and again I come across a quote whose source seems to be unknown: "Not to forgive is as if we ourselves had swallowed poison but expect the other person to die of it." There is much truth in this. In every session I have given in my healing work so far, we have only got completely stuck when the client still had something to forgive in his or her life.

Not to forgive deprives a person of a great deal of energy, on the emotional as well as the physical level, and can downright "poison" and sicken him or her. Once we become aware, though, that those people who give us a hard time and hurt us most are on a higher level our friends, forgiving suddenly becomes much easier: These people make themselves available to us so that we may learn certain soul lessons that we have resolved to deal with in this life.

At this point I would like to refer again to the book *The Journey Home* by Lee Carroll and Kryon, which describes this idea very clearly in the form of a parable with seven angelic beings.

Besides, to forgive does not mean to approve of terrible deeds. Instead, it signifies that we finally release ourselves from the (self-created) prison that we have ended up in due to not forgiving. Forgiveness is essential so that your vibration can increase and you can manifest the life of your dreams.

Always remember: if you walked in the shoes of the person for only two weeks, you could understand everything and forgive with ease.

Here a wonderful story of forgiveness that my assistant Dani experienced not long ago:

Forgiveness and peace

The relationship between my mother and me has always been very ambivalent. Until I was twenty-five I tried everything to live up to her standards, but whatever I did in order to please her and feel her love, she gave me the impression that she did not recognize me as me – in my uniqueness as Dani.

So I gave up and decided to separate from her and look for my own path. I cut my ties with her, but became bitter, and closed my heart to anyone who wanted to enter. I turned my back on God, because I did not want to deal any longer with a god who had given me such a mother. On top of this, I also closed my light channels as I did not believe in anything any more.

What followed was years of drifting, and partying with a lot of alcohol and sometimes drugs, to escape from myself. My fury with regard to my mother grew to immeasurable size. In my self-pity, I felt that my unsettled lifestyle and professional failures were all her fault. Disappointment and grief about this situation ruled me to such an extent that I was constantly sick. Of course, I did not show this to the outside world. For them I was the strong one, always joyful, playful, and tongue in cheek.

When I met Ralf, he was the first person ever to whom I could show all my sides, and who loved me as I was. Thus I was able to begin again to engage intensively with the spiritual world. Suddenly I was meeting people who in a figurative sense always collected me exactly from where I had been standing: in other words, who simply took me as I was. I came to realize that my mother had given her best. That this was not sufficient for me was not her but my issue.

Once this knot was dissolved my whole life changed rapidly. I began to tidy up my life and put the coat of self-pity back on its peg. Archangel Zadkiel became a close companion and friend during this time, as he helped me in a very gentle way to forgive my mother and also myself. After all this had happened, he explained to me that this was not yet the whole journey.

"You have certainly forgiven her but it is only really done once you have also found inner peace with her."

I had never thought about that. I thought, if I forgive, all is good. But that was not at all the case! Somewhere deep within my heart there was still an ounce of anger about being treated so wrongfully. I started my work, and this time it took a bit longer

---

as my ego kept on interfering. When I was finally there I was able to think of my mother without emotions. Finally everything was calm; the hot fury in my belly cooled off. Every morning now, I asked the angels to tell my mother that I was at peace with her and had forgiven her.

After six weeks I received an email from my mother, in which she asked for my peace and forgiveness for everything she had unconsciously done to me. I could hardly believe it. An incredible joy spread within me. Since that day we have been corresponding via email and slowly starting to get to know each other again after eighteen years. Maybe we will also meet in person again one day. The angels will see to it.

ᘡᘡ Activities for today ᘡᘡ

ᘡᘡ Forgiveness list

Create a sacred space for yourself and call Archangel Zadkiel to your side. Ask him to envelop you in his violet light, so that you are connected with the energy of compassion. Take a deep breath in and out in order to absorb the light, and relax.

List the names of all the people who have hurt you, and who you have not been able to (fully) forgive, in order of importance in your life.

ᘡᘡ Forgiveness ritual

Note: instead of this ritual you can do today's soul journey; or, of course, you can do both.

Take yourself to a place of stillness and peace – your sanctuary – and relax. This can be a place that you know or one that you create in your imagination. Archangel Michael is by your side and creates a space of safety around you. Enjoy your surroundings with all your senses and breathe deeply in and out.

Now call for Archangel Zadkiel and ask him to help you to open your heart to compassion and forgiveness. Feel how he sends his loving energy of compassion into your heart chakra. Absorb this energy fully by breathing deeply in and out.

Now imagine that one of the people you have listed stands in front of you. Connect on the heart level with that person and ask Archangel Michael to cut the toxic cords between you with his sword of love, truth, and light. While he does this take three deep breaths. Then speak:

I forgive you, …(name of the person), and release you in peace.
I bless you. I am free!

Now ask Archangel Raphael to enfold you and this person in his emerald-green healing energy, so that you can continue healing, and breathe deeply in and out.

Repeat this procedure until you have forgiven everybody on your list.

Should you still suffer from feelings of guilt, it is also time to forgive yourself.

Ask Archangel Zadkiel once more to send his love and compassion into your heart, and absorb them by breathing deeply in and out. Then ask Archangel Michael to also cut through the energetic cords that are attached to you due to unpleasant thoughts and which do not consist of love and light. Take three deep breaths during this procedure and then speak:

I forgive myself. I am blessed. I am free!

Finally, ask Archangel Raphael to envelop you in his beautiful emerald-green healing light. Once again, take a deep breath in and out.

Give thanks to Archangel Zadkiel, Archangel Michael, and Archangel Raphael.

Sometimes forgiveness does not succeed the first time round. There is no need to be worried or to judge yourself; you just need to repeat the exercise a few times.

Soul Affirmation

First ask Archangel Zadkiel to enfold you in his blue-violet light. Then take a deep breath in and out, before you say (ideally aloud):

I love to forgive because it sets me free.

Soul Journey

Have pen and paper ready before you begin. You might want to take some notes during or directly after your journey.

With your eyes open take a deep breath in, and then slowly exhale while you close your eyes in slow motion and order your brain to automatically move into the Theta state. Breathe deeply in and out, and relax. Let your thoughts go by like birds flying past. Just let them go and enjoy feeling your breath that continually links you to the breath of God and nourishes you.

With each breath you take you move more deeply into a state of relaxation.

Feel, see, or imagine how you are being surrounded by an intense violet light that very gently pervades and purifies all layers of your aura. You feel clearer and lighter as the light reaches into the very deepest of your cells and purges these too, so that you become more and more aligned with your divine blueprint, the perfect structural design of your body, your cells and your DNS. Enjoy the feeling of purification on all levels.

Then you discover that you are in the middle of an enchanting garden. Flowers of all kinds and shapes cast a spell on you with their delicious aromas, and countless butterflies start dancing around you. You are watching them, knowing that they are a symbol of your transformation, when a mighty angel appears in front of you. It is Archangel Zadkiel. Instantaneously you sense the unconditional love and the unending compassion that emanate from him, and you feel wonderfully secure.

Then Archangel Zadkiel looks up, gives a sign, and within light seconds a beautiful carriage appears by your side, decorated with crystals in rainbow colours and with seven gloriously white unicorns harnessed to it. Zadkiel extends his hand and helps you to take a seat in the carriage. He joins you as well and then speaks to the unicorns in a language unknown to you; they soar up into the air with the carriage and you inside, through the seven levels of illusion, until they reach the crystalline plateau on which an ethereal temple is located. Its unique task is to help people forgive with grace, ease, and joy.

Zadkiel again holds out his hand and helps you out of the carriage. Together you enter the temple, lit by the brightest light. Zadkiel asks you to take a seat on a crystalline throne while he touches your heart on the deepest level and wraps it in compassion.

At this moment Angel Mihr, Archangel Michael and various people you still have to forgive appear in front of you.

Angel Mihr wraps you in his dark-green light of healing and insight, and the first person stands in front of you. As you gaze into her eyes until you see the bottom of her soul a deep understanding for this person arises, and with the help of Angel Mihr you are able to become aware of the soul lessons that you might learn thanks to this person.

Thus you suddenly find it very easy to forgive. You ask Archangel Michael to separate the toxic cord between you and this person with his sword of love, truth, and light and take three deep breaths. Afterwards say from the bottom of your heart:

"I forgive you, [name of the person], and thank you for the lesson that I may learn thanks to you. I release you in peace and bless you. I am free!"

Now take a deep breath in order to completely let go.

If you like you can forgive more people in the same way. Maybe you would also like to release your own feelings of guilt and shame.

Again Zadkiel touches your heart, so that you seem to be overflowing with compassion. Now view with the eyes of compassion what you would like to forgive yourself for. You know that you can achieve this here at this sacred place. Thus you ask Archangel Michael to separate with his sword the toxic cords that are attached to you due to negative thoughts about yourself and others in connection with the same subject. While you take three deep breaths in order to release, Mihr discloses the soul lesson that you have created for yourself in order to grow even further.

Suddenly you find it very easy to forgive yourself, so please speak: "I forgive myself. I am blessed. I am free."

Take one more deep breath in order to also release on the physical level.

A deep peace and an infinite feeling of happiness spread through you, when the three angels – Zadkiel, Mihr, and Michael – take you by the hands and step out of the temple with you into the clearest air that you have ever experienced. Deep gratitude flows through you, as you know that you have left countless burdens behind in this first part of the journey.

Suddenly you understand the language of the unicorns and notice that you would now like to ask them to return to earth with you. You give thanks to the angels, take your seat in the carriage and right away the seven-unicorn vehicle rises into the air with you. This time you do not fly upwards but gracefully downwards to the earth. You alight very smoothly and, sliding out of the carriage, you feel infinitely light. Now reconnect with the ground underneath your feet, with Mother Earth, stretch your body, and return to the here and now. Open your eyes once you are ready.

Part 2

Raising the Vibration

∼ Day 12 ∼

GET YOUR PRIORITIES RIGHT AND LIVE THEM, WITH THE SUPPORT OF ARCHANGEL METATRON

*Every visible thing in this world
has an angelic power placed over it.*
St. Augustine

"*Greetings, beloved soul. I AM Archangel Metatron. There might be times when your life seems to be just passing you by, and you ask yourself whether you are on the right track since you do not seem to have any power over what is happening. This, however, is an illusion. At any time and in any place you can be the master of your time. You just need to take a conscious decision to, each day, become aware anew of your true priorities.*

Your life does not choose you, but you choose your life. This might sound hard when the blows of fate afflict you, but this is how it is. Even in those times you have the choice to reflect upon what you want to focus on and prioritize, beloved being. Recognize this and from now on choose wisely. At every single moment I am available to support you with help and advice, if you so wish. Now feel how I surround you with my wings and envelop you in crystalline clarity, so that you may recognize what can be recognized."

Archangel Metatron
angel of the children of the New Age, of priorities and of focus
Aura colours: green and pink
Crystal: watermelon tourmaline

My friend Johanna experienced huge relief thanks to Archangel Metatron:

Unexpected lesson

Each year, the months from April to June are very work-intensive for me. As well as my full-time job as a piano teacher I accompany the ballet exams at the Royal Academy of Dance. This, in short, means that I have to rehearse 300 short pieces, have several rehearsals with the ballet students, and throughout the exam period play about seven to eight hours piano each day.

I have been doing this for twelve years, and thus have a lot of experience of it; but what had always happened so far was that in the end, in some way or other, the stress would become too much for me to handle. My body would then enforce a time of rest – be it in the form of unbearable backache that made it impossible for me to rehearse, so that some of the pieces were not well enough prepared; or through sudden concentration problems during the exams, which created awkward moments for me as much as for the dancers.

As this year I had taken on the same exam job for two ballet schools on top of the Royal Academy, I had resolved to tackle this with the support of the angels, since I could already see that I might be unable to cope. Thus I asked Archangel Metatron to help me with the timing of my days and with the discipline necessary to manage this workload.

I went in to meditation and connected to Metatron's energy, surrendered my worry to him, and then let it go. Since I am by now used to communicating with the angels it did not take long until I was virtually showered with information. And what I got to hear was so decidedly different to my expectations and to the way in which I so often tried to master stressful situations that I had to laugh!

Metatron explained to me that my view of the situation would not solve the problem. I did not need more discipline, but in some respects less. I needed more fun and relaxation. But how could that happen within the context of a sixteen-hour work day, every day? In my family, and also as a pianist, I have been trained to believe

---

that only hard work could lead to good results; thus I tend to organize my days in a very performance-oriented way, to a degree that often does not allow any space for undesigned unwinding, enjoying life, and so forth.

The result? The good discipline becomes a corset, so an imbalance in the soul occurs. The soul again takes the necessary measures herself – usually at a particularly inopportune time. I either procrastinate over urgent tasks, or I cannot fully concentrate under pressure, or I develop physical symptoms that prevent me from working, until balance is restored.

Metatron explained that I could direct and control these measures by choosing completely new priorities. They looked like this:

He placed meditation, keeping open my spiritual channels, and my work as ANGEL LIFE COACH® first.

He asked me to list, leaving aside my musical work, all the projects that were currently buzzing around my head and to do a ritual for their manifestation, in order to then let them go and clear my mind. I followed this advice and noticed immediately how beneficial it felt to finally surrender all these ideas to the angels. It put me into a downright good mood. Plus, as confirmation of this priority I immediately received enquiries from two clients requesting a reading.

The next step concerned the work itself – in this case practising piano and the time I would dedicate to this. That meant: essential practising – yes; mechanical practising – no, not a single minute. He explained to me that I spent too much time on repetitions; this was partly from habit, partly from worry that I would not be prepared enough.

Thus I practised during this time as efficiently and effectively as possible; I tried to limit myself to the minimum and noticed very soon that because of this new approach I had much more spare capacity during my rehearsals to fully feel my way into the music. I was more in the flow; therefore I did not tire so easily either.

Interestingly enough, I also finished my preparations more quickly, so that I still had spare time. I now got the strict order to spend this time doing something that had nothing to do with work. A difficult task, since as a pianist you feel that you have never really practised enough, and also genuinely love making music. But Metatron reminded me that I could only be a hundred per cent confident of my ability to concentrate during rehearsals and exams when I also spent time doing something else and enjoying my downtime. So I stuck to this.

Metatron particularly emphasized that I needed to do some yoga exercises regularly in the morning and in the evening, because I spend so much time sitting; and to tap my emotional balance points (with the help of the corresponding angels) prior to every rehearsal and every exam, in order to get the energy moving. Furthermore, there were quite a few rules with regard to sleeping, eating, and drinking, in which the first command was: You have to take care of yourself, and you are supposed to have fun!

At the moment I am in the middle of this intense period, but despite all the exams and piano students I do still have some spare time – for example for writing down this story – and enjoy every new day in which I am able to play piano for eight hours without concentration problems or back pain!

Reflection

Use today to observe precisely which activities you spend your time on; write them all down, with exact time specifications.

Activities for today

Reflect on how you use your time

Remember to first create a sacred space before you answer the following questions in writing.

Call Archangel Metatron to your side and ask him to accompany you throughout the whole day and surround you with his green and pink light, so that you are connected with the frequency of healing. Breathe deeply in and out in order to take the light in, and relax.

- How do you spend your time?
- Do you make time for your priorities? Or do you allow yourself to get distracted from them?
- Do you surf the Internet endlessly (Facebook etc.) instead of applying yourself to your priorities?
- What actually are your priorities?
- How much time do you dedicate to meditation, prayer, affirmations, yoga, fitness, and such?
- And how much time do you grant yourself every day in order to work on your goals?
- What about "Aloha"-time (i.e. time in which you relax and enjoy life – see day 16)?

Day 12

Activities for today and for the future

Use Metatron's cube

If you do not yet have a picture of Metatron's cube, it is time to get yourself one (you can search for it on the Internet and print it out), as this cube contributes much towards strengthening your focus and allowing you to concentrate on the essential. (*The Flower of Life* by Drunvalo Melchizedek covers this in great detail.)

Become aware of your priorities

Every morning before you begin your day, connect with Archangel Metatron. Ask him to surround you with his green and pink light, breathe in and out deeply, and recognize, with his help, the three priorities for your day. It's best to note them down in your diary (even after you have completed this twenty-eight-day programme); in addition, place them in a strategically important location – the bathroom mirror, your desk, your mobile phone etc. – and act accordingly.

Soul Affirmation

First ask Archangel Metatron to enfold you in his green and pink light. Then take a deep breath in and out, before you say (ideally aloud):

I am always aware of my priorities and act accordingly.

Soul Journey

Have pen and paper ready before you begin. You might want to take some notes during or directly after your journey.

> *With your eyes open take a deep breath in, and then slowly exhale while you close your eyes in slow motion and order your brain to automatically move into the Theta state. Breathe deeply in and out, and relax.*
>
> *Let your thoughts go by like birds flying past. Just let them go and enjoy feeling your breath, which connects you with the breath of God and nourishes you. With each breath you take you move deeper and deeper into the relaxation.*
>
> *You realize that you are at a place of iridescent beauty. Flowers of all*

113

kinds and shapes exude their delicious fragrances, which immediately transport you to a state of peace and equanimity.

Surrounded by a bright, clear green and pink aura, a tremendous angel now appears in front of you. It is Archangel Metatron. His presence is full of power and crystalline clarity, and you feel your frequency changing and increasing in his presence.

He guides you to a nearby temple that shines resplendent in brightest sunlight. Together you enter the sacred space, and in the middle of the floor you discover an enormous mosaic that depicts Metatron's cube. You are magnetically attracted by this mosaic and stand in its centre. What happens there is very difficult to describe in words. It is as if, out of the mosaic in the floor, a magical force rises and pervades in spiral form all your ethereal bodies and your physical body. It happens at the speed of light in such a powerful way that you do not have time to hold on to any thoughts. A crystalline clarity begins to spread through your whole being. All your cells vibrate in a sacred rhythm that connects you again with your divine blueprint.

Then Archangel Metatron speaks to you: "Beloved being, now it is time to truthfully recollect yourself and to become conscious of your true priorities. Listen carefully and recognize! You might be aware of your priorities for the next two weeks or for your whole life. It is also possible that for now you will only become aware of the priorities for today. Whatever happens does so in accord with your inner wisdom. Listen with all your senses!"

Images, sounds, thoughts, or feelings might emerge in you that point you towards your true priorities.

After a while the spiral wave that has infused your whole being dissolves and you recognize again where you are.

Now Archangel Metatron passes you one of his beautiful cubes that shimmers in all rainbow colours and says: "Take it with you. It will not only help you to recognize your priorities but also strengthen your concentration and your focus, so that you may accomplish them."

Full of gratitude, you accept the magical cube and feel the infinite vibrations radiating out from it.

Holding the cube in your hand, you leave the sacred place with Metatron and feel again Mother Earth underneath your feet. Sense her rhythm through the roots that connect you to the centre of the earth. Take three deep breaths and return completely into the here and now. Open your eyes.

Now write down what you have realized.

~ *Day 13* ~

BOOST YOUR CONFIDENCE
AND COURAGE WITH
ARCHANGEL ARIEL

As pillars support whole houses,
so the divine powers support the whole world:
They carry it and bestow beauty upon it.

Philo of Alexandria

"*Greetings, beloved human being. I AM Archangel Ariel. Always remember that only love is real. When you are conscious of this, not only on the level of reason but also to the bottom of your heart, your fears fall away like shadows behind you. What is it that distresses you so much? That you might fail and would not be loveable? Believe me, beloved child, these are only illusions, for on the true plane of life the point is to fulfil your soul lessons. In this you cannot fail – it is only a question of when you will fulfil them, because people always do. Time is flexible and can change, so let go and dare to live your life in all its magnitude. That is what it is about!*

Be aware that we love you unconditionally for all eternity and that you are infinitely loveable, whatever you do.

115

Unite with me and with my light, and recognize that deep within yourself you are full of courage and trust. Only by spreading your wings can you start to fly. So, what are you waiting for?"

Archangel Ariel
angel of trust and courage,
of manifestation and abundance
Aura colour: pink
Crystal: rose quartz

My friend Patricia, also a member of my team and a powerful shaman, had the following wonderful experience with Archangel Ariel:

A magical moment of manifestation

I was in Rome for the third time, to facilitate a workshop with my co-trainer and friend Chris. Since I prefer to speak in the language of the country I work in, I prepared my part in Italian, word by word. I read through the prepared text a few times in order to be able to speak to my audience without having to read from a piece of paper.

It was near the end of the day when my co-trainer leaned over and asked: "What would you think of us holding the meditation together, instead of me by myself? We will call it "M3" ("Magical moment of manifestation"). I will start, you continue, then I speak again and so forth. It will be magical and very special!"

I looked at him as if he was completely mad and asked how he pictured that happening; after all, I had not prepared anything and did not yet have a good enough Italian vocabulary to speak spontaneously. He returned my gaze as if I was the mad one and responded:

"You are the one who tells me about angels. Don't you know any angel who can help you with this?"

I looked at the rose quartz ring on my finger and said: "Give me a few minutes!"

Sitting on stage, I closed my eyes and called for Archangel Ariel. I asked her to give me courage and to manifest within me, as this meditation was supposed to be about manifestation, and to lead me through it.

I did not feel any direct answer but as I trust Ariel I looked at Chris and said: "OK, let's do it."

The windows and doors of the room were closed for warmth. Chris started to lead the group into meditation and, at a certain point, stopped so that I could continue. At that moment, I felt a gentle wind around me and I whispered: "Archangel Ariel is here. She will lead us in this meditation and in this magical moment."

I spoke Italian as I never had before while Ariel's wings and courage enfolded me. Chris and the audience were as utterly entranced and absorbed as I was by one of the most beautiful and intense meditations that I have ever facilitated. For me, this meditation was also absolutely M3, a magical moment of manifestation!

Ever since this experience, I always call on the angels before any workshop, seminar, any meditation or trance dance, and ask them to spread their support wherever it is needed.

∽ *Reflection* ∽

Time and again I meet people who, due to lack of trust and courage, do not dare to take steps to manifest the life of their dreams. What ultimately deters them is fear.

But what actually is fear? It seems that it exists in thousands of forms. A wise man and wonderful teacher of mine, Maestro Sergiu Celibidache – one of the most exciting conductors of the last century – once spoke about fear in one of his lectures in a way that truly opened my eyes. He explained to us that there are really only two fears, on which all others are based: the fear of not being loved and the fear of death.

You might think this cannot be true, but when you trace back every single fear, you will find that you can ultimately trace each one back to one of those two fears. Take, for example, the fear of failure. What lies behind this one? The fear of disappointing someone, or of being judged, and thus no longer being loved. But if you look at this more closely, you will realize that the people who wholeheartedly love you will love you just as much when you fail; the other ones do not really love you. Besides, you know as well as I do that you are always surrounded by angels, who love you unconditionally. This means that fear of failure is as unfounded as the fear of not being loved.

What about the fear of death? This is not very real as, deep within, you know well that death is only a transition into a higher dimension, another birth. (More on this on day 19.)

I know this might sound too simplistic, but it really is as simple as this. I had to face thousands of fears during my healing process, and I have noticed that Maestro Celibidache was absolutely right with his talk about the two basic ones. This does not mean that I no longer have any fears; but today I know that they are not real, and thus I can deal with them quite differently. This is where trust and courage come into play.

ᘓᘓ *Activities for today* ᘓᘓ

ᘓᘓ *Face your fears*

Remember to first create a sacred space for yourself before you answer the following questions in writing.

Call Archangel Ariel to your side and ask her to accompany you throughout the whole day. Ask her to envelop you in her pink light, so that you are connected with the frequency of love, trust, and courage. Take a deep breath, in and out, in order to absorb the light and relax.

- What are your worst fears? Screen them and trace them back to one of the two fears mentioned above.
- What is the worst that could happen to you in connection with these fears? Is it really as bad as your fear suggests to you? Or is it much less harmful than you had thought?

Remember that you have Archangel Ariel by your side throughout the whole process. At any point you can breathe in her light once more and take time to relax again before you continue.

- Which fears keep you from realizing your dreams? How real are they, in truth?

Bear in mind that being courageous does not mean to no longer have any fears, but rather to dare to do something despite them!

- Is there someone that you would like to speak to because you think she or he could help you on your path towards realizing your life dreams? If so, why have you not done so yet? Are you afraid to be rejected?

By now you know that behind this hides the fear of not being loved – a fear that is not real. So, what have you got to lose? If you do not ask then the outcome is a definite "No". If you do ask, however, the answer could also be "Yes". What do you think: is it better to pluck up courage or not? The answer is clear. So, go for it (and win)!

Only when you move out of your comfort zone will you create the resonance to achieve what you wish for. Do it now!

✑ *Soul Affirmation* ✑

First ask Archangel Ariel to enfold you in her pink light. Then take a deep breath in and out, before you say (ideally aloud):

I face my fears because I know that in truth they cannot harm me. With every minute I trust more and more and dare to jump into the unknown.

✑ *Soul Journey* ✑

Have pen and paper ready before you begin. You might want to take some notes during or directly after your journey.

With your eyes open take a deep breath in, and then slowly exhale while you close your eyes in slow motion and order your brain to automatically move into the Theta state. Breathe deeply in and out, and relax.

Let your thoughts go by like birds flying past. Just let them go and enjoy the sense of your breath that continually nourishes you. Become aware of how great your trust is in the infinite strength of your breath that keeps you alive. Enjoy it, and relax with each breath you take even more deeply while Archangel Ariel envelops you in luminous pink light that links you with the deeper layers of trust. Feel how this gentle yet at the same time powerful light permeates every single fibre of your being and makes you feel safe and secure.

You realize that you stand together with Archangel Ariel at the foot of a very steep, sacred mountain. Then Ariel takes your hand and you jointly soar up into the air towards the mountaintop. Once you arrive at the summit Ariel prepares a camp on the craggy rocks, so that you can sit down comfortably. She sits next to you and asks you in her warm deep voice:

"Beloved child, what are the anxieties and fears that prevent you from living your dreams? Please do some serious soul-searching and tell me about them."

Listening to your response, her loving words are: "It is now time to free you of all your fears as they are nothing more than an unending illusion."

And right away Ariel begins to dissolve your fears very gently from your whole being. It feels wonderful!

Then you again hear her voice at your ear: "Now, what are the dreams of your lifetime? Tell me."

After you have disclosed them to her Ariel extends her hand to help you get up.

"Beloved being, it is now time to fly with your own wings!"

She guides you to the edge of the mountain. "Spread your wings. Are you ready?"

What a heavenly feeling it is to perceive how your wings open! Right away, Ariel gives you a gentle push and you truly start to fly. What a miracle, and yet so familiar.

While you sail along, visualize your dreams with all your senses, let them go and then see them fly too.

Now it is time to return to the here and now, and to realize your dreams full of trust and courage. Take three deep breaths in order to deeply anchor what you have experienced, stretch your limbs, and return fully into your body. Once you are ready open your eyes.

Day 14

INCREASE YOUR SELF-LOVE
AND SELF-CONFIDENCE WITH
ARCHANGEL CHAMUEL

If I speak in the tongues of men and of angels
but have not love, I am a noisy gong or a clanging cymbal.
And if I have prophetic powers, and understand all mysteries and all
knowledge, and if I have all faith, so as to remove mountains,
but have not love, I am nothing.

Corinthians 13,1+2

"Greetings, beloved human being. I AM Archangel Chamuel. In your search for love you often forget the truly essential: that is, love of yourself.

How can there be a kindling of love for you in another person, how can someone cherish you, if you speak harsh words bereft of any self-love to yourself in front of the mirror and elsewhere? I think you realize that this is not possible.

Should you take the time, though, to learn to love yourself more and more, your vibrational frequency and your resonance will change too. That way you will draw to you people with a similar frequency, who are able to show you the love that you are longing for. I do not speak here of romantic love only.

Call me to your side as often as you like, so that I can envelop you in the subtle

121

green and pink light of love. Breathe in love and breathe out any kind of self-judgement. Repeat this several times and send out the intention to from now on draw breath in this way. Then move in front of the mirror and look deeply into your own eyes. At some point you see your soul and recognize who you actually are: a being of light and love. From this moment onwards, you will find it increasingly easier to love yourself. Do this every day, and you will not have to wait long for changes in your life. Let 'love' be your mantra, and love will be yours."

Archangel Chamuel
angel of self-love and self-confidence, of opening the heart,
of personal and global peace, of finding things, places etc.
Aura colour: subtle green and pink
Crystal: green fluorite

⸂ *Hard school* ⸃

It is a bit tricky, self-love. When we feel at ease with ourselves and everything works well, we are convinced that we actually love ourselves. But by now I know that this is not necessarily the truth. I had to learn this the hard way myself.

When I received the diagnosis of having only between three days and three weeks to live, my love for myself had already been reduced to a small shadow, since within that one week I had already lost my partner, my house, and my place to study in California. When on top of that I saw all the sad figures with yellowish faces and bald heads in the corridor of the oncology ward, and realized that I would soon look the same, I had the feeling of being in an endless nightmare.

Thanks to Louise L. Hay's book *You Can Heal Your Life*, as well as other insights, I managed to step out of my life as a victim by using affirmations and prayers. Even when I had lost all my hair, eyelashes, and eyebrows I still succeeded in stepping in front of the mirror and saying to myself: "I love myself as I am," exactly the way Louise L. Hay suggests in her book. But when I gradually started looking puffed up as well, because I had to take hormones, there was really nothing at all left of any love for myself. I felt like a picture of misery, like the ugliest duckling in the whole world. I completely freaked out, which is absolutely not my style.

It took quite a while before I again stepped in front of the mirror and continued with the affirmations. This was only possible for me when I realized that my love for myself has to be entirely independent of my exterior looks and the thoughts others might have about me. This gave rise to the next insight: that I had to learn to feel complete by myself, just as I was. I started to work on this as seriously as I did on my healing.

And lo and behold, a few months later I felt entirely comfortable in my skin, even without hair, eyelashes, or eyebrows. I was grateful to still be alive and utterly content with myself. It was the first time in my life that I had felt absolutely whole even without a man by my side, because I really loved myself as I was.

Reflection

How often do we think or say something negative about ourselves? This though is exactly what strengthens our negative belief patterns, which suggest to us that we are not loveable. As Chamuel and all other angels say, this is not at all true. So it is really time to love yourself!

Spontaneously, without thinking too much, allocate a number on a scale of 0 to 10 to the following questions, with 10 signifying the worst state possible and 0 the most wonderful one that you can think of:

- how great is your self-confidence?
- how much do you love yourself?
- how do you rate your ability to love others?

Activities for today and for the future

Connect with the love for yourself

Take yourself to a place of stillness and peace, your sanctuary. This might be a place that you know, or it might be one that you create in your imagination. Call Archangel Michael to your side and know that you are completely safe and protected.

Close your eyes and perceive your paradise place with all your senses. Feel the earth underneath your feet, listen to the noises around you, enjoy the smells and the wonderful surroundings.

Now call Archangel Chamuel to you and ask him to send his subtle green and pink light into your heart chakra. Very gently, bit by bit, dissolve everything in there that prevents you from truly loving yourself. Take three conscious breaths in order to let go.

After a while, Chamuel sends pure angelic love into your heart chakra. Absorb it completely and then speak (ideally aloud): "I love myself", and repeat this at least three times.

Take three further deep breaths, stretch yourself, and open your eyes again.

Either immediately afterwards or later, stand in front of a mirror. Look into your own eyes until you eventually perceive your soul. This is the moment in which there is no reason left not to love yourself, since you see your true essence, which is nothing other than light and love.

Now speak again, aloud, while you continue gazing into your own eyes:

I love you. I truly love you!

Enjoy the feeling.

From now on (today and for the rest of your life), whenever you see yourself in a mirror or come across yourself mirrored in a window or suchlike, say: *I love you. I truly love you!*
Negative thoughts or statements about yourself are off-limits from now on. Should they still appear, call Archangel Chamuel straight away and ask him to send his light into your heart chakra (see above).

Speak the Mantra "Love"

Repeat the mantra "Love" until you vibrate, full of love. It really works!

Create a "self-love list"

Now write down everything that is loveable in you. For example: "I am loveable because I can listen to others very attentively."

Keep adding to the list as soon as you think of something new. Carry the list around with you and read it immediately whenever you think that you are not loveable (ideally in a loud and clear voice).

Update your wardrobe

Jointly with the Archangels Chamuel, Jophiel, and Haniel, clear out your wardrobe and from now on wear only clothes that you feel completely comfortable in. Anything else sabotages your feelings of self-worth.
After you have also worked with the soul affirmations and the soul journey, move back to the questions under "Reflection" and answer them once again. Chamuel and I are convinced that the numbers will have already changed to the positive.

ᘒ Soul Affirmation ᘒ

First ask Archangel Chamuel to enfold you in his subtle green and pink light. Then take a deep breath in and out, before you say (ideally aloud):

I love myself exactly as I am. I am perfectly loveable.

ᘒ Soul Journey ᘒ

Have pen and paper ready before you begin. You might want to take some notes during or directly after your journey.

With your eyes open take a deep breath in, and then slowly exhale while you close your eyes in slow motion and order your brain to automatically move into the Theta state. Breathe deeply in and out, and relax. Let your thoughts go by like birds flying past. Just let them go and enjoy the sense of your breath that continually links you to the breath of God and nourishes you. With each breath you take you move more deeply into a state of relaxation.

Feel, see, or imagine yourself being wrapped in delicate pink light that gently caresses your aura and your whole being. Enjoy sensing the frequency of love that surrounds you and relax even further.

You stand in a paradise garden underneath a cherry tree, whose pink blossoms emanate a delicious aroma, and feel a sense of well-being welling up in you. A luminous angel appears in front of you. It is Archangel Chamuel, who, full of love, gazes into your eyes. You feel immediately perfectly safe and secure, loved and accepted, just the way you are. Chamuel asks you to lie down under the flowering cherry tree whose branches move softly, almost protectively above you in the breeze. You feel Mother Earth underneath you and become aware of her heartbeat that connects with your own and nourishes you.

Then Archangel Chamuel kneels down next to you and, full of tenderness, begins to work on your heart chakra to relieve it of its shadows. Keep breathing deeply in order to let go.

With his pale green healing energy he also gently dissolves all negative emotions from your whole being, which have developed because of your belief patterns that you are not loveable. You notice how your heart chakra opens wider and wider like a wonderful lotus flower. You also feel how your whole aura becomes brighter and lighter. A heavenly feeling! You feel unconditionally loved and know that you are connected with the frequency of love. Shivers of delight permeate your whole being while Chamuel extends a magic mirror to you, in which you recognize all those characteristics in you that are loveable. Take your time and enjoy it!

When you have seen enough and return the mirror to Chamuel you notice that a circle of graceful animals has assembled around you. They have been attracted by the frequency of love that you radiate and look at you lovingly. A deep feeling of happiness flows through you as you know that you have truly changed your resonance and connected with your self-love. Maybe one or more of the animals has a message for you. Listen with your heart and know that from now on you will always attract more love.

Place your hands on your heart chakra, say, full of enthusiasm: "I love myself and my life, and my life loves me!" and open your arms as if you wanted to embrace the whole world. Enjoy the feeling and give thanks to Archangel Chamuel for the healing. He enfolds you in his wings before it is time to return to the here and now. Take three deep breaths in order to deeply anchor what you have experienced.

Connect yourself with Mother Earth and feel the roots underneath your feet, which link you to the crystal in the middle of the earth. Stretch your limbs in order to fully return into your body, the temple of your soul, and open your eyes.

Now write down which of your loveable characteristics you have seen in the mirror and compare this to your notes from before. Could you discover any more?

Day 15

EXPERIENCE THE POWER OF SOUND WITH THE HELP OF ARCHANGEL SANDALPHON

Music is well said to be the speech of angels.

Thomas Carlyle

"Greetings, beloved soul. I AM Archangel Sandalphon. It is my great wish to bring you even more in touch with the true power of sound, since in sound lies a hidden might that can only be compared to the power of love that overcomes all boundaries. The people of the old civilizations knew of this potency. Thus they were able to construct the most magnificent buildings and stone circles with the help of sounds and no machinery, and without applying any physical strength.

In these days of light increasing, this knowledge is rising more and more to the surface, so that today there are again people who perform true miracles in this way.

The issue for you, though, is not that you are supposed to transport stones with the help of sound, but that you work on expanding your consciousness in order to use this divine power for yourself, your life, and the healing of the world.

Music is truly a miracle cure on all levels. It is able to heal the soul as otherwise only love can do. It is also able to give comfort, ease pain, spark happiness, and increase the vibration of every person in such a way that, with its help, miracles can be created. Recognize its power and use it wisely."

Archangel Sandalphon
angel of music, voice, serenity
Aura colour: turquoise
Crystal: turquoise

The power of sound has a very special meaning for my husband Hubert. Here is his story:

Sandalphon's temple

The evening sun of a magnificent summer's day floods the steps leading up to the entrance portal. People in festive attire are arriving, ascending through tourists and visitors, dates are meeting, couples waiting.

I am sitting on the warm stone steps with my espresso-to-go and am full of joyful anticipation. Munich hosts an annual opera festival, and after a long time I am once again attending a performance: Verdi's wonderful opera Falstaff, a musical adaptation from Shakespeare's comedies; a cheerful and perhaps rather unusual subject matter for opera, which generally lives on love, pain and drama.

I remember this evening so clearly because it was the beginning of a development that changed my life. I grew up with classical music and have loved the opera since I was a child, but there was a long phase in my life when I withdrew and hardly attended any performances. Falstaff initiated my rediscovery of the power of music.

An evening at the opera has a clearing, purifying, and exhilarating effect on me. Even after a long working day, and when I have standing tickets and spend several hours on my feet in the upper circles I never feel tired, but animated, exhilarated, and full of energy and strength. I am optimistic and confident; after a fulfilling opera evening I can often still write creatively and with concentration on my book projects, with ideas springing forth.

Where does the fascinating energy of music come from, that inspires me and provides me with all the strength that I need? Music is the language of the heart. When I am at an opera my everyday consciousness is switched off; my ego does not have any opportunity to distress me with troubles, concerns, or anxieties. At the same time my heart can open to the beauty of the music. Even when the subject matter is

---

rather dramatic or demanding, the beauty and love coming from the music radiate directly into my heart.

Since I have taken up going to the opera regularly again, my life has changed dramatically for the positive. I have been able to realize projects that had not functioned for a long time; professional changes and developments have become possible, and I have finally found the creativity, resourcefulness, and discipline to work on my books.

I buy my ticket way ahead, so that there can be no excuse for not attending an evening. Opera days are sacred to me. When I arrive, walking through the pedestrian zone at the Max-Joseph-Platz, and walk up the steps to the main entrance, the curtain of everyday life falls behind me and I immerse myself in the world of music and beauty. This is no escape: quite the contrary, it is time out, almost like a short holiday. For me, the opera is "Sandalphon's temple". Here I can connect myself directly with energy, strength, and beauty, and as behoves a temple I leave it positively changed.

Regular opera visits constitute an essential module in my "project quality of life". I made a decision to again include more things that signify for me good quality of life – irrespective of how much else I have to do, or think I have to do. The amazing thing was that "project quality of life' brought many new things into my life that had not functioned for a long time. Ultimately, things have changed only because I began to feel and radiate more vitality. The music in "Sandalphon's temple" constitutes for me joy and recreation, and is at the same time part of my successful manifestation process. Little else has changed my life over the past few years as successfully as the joy I get from the music at the opera.

Falstaff is Verdi's last opera and one of the few with a happy ending. In its last act, Falstaff finally realizes that he has been set up, and he takes it in good humour.

The great final fugue begins "Tutto nel mondo è burla…" and ends with applause for a magnificent opera evening. I go down the steps and before I "change worlds" again I remain for a moment standing in between the pillars, looking into the glistening satin evening sky. The lights of the houses greet me, people pass by me.

Tutto nel mondo è burla – all the world is folly. With gratitude I walk home.

My friend Gido, who is a fantastic singer, actor, and dancer as well as a phenomenal coach, experienced the following not long ago:

The right sound with Archangel Sandalphon

A few days ago, Archangel Sandalphon again confirmed for me with what lightness and humour the angels work. Several weeks ago I had signed a new contract to take on the leading part in a very well-known musical. It is a role that I have played before, years ago, and that I love very much; but I knew how stressful the part would be, physically as well as mentally and vocally. The show I am talking about here is *Cats* – arguably one of the greatest challenges for any performer as you are pushed to your limits in every sense. The songs demand the voice use all its highs and lows, while each number is fully choreographed, and you must dance across the stage with catlike movements.

Over the past two years I had withdrawn a little from the stage and had instead dedicated my time exclusively to my clients and workshops, and because of this I was not at full fitness. I have to say I felt a bit nervous, thinking about tackling this part, especially with only eight days of rehearsals. But as I now had the angels by my side, I asked them for their support in reminding me of everything and looking after my health. I particularly appealed to Archangel Sandalphon to help me be vocally perfect and not only sound the right notes but also touch people's hearts with the songs; I would do this by using the right shades and tones in my voice, with ease.

Thus I began playing this character; I plunged in one weekend when we had four performances in two days. By Sunday night I hardly knew how to stand or sit. But when I woke up on Monday I felt as well as always and thought: "Looks like I am in better shape than I thought…"

During the first few shows, though, I naturally very much felt the strain, in particular in my voice; but after a few days I started feeling as if I had been playing this role for months.

It must have been during the eighth show when I had a hitherto unknown feeling: I was utterly relaxed, even though I was in the middle of singing one of the most difficult numbers of the evening. I felt afraid that I was only giving half my strength to the song – pretending, so to speak – on the other hand I was intellectually conscious of the fact that this was not true. I gave everything, used my voice to the fullest, and despite this was fully at ease? As I finished my last number in Act 1, I asked the angels what was happening here: am I faking it, am I not giving enough?

Suddenly I heard Archangel Sandalphon at my right side. He said, laughing:

"Well, that's what it is like if you work with us angels. You should all understand how much lighter your lives can be with our help – and in every situation. You have asked for the right kind of help and that you have received. And now enjoy your show with ease and joy!"

I nearly started laughing out loud – which would not have gone down well in the middle of the show. Since then, I have done no show or rehearsal without first asking Sandalphon to look after my sound and to guide me in such a way that I can perform the part with a healthy voice.

My colleagues seem somewhat bemused that I am doing so well on all levels, and that my exertions do not wear me down; but I just smile and thank my angels for this support.

⮞ *Reflection* ⮜

The power of music is now undisputed. Next to smell, it is the sense that reaches the limbic system (the emotional centre of the brain) the fastest and can evoke great mood changes within the shortest time.

As is well known, the music an expectant mother listens to during pregnancy affects the unborn child. Some girlfriends and course participants have told me that they had angel music (such as *Snowflake* by Lajos Sitas, *Angel Love* by Aeoliah) playing in the background while giving birth. This way, they found that not only was the birth easier than usual, but also the baby was met with familiar sounds as soon as it made its way out of the warm, sheltering womb of its mother, and its entry into the world was less harsh.

Music is also used by some doctors and dentists for relaxation and alleviation of pain during operations, since the world is gradually realizing that the power of sound has no limits. This was generally known and accepted in the past.

As described in the passage about my "Burning Desire" (see day 1), I have also experienced the power of music very clearly within my own body. Without it I would probably not be on earth now. When I was ill, playing piano on stage and listening to music on my CD player were my life elixirs; I needed the sound as I need the air to breathe.

Now ponder in which situations the power of music has already helped you and write them down.

⮞ *Activities for today and for the future* ⮜

⮞ *Choose music to strengthen your aura*

As you know, there are many very different forms of music. Some sounds instantly shift you into a joyful, enterprising mood, others relax you, others again move you to tears, and much more.

Today, though, the aim is to choose a piece of music that you definitely feel strengthens and thus also protects your aura. A CD that I especially value in this context is *The Heart of Healing* by Karen Drucker, a very touching and powerfully interpreted affirmation CD. Whenever I am not in my centre I only need to listen to one or two songs and the world is OK again; the lyrics are extremely healing. Listening to this, minute by minute my aura becomes more powerful. My colleagues have also had very similar experiences with this CD.

Now listen to some music that triggers something similar in you. If you do not know what to select, ask Archangel Sandalphon to help you.

ᴄ∾ Sing

In order to have a sonorous voice it is important to sing regularly. This does not mean that you need to start taking singing lessons (unless it is your wish, of course!), but just that you should sing whenever you feel like it. That might be under the shower or in the car when your favourite song or a gorgeous opera aria starts up. The only thing that is important is that you actually do it (and best start today), as then your voice will stay flexible and remain young for longer.

How your voice sounds is highly important for your personal and professional success; the power of sound is not to be underestimated. Research has shown that it is the sound of the voice that determines whether a person listens to us, not, as most people assume, what is actually being said. During a phone conversation only 8 per cent of the content – as opposed to 92 per cent of the sound of the voice – determines whether someone really listens to you; in a face-to-face conversation it is again only 8 per cent of the content, against 37 per cent of the sound of the voice and 55 per cent of body language, that determines whether someone listens to you attentively (figures from Arthur Samuel Joseph's book *Vocal Power*).

This should definitely be an incentive for you to look more closely into your voice. Maybe you would even like to take a few sessions with a voice coach.

ᴄ∾ Listen to your answerphone

Now listen to your voice on your voicemail or your answerphone. How is this for you? Do you like what you hear? Or does your voice sound nearly unbearable to your ears?

Should the latter be the case, it is a sign that you still need to work on loving yourself and on your self-confidence, as your voice is an expression of who you are (if this is the case for you, please repeat the activities from the preceding chapter over the next few days).

Before you think any further, call Archangel Sandalphon to you and ask him to enfold you in his turquoise light, and breathe deeply in and out. Relax.

When you feel calm and relaxed, place one hand on your belly, breathe in through your nose, and allow your belly to expand outward. While you breathe out, you feel how your belly returns to its previous position. Practise this breathing exercise a few times until it feels absolutely natural for you.

Then, in the same way, take another breath in and while you breathe out (without stopping the air in the belly) say: "*I am...* (add your name here)." Repeat it until you like the sound of your voice.[3]

Afterwards – or after you have completed the soul journey – record a new message on your voicemail or answerphone and have Sandalphon support you in this.

⁀✑ *Chant mantras*

Music is sometimes called "the yoga of sound"; thus chanting mantras ranks high in various yoga traditions. Archangel Sandalphon also advises you to become familiar with this important spiritual practice, because by singing mantras in Sanskrit you can bypass your intellect. This way you reach more and more into your heart space, since the repeating sounds transfer you into a kind of heightened state and help you to become purer and clearer. A wonderful feeling!

There are various ways to chant mantras:

- Find a chanting group that meets regularly.
- Attend a yoga class that integrates mantras into the lesson.
- Buy yourself a beautiful mantra CD and chant along.

⁀✑ *Create your own sound mantras*

Archangel Sandalphon asks you to create together with him so-called "sound mantras". These are images of sound, which want to arise within you in order to express your feelings and your being. At the same time, they enable you to get to know new areas of your voice's spectrum and to become freer.

Create a sacred space for yourself before you begin, so that you can experiment within a safe environment. Then become still, turn your attention inside and give space for a sound or sound mantra to arise within you out of your subconscious.

⟵⟶ *Play an instrument*

If you have in the past engaged in creating music yourself, today is a good day to dedicate some time to this desire; if not, Sandalphon asks you to ponder which instrument you have always wanted to learn. Ask yourself honestly whether you would still like to do so. If the answer is yes, take the first steps to finally put this wish into practice – today!

⟵⟶ *Attend a concert or visit the opera*

In order to really truly feel the energy of music it is very helpful to go somewhere where you can hear it live. Choose something that appeals to your taste in music – or allow yourself to be inspired by something new in order to broaden your horizon.

⟵⟶ *Soul Affirmation* ⟵⟶

First ask Archangel Sandalphon to enfold you in his turquoise light. Then take a deep breath in and out, before you say (ideally aloud):

The energy of music carries me, inspires me, and protectively surrounds me.

⟵⟶ *Soul Journey* ⟵⟶

Have pen and paper ready before you begin. You might want to take some notes during or directly after your journey.

With your eyes open take a deep breath in, and then slowly exhale while you close your eyes in slow motion and order your brain to automatically move into the Theta state. Breathe deeply in and out, and relax.

Let your thoughts go by like leaves gliding along a river; do not hold on to them. Just let them go and move more deeply into a state of relaxation. Enjoy the sense of how your breath nourishes you and connects you with the sphere of the angels. A wonderful feeling!

While you become calmer and calmer as you concentrate on your breath, a beautiful, boyish-looking angel, submerged in resplendent turquoise-blue light, appears next to you. It is Archangel Sandalphon.

Full of tenderness, he wraps his wings around you, and you feel how his profound calmness and serenity are transferred to you.

Then he takes you by the hand and rises into the air with you. In spirals you soar higher and higher until you reach the shores of a celestial ocean that sparkles in the sunlight in the lightest shades of turquoise. Sandalphon bids you sit down in the white sand and listen to the sound of the waves. You do as you are asked and become aware of how the sound of the waves calms you and how it allows you to slip into a state of very deep relaxation. Enjoy it!

At last Archangel Sandalphon takes your hand again and helps you get up. Together you walk along the shore until a stunning building, crowned by a huge golden dome, looms in front of you. Reverently you walk up the marble steps with Sandalphon and move into a kind of temple hall, in the centre of which you find a crystalline couch – right underneath the dome, which has been created according to the laws of sacred geometry.

Sandalphon indicates that you are to recline on the couch. As soon as you lie down music starts to sound, seemingly unknown to you yet very familiar on some levels. It feels to you as if you were in a sacred sound-healing chamber while the music begins to cleanse, heal and increase your whole field in waves. Activated by the sacred frequencies of the music, every single one of your cells starts to vibrate. It feels great. Intuitively you know that at this moment old shadows bid you farewell; you can feel yourself becoming so much brighter and lighter.

Then Archangel Sandalphon's sonorous voice sounds at your ear:

"Beloved being, this music does not only contribute to purifying your aura and healing you on the energetic level. It also activates idle strands of your DNS that want to be revived again. Thus you can find your way through the veil on earth and perceive the messages that are carried within your field every single moment. That way you will find it much easier to recognize the relationships between all things."

These words and the sacred sounds fill you with infinite gratitude, and within you emerges a feeling of oneness with All-That-Is.

When you finally slip off the couch again you sense the wonderful transformation of your resonance, and you know that you are no longer the same person as before your visit to this heavenly sound-healing temple. You gratefully look up to the sacred dome and, astounded, you see that a luminous white dove is hovering above you. Waves of bliss flow through your whole being.

Finally it is time to return to the here and now. Together with Archangel Sandalphon you leave the sacred chamber and fly back to the earth. You smoothly land on your feet, begin to stretch your body, and slowly open your eyes.

Day 16

ENJOY YOUR LIFE WITH THE HELP OF ANGEL RAMAELA

O man, learn to dance,
Or else the angels in heaven
will not know what to do with you.
St. Augustine

"*Greetings, beloved being. I AM Angel Ramaela, the angel of joy. Allow yourself to be enveloped in my bright orange light that immerses you in waves of purest joy, and take a deep breath.*

What is it that keeps you from enjoying your life to the full? That so often has you appear so serious? Believe me, your life is many times easier and lighter when you connect to your true vitality.

Even if it does not seem like this, every single moment you have the choice to either allow yourself to be weighed down by the sorrows and burdens of the past or to decide on ease and joy. In the energy of joy you find solutions that you can only dream of while the energy of doubt rules. Thus immerse yourself in my energy and that of my companions, the dolphins, that you love so much. They are true masters of love, grace, ease, and joy; for that reason your heart opens instantly as soon as you see them or a picture of them.

From now on send the intention out to the universe that you will connect with their energy to that extent that you can leave any comparison and any competition behind, just as they do. It is these two things that deprive you of your joy in living and weaken your vibrational frequency. Instead be happy about the success of each person; that way you also have a part in it, since ultimately all is one.

Immerse yourself once more in the waves of purest joy emanating from the dolphins and me, begin to dance through your life and to delight in the details of every day, and miracles will be part of your life!"

Angel Ramaela
angel of joy
Aura colour: orange
Crystal: aqua aura crystal

Britta, one of my ANGEL LIFE COACH®es, had the following funny and refreshing experience:

Lucy and Ramaela – or the colour orange

"Hello, hello, I am Lucy – and who are you?"

A bold half-metre hand puppet with tousled orange hair, green-orange dungarees, and sweet freckles waves to me at a street party. Within seconds my heart opens and I chat with her for a good half hour. I cannot buy her, she tells me, but I could adopt her. Adoption needs to be well considered, and thus I leave Lucy with heavy heart. But she calls after me: "Hey, I'll wait for you."

And I? I have fallen in love with Lucy.

A few weeks later, my husband and I have arranged for the "adoption" and Lucy moves into our house, into our life. Whenever we are fighting, are angry, or grumble, Lucy explains to us how we could do it in a better way. This small puppet has developed her own character astonishingly quickly, and she also tells us again and again: "I am Lucy Joy, and I have come to bring you joy."

No idea where she got that from. She is right, though: she enriches our life with her intelligent comments, her accurate advice, her bold and heart-opening smile. Wherever we go with Lucy, she always wins people's hearts and puts a smile on their faces. And time and again she stresses how much of a favourite colour orange is for her.

During a seminar in September 2009, Isabelle explains to us the archangels and

---

the colours in which their light radiates. Someone in the audience asks: "And what about the colour orange? Is orange not represented among the angels?"

"Orange? Yes, of course, that is the colour of angel Ramaela, the angel of joy," Isabelle says.

At this moment, we finally understand why our Lucy Joy adores the colour orange so much.

Thank you, dear Ramaela, that you have sent us Lucy Joy with her love for the colour orange!

P.S.: By the way, when questioned Lucy told us: "Sure, Ramaela sent me to you so that I may bring joy to your life."

The paths of the angels are amazing and wonderful.

⟋⟍ *Reflection* ⟋⟍

A quote by the well-known philosopher and wisdom teacher Jiddu Krishnamurti from his book *Total Freedom* has always touched me deeply. It says: "When one child is compared with another this constitutes a hurt. Every form of comparison hurts."

It is so true and so utterly corresponds with what the dolphins told me when I was swimming with them in the open sea. As we are all one, when comparing ourselves with others the following things happen: either we feel bad because in comparison with another person we fare worse, or we do not feel comfortable in our own skin because we put someone down in comparison to us – which immediately affects our vibrational frequency; this is true even when we are under the impression that we are doing better because we are somehow better than the other person.

It is the same with any form of competitive thinking, which ultimately only promotes envy.

In order to continuously increase our frequency, though, it is necessary to free ourselves more and more of these rivalries and to become like the dolphins.

Now create a sacred space for yourself, before you answer the following questions in writing.

Call Angel Ramaela to your side and ask her to accompany you throughout the whole day and to surround you with her orange light, so that you are entirely connected to the frequency of joy. Take a deep breath in and out in order to absorb the light, and relax.

Now think about which people you compare yourself with, and with regard to which people you feel competition or even envy. Be honest with yourself! Even if you have such feelings, there is no reason to judge yourself for it since, as you know by now, we all consist of light and shadow.

ᐠᐤ *Activities for today* ᐠᐤ

ᐤ *Bless your former "competitors" and be happy about their successes*

After you have answered the question about "competitors", bless everyone who has come into your mind.

Then write down how happy you are about all the successes of the people you consider successful. For example: "I am very happy about Margareta's success. I think it is fantastic how her school has expanded in the past few years."

In this way, you create an entirely different resonance that helps you to become freer and attract more and more success yourself.

ᐤ *Make a date with friends*

In order to love life you need regular, fun meetings with friends. Today is such a day. Go out for a meal with your best friend. Enjoy a funny film with a group of people. Or do whatever brings you fun.

ᐤ *Dance*

It is well known that dancing encourages vitality. Time and again I experience in my workshops and trainings that some participants have a bit of a strange, nervous look on their faces when the lively rhythms start to sound through the workshop space and I ask them all to dance. Only a few minutes later though, most of them are enjoying it and many pairs of eyes begin to shine more and more.

As the angels say, you cannot hold on to anything when dancing; thus sadness, frustration, lethargy etc. all dissolve by themselves. Now dance round your flat or house to your favourite songs. Or make a dance date with friends; that way you can do two activities at the same time.

↝ *Activities for the future* ↝

↝ *Aloha time*

Aloha[4] is a wonderful Hawaiian expression for love, respect, appreciation, compassion, understanding etc.. It is at the same time a form of greeting, and much, infinitely, more. It is also an attitude towards life and life philosophy.

Aloha also means to honour and enjoy life. But words just do not suffice to describe Aloha. Only one thing is certain: with Aloha you live more easily!

During a holiday on Maui, Hawaii (Hawaii is also called "Aloha state", by the way), my husband Hubert and I realized once again that life proceeds at a different pace here: it moves more slowly, it's more relaxed – and at the same time more in the flow. Thus we created the expression "Aloha time" and tried to do as the Hawaiian people do.

And something amazing crystallized out of this: the more we gave ourselves space to enjoy life and start things slowly, without stress, the more creative and productive we became. In the preceding days, I had still felt quite stressed: My calendar *Himmlische Begleiter 2012 (Heavenly companions 2012)* would have to be more or less finished after our trip to Hawaii, and most of the work was still ahead of me. With Aloha time (naturally fully approved by the angels), though, it suddenly worked out and I completed it very easily.

Allow Aloha time to become an important part of your existence! Our times are so fast-moving that it is no wonder that we find it difficult to notice and recognize all the many signs of the angels.

Do not allow your everyday life to be too dominated by times, schedules, obligations, BlackBerries, iPhones etc., but live slowly and enjoy your life. This way you create time in which creative ideas and other messages can get through to you, that help you to walk your own path and realize the dreams of your life.

↝ *Soul Affirmation* ↝

First ask Angel Ramaela to enfold you in her bright orange light. Then take a deep breath in and out, before you say (ideally aloud):

I allow myself to enjoy my life to the full. I love my life, and my life loves me.

⌦ *Soul Journey* ⌦

Have pen and paper ready before you begin. You might want to take some notes during or directly after your journey.

With your eyes open take a deep breath in, and then slowly exhale while you close your eyes in slow motion and order your brain to automatically move into the Theta state. Breathe deeply in and out, and relax. Let your thoughts go by like leaves gliding along a river; do not hold on to them. Just let them go and move more deeply into a state of relaxation.

You find yourself at an untouched tropical, white, sandy beach. Your soul enjoys the beauty of nature. Feel the warm sand underneath your feet and the delicate beams of the morning sun on your face. Enjoy listening to the sound of the waves and the cries of the seagulls that circle above you.

Next to you an exquisite-looking angel now appears. It is Ramaela, the angel of joy. She is surrounded by the loveliest orange light that you have ever seen. Its effect unfolds the moment Ramaela embraces you with her wings: you feel suddenly flushed with such joie de vivre *that your frequency instantly rises.*

Full of joy, you look out to the ocean that glitters and shines in the most brilliant hues of turquoise, and you spy countless dolphins on the horizon performing artistic jumps. Your heart positively dances with joy when all at once a bluish-silvery lustrous dolphin, a so-called angel dolphin, swims towards you.

In the presence of Angel Ramaela you feel so safe and secure that nothing can stop you from moving towards this special dolphin in the sea. As soon as you approach the dolphin he starts to scan your aura with his sonar. It feels strange, but at the same time extremely healing. He indicates clearly that you are to just let yourself drift in the water while he swims in circles around and underneath you, always accompanied by the clicking sounds that are by now familiar to you. In this way he very gently relieves you of any comparisons, any feelings of competition and envy. It feels simply wonderful.

Eventually his head emerges right in front of you and the angel dolphin looks into your eyes in his inimitable way, full of the purest love, so that your heart brims over with joy. Suddenly all the other dolphins are nearby and start to play with you. They dive and jump in magnificent formations around you, and you feel how your heart chakra opens wider and wider while you start to swim with them, utterly enchanted.

All that has hitherto prevented you from enjoying your life to the full dissolves into thin air, practically by itself, now that you have become completely one with the energy of the dolphins that radiates only infinite love, deep joy, grace, and lightness. Suddenly you realize that you feel so much at home with them because they embody your very own essence.

Telepathically you ask them to activate those strands of your DNA that help you always to be connected to this deep zest for life. And again you hear their clicking sounds and feel how you become even brighter and lighter, just as if you were already in heaven.

At this moment, Angel Ramaela appears above your heads, surrounded by her luminous orange light, and gives you a sign that it is time to swim back to the shore. Full of gratitude, you take leave of these very beautiful animals and you know that you are no longer the same. With shining eyes and heart vibrating, full of joy you leave the water to be wrapped in a soft towel by Ramaela. You gratefully dry yourself and decide from this point onwards to live your life full of grace, lightness and joy – just like the dolphins.

Now take three deep breaths in order to anchor within you what you have experienced, stretch your body, and slowly open your eyes.

·⊷ Day 17 ⊶·

CREATE A WONDERFUL PARTNERSHIP WITH THE HELP OF ANGEL SOQEDHAZI

We are each of us angels with only one wing –
And we can only fly by embracing one another.
Luciano de Crescenzo

"Greetings, beloved soul. I AM Angel Soqedhazi. Once you start seeing yourself and all others with the eyes of love there is no longer any impediment to a wonderful partnership. Because in this moment, you have realized that it is your individual essence that is of importance. In this moment, you become aware of the things that unite you and leave everything behind that separates you. This way you enable the true unison of your souls to emerge, so that your essences can connect and unite in deep love. Only such love truly deserves its name. Everything else is just desires and conveniences. Beware of them, since they cut you off from your true power. Thus connect now with me and with the infinite power of love, so that you yourself turn more and more into a partner whose resonance attracts nothing else but a wonderful partnership; since that is what you truly deserve!"

Angel Soqedhazi
angel of partnership
Aura colour: pink-golden
Crystal: pink topaz

Stephanie, a friend and among other things also an ANGEL LIFE COACH®, experienced a wonderful event:

A dream comes true

I am calm, inwardly expanded, deeply grateful, happy, and full of trust. Warm rain rustles lightly through the olive branches here on Mallorca, and far down I hear the regular swell of the sea.

Isabelle asked me to write down "our" story, because it is definitely a story that the angels and in particular Angel Soqedhazi contributed to. In order to understand the miracle of this story I should start at the beginning – was I then already guided by the hands of angels?

On 6 December 2008, I met a man – Holger – and at the moment we met my heart opened. Was it love at first sight or had I met my soul partner here? Was it fate or "just" my longing for a relationship and partnership?

It was like a sense of recognition, a feeling of familiarity, a merging on a soul level – as if we already knew each other from a previous lifetime. For the first time in my life I felt that I was completely accepted and loved, just as I am. A wonderful feeling!

Rose-coloured clouds carried us, in particular me, into the fairytale heaven of love – and I consciously put all the ominous signs that arose in front of both my inner and outer eye, to the side.

An abrupt ending – like a fall from light into darkness – seven months later.

Were the challenges in the outer environment too big, the old and new responsibilities in life too heavy, the own story not dissolved yet: children who need their father, substantial job challenges, a serious illness in the family, the path to our own roots of steadfastness in life, or the distance between Munich and Karlsruhe? Was the love not deep and strong enough, or was everything just appearance? Were we not free or mature enough for a new love?

Whatever the reasons, the bond was abruptly severed, and I have accepted it. There was no more clarifying conversation, and I was lost in separateness. In addition to pain and deep sadness these questions kept coming up: how can such a wonderful thing first appear and enter my life, as though it was given to me by angels, fate, or coincidence, and then dissolve into nothingness? My doubtful questioning saw me sometimes even quarrelling with the angels.

But help is always there when we ask for it. Such I was also given to experience; was held, guided, and supported by inner and outer helpers. Healing could happen – forgiveness from the depth of my heart was possible.

To my ever-recurring questions: "What else is it that I am supposed to learn? How to develop myself further? And when does my heartfelt wish for a loving, equal relationship come true?", I always received the same answer, whether through readings, by angels, and more and more often also from my own inner guidance:

"Nothing – you do not need to do anything, everything happens with perfect timing. You are wonderful and unique and loveable exactly the way you are."

For nearly two years I have been regularly listening to Isabelle's *Angel Trance Meditations* when going to sleep. I choose them intuitively and stay for a while with the topic. I have usually fallen asleep by the time the meditations reach the stage of the prana breathing, or sometimes the stage of strengthening the chakras, and am thus never consciously "present" when the individual angel appears on the journey, accompanies me, and acts upon me in a healing loving way. I know, though, that the messages still anchor themselves deep in my unconscious.

I feel how free, light, and happy I have been for at least a year now. I do not only believe but really feel that everything does happen at the right moment.

Since about November 2010, I had been listening to Angel Soqedhazi (Angel Trance Meditation no. 14) when going to sleep, to open up again to a new, truly deep partnership and love, and to invite this energy into my life anew.

In February 2011, driving to a health and healing event, I wanted to inform one of my clients about this presentation but "accidentally" (an angel at work?) dialled Holger's phone number instead…

Out of an amiable small talk suddenly emerged the question: "Do we want to meet again? We do still have a conversation pending, don't we?"

Now, I did not really want to go back into old stories – at the moment I felt genuinely light, free, and simply happy in my life. I wondered whether he wanted to disengage himself, through a clarifying chat, in order to be free for his new relationship, or whether he wanted to ask my forgiveness for what happened back then.

I was curious and asked the angels every day for guidance, if they would please see to it that in case of a potential meeting the best should happen for both of us.

Two months later Holger walked in through my door and it was as if we had lovingly said goodbye to each other only two weeks ago, and not nearly two years ago.

It was magic: the bond was re-established as if through angels' hands, the intimacy just simply present. Had time stood still? Is such a thing as this a miracle or just life?

Both of us continue to move forward. I am sure that Angel Soqedhazi and all the other angels guide us, and the two of us have the courage to move into this light-filled opportunity of love lived that presents itself to us. Now is the moment!

And just at this moment, as I write these words, I am calm, infinitely happy and grateful, connected with myself, with the light and the love and the man of my heart, just trusting that the best will happen.

And all the angels are around. Thank you!

Gabriele, one of the listeners to my radio programme, also manifested her soulmate with Angel Soqedhazi's help:

My soulmate on the Camino
For some time I had felt that I was losing energy. Especially in the mornings when I got up, I felt very tired out and did not know why. Since I started meditating every morning and often also in the evenings with Isabelle's Angel Trance Meditations, I have been pretty much able to keep up my vitality during the day.

In March though, out of the blue, I had a burnout, with the accompanying symptoms of tinnitus, panic attacks, and pain in the lumbar spine. And so I finally started thinking about my life and, through this and also with the help of my therapist, reached the decision that I should end my marriage as quickly as possible. I also decided to walk the Camino de Santiago in Spain for a month.

Before I went on the journey I did a meditation and afterwards wrote affirmations intended to accompany me all day while on the Camino. I also "created" my soulmate: I described him as accurately as possible and always placed a "thank you" at the beginning of the sentence, as if this man was already in my life. I wished for example that he be spiritually open, wanted to build up a healing centre with me, that he could cook and dance, that he were tall with blue eyes, and so on. Thus I wrote: "Thank you for my wonderful soulmate. Thank you that my soulmate is tall and has blue eyes. Thank you for..." etc.

Two days before the start of my journey the angels arranged for my flight home to be a few days later than I had originally booked, and I felt that there is a reason for everything.

When I finally started my journey on the Camino I frequently communicated with the angels while I walked, and also diligently spoke my affirmations. It felt great.

After only fourteen days my desired soul partner emerged on the path – emerging all of a sudden from behind a donkey! And we met again... already in our second meeting we felt a strong primordial familiarity on a level that neither of us had experienced before.

It was a wonderful sense of being reunited! We understand on a mental level what the other says, without any words needing to be spoken. And the really incredible thing is that he fulfils all my wishes – without exception. An absolute dream!

Ever since this day I very, very often thank Angel Soqedhazi, who is responsible for help with seeking a partner.

Reflection

There is about as much again to say on this topic as I said on day 5: I could probably fill a whole book with it! Together with Angel Soqedhazi I have limited myself to the essentials; we are both convinced that you can from these activities create a wonderful relationship.

Today's Activities for Couples

Devote more time to your partner

Give some thought to what gives great pleasure to both you and your partner, and then agree on which of these activities he/she would like to do together with you. Do it – today!

Write a "love list"

Create a sacred space for yourself, call Angel Soqedhazi to your side, and ask her to accompany you throughout the whole day and envelop you in her pink-golden light, so that you are completely connected with the frequency of love. Breathe deeply in and out in order to absorb the light, and relax.

Now write down everything that you love about your partner and communicate this to him/her in your own unique style (for example through a wonderful handwritten letter, on your date today, in small regular "bites"...).

Make a commitment

If you have had a rather casual approach to your relationship up to now, then today is a good day to tell your partner that you would like to get involved with him/her on a deeper level and that you would like to "come out of the closet" with regard to your connection to each other; that is the only way that your partner will feel truly safe and be able to trust you to the extent that a wonderful fulfilled relationship becomes possible.

This could mean that you suggest moving in together, getting engaged, getting married, having children, or whatever deep involvement means to you both.

If you have already made a clear commitment you might want to expand it a bit. A relationship should lend both partners roots as well as wings. On the one hand, this means that each must be able to deeply trust the other and if necessary also lean on them. On the other hand, each partner also needs the freedom to realize their own dreams. Have you already made this commitment? If not, today is a good moment to do so.

∙◇ Leave a relationship that sabotages you

If you have for some time had the feeling of being in a relationship that does anything but support you, today is the time to take a decision: to either, one last time, try everything in order to transform the relationship into a fulfilling partnership, or to finally implement the separation.

∙◇ Future Activities for Couples ∙◇

∙◇ Appreciate your partner

It is important to acknowledge your partner's successes, and to express this out loud.

Men in particular have historically been judged almost exclusively by their "successes" – earning ability, career progression, material goods and so on. Thus it is not really surprising that many men still feel that these are the most important or only aspects for which they might receive praise. Try to express to your male partner what you appreciate about him and see as positive – independent of any material "achievements".

Women are often still seen as the guardians and preservers of the home, skilled at creating an atmosphere of beauty and security. Even though your partner may make this look easy, it will make her feel happy and appreciated if you tell her that she has made the dining table into a true feast for the eyes and that she has prepared a delicious meal. Take note of the creative ideas she uses to shape your home into a wonderful place. Praise everything that you like about her.

Whether man or woman, take care to appreciate and praise your partner for whatever positive aspects you see in them and for anything positive they have done.

✑ *Give thanks*

Even if you are of the opinion that it is self-evident that your partner should pull his weight at home you should regularly thank him for his support. In the not too distant past domestic chores were often perceived as unmanly; this is more deeply ingrained in the human genes than you might be conscious of. Besides, your partner will be much more willing to help if you do not criticize him, even if he does something that does not quite match up to your own standards.

There are most likely countless other reasons why you could praise him. So do it!

Many a relationship suffers from exactly this: that one person takes everything for granted. To express gratitude, genuinely, from the bottom of your heart, creates a wonderful frequency that also helps to overcome the various smaller difficulties a relationship comes across with grace and ease.

Suffice to say that a man should appreciate and thank his partner, not only for extraordinary things but also for regular, "small" favours and tasks.

Angel Soqedhazi's message is:

"If people could learn from the outset of their lives to express their gratitude with all their heart – for everything wonderful and also for all they take for granted that happens for them through others –, far fewer relationships would break up. Thus I ask you to allow voicing gratitude to become an ever-present part of your life."

✑ *Listen carefully*

Your partner will be overjoyed if you regularly make space to consciously listen to her, without necessarily immediately handing out advice or proposals for solutions. Women like to talk about things they have experienced or are engaged in because they get clarity in an intuitive way, through narration or talking for its own sake. If you instantly jump in with a piece of advice – even though it is well-meaning – you might deprive your partner of the opportunity to find solutions in her own way.

Many ancient cultures honoured the fact that men and women clarify and deal with things differently: men and women came together in separate groups, to talk about things exclusively with people of the same gender.
In a partnership, however, it is also important to share your own concerns with your partner.

Rather than pestering your husband with questions, simply allow him the space to talk when he is ready to. Here too it is important to listen sincerely and not bring in your own problems right away, once you have established deeper communication between the two of you.

✐ *Pay compliments*

It is very important that you consciously see, or look at, your partner. Too often, after a certain time a man in a relationship stops noticing all the things his partner does in order to appeal to him. Continue what came so naturally at the beginning of a relationship: namely, tell your partner how beautiful her hair is, how sexy she looks in her new outfit, and so on.

Compliments are important for both genders, not just women: I often notice how happy it makes men when I pay them a compliment. If it is true, tell your partner how much you appreciate it that he is solid as a rock that you can always lean on, when you want to let go for a while, or on how much you trust him.

Men definitely like it too when you compliment them on how they look or on some garment they wear which you particularly like.

I think one of the nicest compliments that you can receive from a partner is: "I feel entirely safe with you because I feel that you love and accept me as I am, so that I can be fully myself with you."

✐ *Plan regular dates with your partner*

In order to keep a relationship alive, you need to take regular time for joint adventures, just as you probably did at the beginning of your partnership. Make a date for just the two of you, without any children, at least once a week (if you do not live too far apart) and go to a restaurant together, to the cinema, to a concert, go dancing, do sports, or something else that you both love doing together.

With long-distance relationships this frequency is not always possible, of course, but long distance has an upside: over the years I have found that couples who live far apart very often use the precious time they have together much better than couples who live everyday life together.

✐ *Arrange joint downtime in special places*

Regular dates are not sufficient on their own: in order to really spend time with each other you need to plan-in longer periods of downtime together (without children, as above).

Plan trips or holidays to places that attract both of you. Go in for things that you both have fun with. And should time be scarce, then just spend a night in a nice hotel. Come up with some ideas!

⚬〜⚬ Say or write regularly: "I love you!"

At the start of a relationship, while both partners are on a pink cloud, it comes very naturally to tell the other one how much you love him or her. With time this often decreases, and contributes to the feeling that everyday life is no longer as beautiful as it was in the beginning.

Be imaginative and continue to declare your love from the bottom of your heart time and again, so that your affection remains fresh and alive.

A friend of my mum's was exuberantly happy when, on holiday with her girlfriends, she found in her suitcase – hidden tucked away between her things – many small slips of paper on which her husband had written: "I love you."

⚬〜⚬ Today's Activities for Singles ⚬〜⚬

⚬〜⚬ Look at your past

Now create a sacred space for yourself before you answer the following questions in writing.

Call Angel Soqedhazi to your side. Ask her to accompany you for the whole day and to envelop you in her pink-golden light, so that you are completely connected with the frequency of love. Take a deep breath, in and out, in order to absorb the light, and relax.

- Are there one or more ex-partners who you have not forgiven yet? If so, go back to day 11 and perform the forgiveness ritual, or listen to the soul journey.
- Are you still in love with someone even though you know that they are not your soulmate, or that a relationship will never be possible? If so, it is time to finally let go of this person if you would truly like to manifest a new and wonderful partnership for yourself. This does not mean that you are not allowed to like this person any longer; your resonance however has to radiate that you are ready for your dream partner – which cannot be the case as long as another person resides in your aura in a similar way. Go back to day 3 and do the exercises "Release your past" and "Recognize your soul lessons", as well as the soul journey.

⚬〜⚬ Love Yourself

Ask yourself with an honest heart whether you love yourself the way you are.

If so: fantastic – this way you already are a magnet for true love!

If not: please go back to day 14 and choose the activities that help you with this. Maybe you would also like to listen again to the soul journey.

Create your dream partner wish list

Again create a sacred space for yourself before you write your list. Now call Angel Soqedhazi to your side and ask her to envelop you once more in her pink-golden light, so that you are completely connected with the frequency of love. Take a deep breath, in and out, in order to absorb the light, and relax.

Contemplate how you imagine your soulmate and write a detailed list: Ideally it should not only give their looks and skills, but also take into account their behaviour in various everyday situations – for example with regard to their humour, their eating habits, during lovemaking. In order to charge this wish list with manifestation power it is very helpful to write the sentences in a particular way, like this:

> THANK YOU (or: I am so grateful) that my partner loves me exactly the way I am.
> THANK YOU that my partner is always truly aware of me.
> I am so grateful that my partner knows how to dance so well.
> THANK YOU that I can grow spiritually together with my partner.
> I am so grateful for our wonderful, exciting love life.

Gratitude is one of the strongest magnets for manifestation, as you can see from Gabriele's story (see page 146).

I manifested my husband with the help of a long list, as did one of my girl-friends. Her list was so long, in fact, that her best friend said at the time: "You will have to create this man yourself; it is just not feasible that such a paragon exists!"

My girlfriend though was absolutely convinced of it, and it did not take long until just this very man stood at her door, looking exactly as she had desired. The only skill this dream lover does not have – he is no dancer. But, funnily enough, even though my girlfriend had wanted to ask for him to be able to dance well, she forgot to put it on her wish list! Today the two of them are very happily married.

Now write your wonderful list together with Angel Soqedhazi and Archangel Chamuel (an angel responsible, among other things, for help with finding something). By the way, my girlfriend with the long list and the soulmate told me: "It is important to take about two weeks to make up this list because you will keep remembering things that are important to you."

Once you feel that your list is complete, place it in your angel box with the following words: "This or something better may manifest to the highest good of me." And then let go of any attachment to the outcome.

ᨳ *Prayer – channelled from Angel Soqedhazi*

Dear angels, thank you that you help me to see myself and everybody with the eyes of love and thus to be able to better understand and forgive so many things.

Thank you that you support me in releasing my past experiences in relationships, which have hurt me or made me insecure, and in healing my heart, so that I can begin completely anew, full of enthusiasm.

Thank you because you have given me the knowledge that my soulmate exists and I am already communicating with him or her on the level of the higher self.

Thank you that with your help I dare to be authentic and to show myself as I am.

Thank you that you help me to strengthen my trust every day, so that I find it increasingly easier to let go and thus be "in the flow".

Thank you that you give me signs and messages as to how and where I can meet my soulmate - signs that I simply need to follow for them to come about.

Thank you that with your help I radiate more and more love and become a magnet for my soulmate.

Thank you because you remind me that love is always the answer, so that I can live a relationship with my partner that is fulfilled on all levels, and full of grace, ease, and joy.

THANK YOU!

If you would like to find your soulmate you shouldn't just say this prayer today: write it on a piece of paper or into your diary, and later maybe also into your little book of gratitude (see day 20), so that you always have it with you and can pray at any time.

ᨳ *Future Activities for Singles* ᨳ

ᨳ *Be ready for a partnership*

Create a sacred space for yourself before you start thinking about the following questions.

Call Angel Soqedhazi to your side and ask her to enfold you in her pink-golden light, so that you are completely connected with the frequency of love. Take a deep breath, in and out, in order to absorb the light, and relax. Consider your life and note the answers to these questions:

- Is there space and time in your life for a relationship? If not, what can you change?
- What does your home look like? Is it full of good atmosphere, so that you could invite round a potential partner at any time? Is your bed big enough? Or is it time for a clear-out, time to tidy up, and redecorate your living area?

If you lived with your ex-partner in your present home it is necessary to finally cleanse it of old energies, be it with a smudging ritual, a purifying room spray and Archangel Michael, or with another purification ceremony.

Maybe you could also investigate feng shui in order to find out which corner of your home and your bedroom holds the so-called relationship or marriage area. It is very beneficial to put up pictures or sculptures of couples in this corner; they could depict human lovers or be something else – like a sculpture of interlocking dolphins.

In order to attract love it is also very helpful (and beautiful) to regularly bring fresh flowers, in particular roses, into your home. Remember, pink roses are conducive to heart-opening and tenderness, while red roses symbolize fervour and passion.

Check your appearance

If you wish for a beautiful and attractive partner you have to correspond to this resonance yourself.
Would you like to change anything about yourself, for example your hairstyle or your overall style, clothes or anything else? If so, get started!

Be a wonderful partner yourself

Create a sacred space for yourself, call Angel Soqedhazi to your side, and ask her to enfold you once more in her pink-golden light, so that you are entirely connected with the frequency of love. Take a deep breath, in and out, in order to absorb the light, and relax.

Now have a look at your soulmate wish list and consider which of the characteristics that you find particularly important for a relationship you embody yourself. Of course, I do not mean things like having blond hair yourself if you wish for a blond-haired partner, but rather, for example, that you should be faithful yourself if you wish for a faithful partner.

Recognize which characteristics you already live and which you should embody more strongly, so that you can create the resonance to attract your dream partner. As soon as you have found these characteristics, contemplate how with the angels' help you can put this into practice, and do so step by step.

 *Be yourself*

Often when getting to know a partner we try to show our best side, and might subtly play to the gallery in order to attract attention. Occasionally we might use certain seduction skills, intended to induce the other person to act in specific ways. This, however, is not particularly helpful, as Angel Soqedhazi told me during a workshop in Bologna:

> *"If you present yourself as different to how you actually are you can never attract a partner who truly suits you. Only if you are authentic and show yourself as you are will you find a person who will not just share the sunny side of life but will walk with you through thick and thin. Show your strengths as much as your weaknesses, but leave your manipulative seduction skills aside; this does not mean that you are not allowed to be charming – it is a fine line but you know well in yourself which part of you is artificial and which one is authentic. Be yourself from the start and you spare yourself many unnecessary acquaintances."*

What can you change in this sense? Write it down.

Visit unknown places

If you have not yet encountered your soul partner it is time for you to go to places that you have not visited before; if you always go to the same places you always meet the same people.

Give some thought to places you have wanted to visit for a while – maybe that was a small poke by your angels – and go there.

If nothing comes to mind, just ask Angel Soqedhazi. You will receive an answer, be it through signs, a feeling, a picture, a symbol, through words, or through simple knowledge that it is somewhere you need to go.

Soul Affirmations

First ask Angel Soqedhazi to envelop you in her pink-golden light, then take a deep breath, in and out, before you speak (ideally aloud):

ᴄᴏ For Couples

I see with the eyes of love and recognize in every moment the essence of my partner. In this way I create the resonance for a fulfilled partnership.

ᴄᴏ For Singles

I see with the eyes of love and turn into a wonderful partner myself. Thus I create the resonance to find my soulmate and to live a fulfilled partnership.

ᴄᴏ Soul Journey ᴄᴏ

Have pen and paper ready before you begin. You might want to take some notes during or directly after your journey.

With your eyes open take a deep breath in, and then slowly exhale while you close your eyes in slow motion and order your brain to automatically move into the Theta state. Breathe deeply in and out, and relax.

Let your thoughts go by like birds flying past. Just let them go and enjoy feeling your breath that links you with the breath of God and nourishes you. With each breath you take you move more deeply into a state of deep relaxation.

Feel, see, or imagine yourself being enfolded in heavenly beautiful pink-golden light that very gently caresses your aura. It feels as if your whole being is immersed in love. You feel it with every fibre of your being and perceive how all your cells begin to vibrate and dance in the frequency of love. Enjoy embodying love more and more. In addition, your light body unfurls in the colours of love and you sense how you yourself become very much brighter and lighter.

You find yourself at the shore of a lake glittering in the sunlight, and you connect yourself with the energy of water since you know that it helps you to be more in the flow in your own life as well as in your relationships. While you are listening to the murmuring of the gently rolling waves meeting the shore, two graceful, luminous white swans swim towards you. You gaze at them with curiosity and sense clearly the unity between the two of them. You are enthusiastically connecting yourself with this energy when suddenly a heavenly, magnificent angel appears next to you. It is Angel Soqedhazi, suffused in pink-golden light, the highest frequency of love. She surrounds you with her wings and it feels as if you are being embraced by the purest unconditional love. Your cells rejoice, so that you are filled with divine bliss.

Day 17

Suddenly, out of nowhere a golden boat appears in the water ahead of you. Soqedhazi takes your hand in order to help you step into the boat securely. With her by your side the boat starts gliding across the lake, softly rocking, guided by Soqedhazi's strength of intention and accompanied by the two beautiful swans.

In the middle of the lake you see a paradisiacal island, towards which Soqedhazi steers the boat. The island is of breathtaking beauty, so that once you step out of the boat and put your feet on the ground again you just cannot get enough of looking around. Exotic fragrances spread such a delicious aroma that you surrender to fully and simply being and leave any will behind. Together with Angel Soqedhazi you range this heavenly place until you reach a golden hammock; it is put up between two mighty trees that emanate infinite wisdom. Soqedhazi bids you lie down in it. You do as you are asked and enjoy the soft rocking in the warm breeze. On the horizon in front of you the most spectacular sunset that you have ever seen occurs. You feel how you become completely one with All-That-Is. Within and around you nothing exists other than pure love.

All at once your partner – or the partner of your dreams – shows him or herself in a very real vision in front of you. At the same time you hear Angel Soqedhazi's loving voice by your ear:

"Beloved soul, in this state of pure love and bliss now recognize your counterpart with the eyes of love and recognize what unites you. Look at the essence of his or her being that is as whole as yours. At this moment there is nothing that separates you. Do you understand now that true love has nothing to do with being separate and taking over? True love allows the other person to be free and gives you yourself the freedom to become your divine self. How does it feel to be loved in such a way? Are you being loved thus and do you love like that yourself?"

Soqedhazi envelops you with her wings, so that you once again feel this purest form of love with all the fibres of your being. Immerse yourself fully in this feeling.

She speaks again: "Only when you love yourself unconditionally can your counterpart develop these feelings for you too. At that moment when you yourself are the best partner for yourself you will experience the partner of your dreams in the outside world as well; be it in your present partner or a new partner who joins you in your life out of their own volition. Now speak with me when breathing in: "I AM…", and breathing out: "…pure love."

I AM…pure love.
I AM…pure love.
I AM…pure love.

Now breathe deeply in and out and visualize how you live the purest form of love. Imagine how you look into the eyes of your partner and know that you could forever gaze into these eyes. Feel how your heavenly embraces and kisses completely merge your auras and lead you into the state of oneness. Know that this is possible and that I will help you reach this state. Visualize and live it more and more with all your senses. It will manifest as soon as the time is right."

You view the heavenly pictures of the relationship of your dreams – and you know with absolute certainty that you carry everything within you to create this for yourself, when the time is divinely right, with the help of the angels. A great calmness comes over you as you feel that you are on the right path.

Finally it is time to leave the island and start the journey home. Angel Soqedhazi gracefully helps you out of the golden hammock that has felt so heavenly. Together you walk back to the boat that gently rocks in the water.

As soon as you are on the boat you are joined by the two swans again, and flanked by them the boat glides across the lake until you reach the shore.

When you feel firm ground underneath your feet you embrace Soqedhazi, full of gratitude. Take three deep breaths, stretch your body, and slowly return to the here and now. Open your eyes once you are ready to do so.

You might like to write down the insights that you have received during this journey.

Day 18

INCREASE YOUR CREATIVITY AND SACRED SEXUALITY WITH THE HELP OF ANGEL ANAEL

In us there is not only a pleasure,
which we share with the brutes,
But also one,
which we share with the angels.

Thomas Aquinas

"Greetings, beloved soul. I AM Angel Anael. Feel how I enfold you in my dark red light of love and passion and enjoy it.

It is time for you to recognize that sexuality is a wonderful sacred energy, which can support you in your ascension to the higher spheres in manifold ways if you allow it to happen in its natural form. For many centuries the church has made you believe that sexuality is something forbidden, something lecherous, but believe me it is a natural aspect of every person. Only when you are in contact with your sexual energy can you unfold your true power. This, however, does not mean living this powerful energy indiscriminately. You need to choose wisely, so that this precious power in connection with the heart energy leads to a cosmic union, which makes your soul and your body as well as the soul and the body of the other jubilant. In this way your kundalini energy will be directed into channels that raise you above yourself, so that you become one with the cosmos, with All-That-Is."

Angel Anael
angel of sexuality and creativity
Aura colour: dark red (like Baccara roses)
Crystal: garnet

Katarina, a treasured friend of mine, had a tantalizing experience with Angel Anael:

With Angel Anael into my new life

My most intense relationship lasted nearly seven years. In the last three, it was more akin to a badly organized flatshare than a relationship between man and woman. I do not exaggerate when I say that in these three years we had sex – I shall call it that – twice at best. It was not that we were not "affectionate" with each other, but we never got further than cuddling up, unfortunately. Not that I had not wanted it. Quite the contrary: sex and the accompanying feeling of being desired was very important for me. But never mind what I did, which issues I addressed or what I tried – he did not want it. Even worse: he rejected me very harshly.

I started to doubt my female essence. My femininity, my attractiveness, my sexuality…During these three years I also gained quite a bit of weight, which, of course, did not help me to feel any more feminine, more attractive, or sexier.

After we separated, I had the opportunity to take part in a five-day seminar. These five days constituted an important changing point in my life, and this was also when I first heard of Angel Anael. The notes I took about her seemed to be particularly timely: Anael is the angel of sexuality; she helps us to make peace with our body and takes care of the yin and yang balance, and that was what I wished for and gave out. Thus Angel Anael became consciously and unconsciously a part of my new life.

Pretty soon after our separation I started feeling very well again. I was almost ashamed that I was happy with and by myself after such a short time. It was as if my soul started to feel well again in my body; and my body changed. With this new feeling of self-worth my vibrancy changed as well. I felt suddenly conscious again of my femininity and my attractiveness; I had not thought of myself like that for a long time. I also enjoyed the reactions from others, whether men or women.

Three to four months after my break-up I met a special man. Right away we got on so well that we did not notice the hours flying by. We arranged a date, a special one for both of us, for four weeks later. He did not have any time to meet before this; also, we did not live in the same city. In the course of these four weeks we exchanged several emails and text messages every day, followed by phone calls that lasted for hours. And even though our physical contact on the night we finally met did not go any further than a kiss, we both suddenly started to write very openly about our idea of our next meeting, our reunion. It was clear to both of us that we were extremely attracted to each other. At some point during this time we suddenly became able to talk about and picture our sexual desires and fantasies without any feeling of embarrassment. It just started somehow.

When we saw each other again for the first time after a month, both of us were initially a bit shy. We stood in front of each other like two teenagers on their first date. This, though, was followed by the most beautiful intimate hours that I have ever experienced. . . Even though we did not really know each other we both had an incredible trust in the other.

This happened eighteen months back. I can express my whole womanliness and sexuality with this man as never before, but as I had always wished for. When the two of us are together there is absolute trust and deep passion between us. We speak about our wishes and fantasies very openly. We jointly decide how far we want to go. With this man I am currently experiencing the most beautiful, erotic, exciting, and intimate hours. And he gives me the feeling that I am the most irresistible woman in the world for him.

When I sent out my wishes back then I did not know how deep this longing ran in me. Today I am grateful to have heard from Anael.

Reflection

Many years ago I was very surprised to learn that the sexual chakra and the throat chakra are deeply connected with each other. It is rare for only one of these two chakras to become weakened – it is almost always either both of them or neither. This is because both stand for a person's ability to communicate and for their creativity; they just work on different levels.

Sexual energy does not necessarily have to be used on the physical level; it can be wonderfully transformed and sublimated, and flow into a work of art, a book, a composition, or anything creative, since sexuality and creativity are closely connected.

Naturally this does not mean that you should suppress your wish for sexual contact. However, you should not be directed only by your sexuality and allow yourself to be carried away to act in a way where you have lost control.

Many people do not take this into consideration, or even deny it: but people's auras mingle in quite a different way if they have sex with each other than if they, for example, just embrace closely while dancing. Also, sexual partners lodge much longer in the aura than other people. For this reason it is truly more than worth considering with whom – and with how many different people – you share your bed. Besides, the deep intimacy on the soul level that leads to sacred sexuality occurs only when there is total trust between you and your partner – which is not possible if you have constantly changing partners.

Consider this: it is the woman who takes the man inside and who thus already on the first intimate contact moves into a much deeper connection with the man than the other way round. Through his sperm she takes the whole history and genetic information of a man into her system – not to mention the possibility of creating a child through the sexual act. For that reason it happens time and again that a woman completely loses her identity when she exchanges men like her dresses. Similarly, excessive sexual activity can weaken a man's energy and identity too.

Whether you have one, a few, several, or many lovers, an important basic principle is to be honest with those partners, not manipulate them (for example in order to get sex), remain true to yourself and not lose yourself in pursuing sexual pleasure.

Note that in old times sexuality was not cut off from the spiritual path, but in later centuries the Church and wider society has instilled in many of us that sexuality and spirituality are not compatible. As a result of this, many of us still have hidden – or obvious – feelings of guilt around sexuality. It is time to have done with this. We are increasingly discovering ancient scriptures (like the second-millennium BCE Vedas and the Dao), and traditions including those from the times of the Mayan priest class and the female Isis priests, in which are described techniques for experiencing enlightenment through sacred sexual activity.

These are very similar concerns as those we in the twenty-first century have: how to connect and sublimate spirituality and sexuality, in order to experience consummate oneness with All-That-Is and to ascend.

On the path towards our essence, which is nothing other than light and love, it is of great importance that we acquit ourselves as much as we can of the ego and allow our higher self to guide us, with regard to living our sexuality as well as in all other areas.

In order to really enjoy your sexuality and live it on a higher level you have to feel comfortable in your body. Thus take a moment to breathe deeply and consider the following questions:

- How do you feel in your body if you think about it and tune into yourself?
- Can you stand naked in front of a mirror without immediately criticizing yourself?

✑ *Activities for today* ✑

✑ *Perform a mirror ritual*

Create a sacred space for yourself before you begin. Call Angel Anael to your side. Ask her to accompany you throughout the whole day and envelop you in her dark red light, so that you are connected with the frequency of passion. Breathe deeply in and out in order to absorb the light, and relax.

Take off your clothes and stand in front of a mirror. Before you begin to criticize yourself, just appreciate the parts of your body that you find beautiful and refrain from any criticism whatsoever.

Now dress in a way that makes you feel really attractive – as described in the next activity step.

✑ *Choose attractive clothes*

Dress in a way that – for a woman – emphasizes your femininity and – for a man – your masculinity. This means for example that as a woman you would wear a skirt or a dress, and shoes with higher heels; these items make you instantly move in a more feminine way than in flat shoes and jeans. Also stress your personal favourite part or parts of your body, whether that be your décolleté, waist, bottom, or legs. Show off what you have and what you love!

The same goes for men, of course: wear trousers that show your (possibly attractively firm) bottom and your legs, and emphasize the parts of your body you love with the things you wear. If you always wear sneakers it might be time to try a different style of shoes for a change.

It goes without saying that I am not encouraging you to walk around dressed in an extremely provocative or vulgar way. You could send out a wrong signal to the universe and attract people who are on a wavelength that you would not necessarily like to have in your vicinity.

ᵕ✆ *For women: detach yourself from the energies of former sexual partners (method inspired by Diana Cooper)*

It is essential to create a sacred space for yourself before you start with this process.

Ideally, do this lying on your couch or in bed, so that you feel secure. Again call Angel Anael and also Angel Shushienae (angel of purity) to your side and ask them to enfold you in their dark red (Anael) and bright white (Shushienae) light, and to accompany you through the whole process. Take a few deep breaths in order to fully absorb the light of the two angels in you.

Then remember your former sexual partners (if you cannot remember every one it will still work!) and visualize or imagine any sperm of them on the energetic level leaving your body. Take at least three deep breaths while you do this, breathing in through the nose while counting to four and then slowly breathing out through the mouth with an "Aaaaaah" sound. You will feel or know when their sperm has left your body.

Then ask Angel Shushienae to flood your physical body and all layers of your aura with her powerful white light, so that you feel completely pure and centred again. Breathe deeply in and out while doing so, in order to completely absorb the bright white light.

Afterwards give yourself a bit of time before you get up again.

You can do this exercise with regard to your present partner as well, should you feel that you are losing yourself in them.

ᵕ✆ *Take a sensual bath*

Buy yourself beautiful red roses (buy enough to display in your home as well as use in the bath!). Fill the bathtub with comfortably warm water and explain to the flower fairies that you are going to pick the blossoms of some roses in order to take a sensual healing bath. You can also drop some rose oil into the bathwater, place candles on the rim of the tub, and listen to music; anything that makes a bath pleasurable for you.

Before you step into the water ask Angel Anael to envelop you once more in her deep red light.

Enjoy relaxing and following your dreams in the sensual atmosphere of the water.

ᴄ✑ *Receive (and give) a massage*

Massage your partner and/or receive a massage yourself. If you do not have a partner at the moment, book a massage with a professional massage therapist; massage gives you a sensual experience of your body.

ᴄ✑ *Create a sensual atmosphere*

Transform your home into a sensual place: light candles (leave all electrical light switched off) as well as incense or a fragrance light, and choose fitting music in order to create a sensual atmosphere.

If you have a partner you can also prepare a wonderful candlelight dinner for the two of you. Out of this a unique sexual union might arise.

If you do not have a partner, invite a friend for dinner. As you sit at a beautifully and lovingly decorated and lit table, ask to speak only about your uplifting and fulfilled life on all levels that you share with your respective soulmate – just as if this is already your reality; this will create the wonderful possibility for it to happen.

You can also create a sensual atmosphere just for yourself; the wonderful energy you generate can then flow into a creative project.

ᴄ✑ *Activities for today and/or later* ᴄ✑

ᴄ✑ *Go dancing – salsa, Argentine tango, samba, lambada, belly dance*

Nothing makes you feel sensual and erotic faster than dancing one of the above dances. If you don't know any of these styles yet, this is a good time to think about which one of them attracts you in particular and to register for a dance class or workshop.

ᴄ✑ *Practise Kundalini yoga*

Kundalini yoga awakens the "serpent" at the base of your spine, your inner fire, and makes it possible for you to connect with the power of your sacred sexuality. Register for a class or workshop!

ᴄ✑ *Sacred union*

Angel Anael told me that it is very powerful when, at the beginning of love-making, the partners sit lightly dressed or naked in front of each other and first build up a connection without touching the other. If possible, breathe in the same rhythm the whole time – this helps you to synchronize your frequencies.

Gaze deeply and silently into each other's eyes for some time: the eyes are the mirror of the soul and the source for opening towards intimacy. As soon as energy starts flowing between your eyes and your partner's, move your attention first to your own heart chakra and feel it opening. Then concentrate on your partner's heart chakra and create a connection between your two hearts.

Once you become aware of a flow between your two heart chakras, move your attention to your sexual chakra and feel its pulsing. Now connect the energy of your sexual chakra with that of your lover until you can feel an exchange taking place on the energetic level.

Finally, become aware of the energy in your third eye and again establish a connection to your partner's third eye.

When you both perceive the flow of energy between your three pairs of chakras you are on all levels connected with each other: the heart level, the physical level and the spirit or soul level. May the union between the two of you become in this way a sacred experience and allow you to ascend to higher levels.

Enjoy!

If your partner is not open to doing this, you can establish the same connection if you just visualize it yourself. As you know, your brain cannot distinguish between you experiencing or just imagining something: you will get the same results.

✒ *Soul Affirmation* ✒

First ask Angel Anael to enfold you in her dark red light. Then take a deep breath, in and out, before you say (ideally aloud):

I enjoy the sensual aspects of my body since they link me to my creativity and to the sacred power of sexuality.

✒ *Soul Journey* ✒

Have pen and paper ready before you begin. You might want to take some notes during or directly after your journey.

With your eyes open take a deep breath in, and then slowly exhale while you close your eyes in slow motion and order your brain to automatically move into the Theta state. Breathe deeply in and out, and relax. Let your thoughts go by like leaves gliding along a river. Do not hold on to them. Just let go and bit by bit move more deeply into a state of relaxation. Feel how your breath nourishes you with manifold energy and enjoy it.

All at once you are being enfolded in deep-red light that has your blood pulsating in your veins and allows you to become aware of the rhythm of your heartbeat. More and more energy rises within you as you suddenly notice the unknown sounds of an animal next to you. You look around and in the midst of the starry night you see a gleaming black panther not far from you. Its intense eyes glint at you. You might feel a bit anxious to start with, but right away she communicates telepathically with you and lets you know that there is no need to be worried. The only thing she wants to do is help you to fully rekindle the passion inside yourself. Calmed, you walk towards her and stroke her gleaming, velvet coat. It feels great and you know that you have found another friend.

Suddenly she starts moving and you follow her through the barren landscape. As there is not much to see you concentrate above all on Mother Earth underneath your feet, and thus you all at once start perceiving her heartbeat very distinctly. As you continue following the gracefully moving panther your own heartbeat starts to synchronize with the rhythm of the earth; and you feel how with each step you take more energy rises through your feet into your body, so that you run with ever longer strides behind your powerful companion.

All at once you see something glowing in the distance. It is a huge fire. When you get closer you discover that the fire is surrounded by a sacred stone circle. With the panther by your side you reverently enter the sacred place. Next to the fire you then see a breathtakingly beautiful angel with flowing black hair, surrounded by a dark red aura. It is none other than Angel Anael. She steps towards you and speaks in her deep, sonorous voice:

"Beloved soul, be welcomed! This fire by my side will help you kindle your inner fire and the fires of your passions that in parts still slumber within you. Only when all your fires are ablaze in a sacred way will you have your complete strength at your disposal. Allow me to help you with that."

She takes you by the hand and moves with you towards the fire. You sense that she intends to run through the fire with you and briefly hesitate. Instantly you again hear Anael's deep, calm voice by your side:

"There is no reason to be worried. I will not do anything that could even slightly harm you. Trust me!"

Together you approach the fire – and all at once it separates so that you can walk through it. Very slowly you move between the glowing hot firewalls, metres high, until Anael stops with you in the centre of the fire and speaks:

"Now unite with the energy of the fire so that you yourself become fire. At the same time I will be working at the base of your spine to very gently awaken the dormant serpent there, so that the kundalini energy can rise within you."

You engage more and more with the energy of the fire and feel how you become one with it. At the same time you notice how an energy, familiar from time immemorial, starts to rise up your spine. A cosmic feeling that awakens all your senses in a way you have not experienced for a long time. An ecstatic feeling of happiness pulsates in the eternal cycle of the primordial force within you and you know, feel, see, hear, smell that you are reconnected with your sacred passions and can sublimate them on your path of ascension in various ways. Take a deep breath in order to anchor all this within you.

Angel Anael has witnessed your transformation with bright eyes full of joy. Now she takes your hand again and guides you out of the fire to the other side, where the panther already awaits you, standing erect on two legs. You sense that the animal would like to embrace you, and step towards her. As you hug you feel how she too transfers her power to you, so that you will emerge even stronger from this journey.

Full of gratitude, you say goodbye to Angel Anael with another intense embrace before you start on your way back with your friend, the panther.

While you walk you notice the heartbeat of Mother Earth even more distinctly; it is perfectly aligned with your own. You know that from now on, through your connection with her, you can always strengthen your root chakra again very quickly.

Stretch your limbs and enjoy becoming aware of your body and the fire within it. Open your eyes once you are ready for it.

Day 19

BE AT PEACE WITH DEATH
THANKS TO
ARCHANGEL AZRAEL

One who knows to live with the angels
lives differently to one who is refused this comfort.
Without angels we are many God experiences worse off.

Gerhard Adler

"Greetings, beloved soul. I AM Archangel Azrael. It is my greatest wish to have you know that death is only another form of birth. You just leave your physical shell of this current existence on earth and move to a higher level on which you will be received by us angels, ascended masters, and the council of the wise ones. Together with us you review your last life and recognize which of the soul lessons taken up before you went to earth you have fulfilled, and which went right past you without you taking them in seriously.

After we have illuminated everything you first receive healing before you undergo further training on these levels, which prepares you for the soul lessons of your new life. You are also allowed to realize that the 'enemies' from your last life are anything but enemies because, as you already consciously know on the mental *level, things are not as they appear. You will also unite with all the members of your soul family who are on our side of the veil. So, beloved being, as you can see from this, there is truly no reason to be afraid of your death.*

Naturally it is different when a person who you love dies before you. But here too I can comfort you. With every month, yes, nearly every week passing, the veil to our side becomes thinner, so that it becomes increasingly easy to communicate with deceased loved ones. I help you with joy in this. Be blessed."

Archangel Azrael
angel of comfort, who helps to accompany the dying into the light
Aura colour: creamy white
Crystal: creamy calcite

⠂⠀ *On the other side of the veil* ⠀⠂

A few weeks before I turned eight my father's best friend, Albrecht, died in a tragic landslide on Mont Blanc.

I was extremely affected by his death as he had been like a second father to me, so I instantly became very ill. I actually had only the measles but on top of that I developed a fierce fever. It rose higher and higher, to the extent that finally it went off the scale of the thermometer and I slipped into a coma.

I remember well that I suddenly saw a tunnel that radiated in the brightest light I had ever seen. Driven by some inner impulse, I practically ran through the tunnel until I arrived on the other side. In front of me stretched a meadow, which seemed to me like paradise: the flowers looked so much more radiant and intense than on earth that they deeply touched my soul. Infinite peace and the feeling of finally being at home overcame me. Sunrays caressed my face, so that I was spinning around my own centre in sheer delight when I suddenly saw Albrecht standing in front of me. He looked very beautiful, completely safe and unharmed, and surrounded by a radiating crown of light.

Full of joy, I flung my arms round his neck and called: "How lovely to see you again! It is great here. I'm staying with you!"

Albrecht carefully loosened my arms from his neck, looked me in the eyes with a loving, wise smile, and said: "My dear Isabelle, that is not possible, because that would break your parents' hearts. Besides, you still have something to do on earth."

Grudgingly I answered: "But I don't want to! I like it much better here."

"This is not for you to decide, this decision lies in God's hands."

Then I knew that there was nothing else for me but to return to earth.

I tried to delay saying goodbye but eventually it was time to return to the other side of the veil.

Probably at about the same time, I awoke from my coma and said to my mum who had watched over me: "I am returning from far away and I have met Albrecht. He said that I needed to come back so that you would not be so sad."

My mother instantly burst into tears as she realized that I had had a near-death experience and only due to God's intervention was I still alive.

Years later, when I became ill with life-threatening leukaemia, many people were amazed that the idea of possibly dying any day did not terrify me. I know that it is this wonderful experience on the other side of the veil that allowed me to stay calm even when facing death

Pilar, one of my ANGEL LIFE COACH®es, has a very moving story:

Angelic goodbye from Papa

At the beginning of March 2011, my sister Antonia and I were making plans to visit our father, who was in hospital in Spain. Following an operation in February it had transpired that he had end-stage cancer. We wanted to say goodbye to him and take letters from and pictures of my children to him. I asked the angels to accompany us on this journey, to arrange it in a kind way, and to help us come to terms with the situation.

On Isabelle's courses I had learned that Archangel Azrael is responsible for preparing souls for transition from earth and to support the bereaved. Thus I asked Archangel Azrael in particular to be with my father, as well as with me and my whole family.

We booked our flight and a rental car. Everything went well: we had a good flight from Frankfurt to Madrid and, as we were sitting in the car preparing to drive to Cáceres, I asked the angels for a sign, even though we knew and also felt that they were accompanying us. When we set off, the first car we noticed had a '4' on the numberplate – 4 is the number of the angels. Antonia and I had fun checking the numberplates of all the other cars. We were again assured that the angels were with us, since all the numberplates we spotted either had at least one number 4 or the total of the numbers came to 4.

Eventually we arrived at the hospital where our father was. We went to his room and I noticed instantly that the walls were painted a soft creamy hue, like vanilla ice cream. I felt a warm embrace and knew that Azrael was present. Our father was very happy to see us. While we were having a very nice time talking, a nurse came into the room. Usually I do not pay attention to these things but on this occasion I looked at her name badge and saw that it said "Angela". I had to smile: the angels were taking great care to show us their support.

The next day I spoke with the attending doctor and was not surprised this time to read on his name badge the name "Angel Maria". He told me that my father did not have much longer to live. The words hit me hard; nevertheless I was enveloped in comfortable warmth. I could feel myself being embraced by two huge angel's wings that gave me protection and comfort.

Two days later we were told that the end was near for our father. His siblings, Antonia and I were now with him constantly. To the right side of my father I noticed something that made me sad and very happy at the same time: Archangel Azrael was lovingly looking down on him and on us. He was very big – his head nearly hit the ceiling. At first he had his wings only slightly spread, but when we all were inside the room he unfurled his wings completely and we were then all embraced by them. Azrael was now constantly with my father and his creamy aura radiated around him.

When my father died I was with him – it was a very peaceful moment. My father was asleep and just stopped breathing. I told the nurses and from then on everything happened very quickly. A doctor came, shortly afterwards someone from the funeral parlour arrived, and then my father's body was driven to his birthplace for the wake.

We were obviously all very sad and affected, but still composed. I felt a great calmness and gratitude because my father had not suffered; he went peacefully and calmly.

On the day of the funeral my father's coffin stood at the front of the church. We as family sat on the front benches, and when the priest delivered his sermon I again saw Archangel Azrael, directly behind the priest. At the very moment when the priest spoke about my father, Azrael "merged" with him, and the words that reached us were very comforting. The voice and the attitude of the cleric changed as well and became more pleasant and tender.

I am very grateful to Archangel Azrael for his support. We have lost our father but Azrael has enabled us with his presence and his love to cope with the loss of this beloved person in the most loving and painless way possible.

Reflection

Even if you do not know for sure whether you have seen or heard the presence of a deceased person yet, you may well have at some point had the feeling that someone who has died softly touched you, or left an impression on your bedclothes, or something similar. Or maybe you have suddenly and briefly perceived the fragrance you associate with this person.

 *Activities for today*

Note your experiences with the deceased

Contemplate this in a sacred atmosphere of candles, music, and pleasant fragrances. Ask Archangel Azrael to be with you and to enfold you in his creamy white light that you breathe in deeply. Then write down what you remember.

Write a letter to a deceased person

If there is still something that you would have liked to tell one or more deceased people, then just write one or more letters. You can be sure that your words will be received and that you will obtain an answer one way or another.

Soul Affirmation

First ask Angel Azrael to enfold you in his creamy white light. Then take a deep breath, in and out, before you say (ideally aloud):

Death is simultaneously an ending and the beginning of a new birth. I am immortal.

Soul Journey

Have pen and paper ready before you begin. You might want to take some notes during or directly after your journey.

> *With your eyes open take a deep breath in, and then slowly exhale while you close your eyes in slow motion and order your brain to automatically move into the Theta state. Breathe deeply in and out, and relax.*
>
> *Let your thoughts go by like birds flying past. Just let them go and enjoy feeling your breath that links you to the breath of God and nourishes you. With each breath you take you move further into a state of deep relaxation.*
>
> *Feel, see, or imagine yourself being wrapped in crystalline light that pervades your whole being and connects you more and more with your light*

body. Feel how you become someone without boundaries – an infinite being between heaven and earth.

You are feeling completely permeated by light when in front of you appears a wise, loving angel who is surrounded by a cream-coloured aura. It is Archangel Azrael. He emanates such benevolence and kindness that you trustingly surrender to the proceedings awaiting you.

At this moment you are both being held within a crystalline pillar that fully surrounds you and seems to reach up into the sky. Archangel Azrael takes you by the hand and very slowly you begin to ascend within the crystalline pillar. You float higher and higher through the various dimensions until you reach the end of the crystalline pillar and a place as beautiful as paradise looms in front of you. You cannot believe your eyes: that which presents itself to you is of such indescribable beauty that you are speechless. Enjoy the view with all your senses.

Once you have taken it all in countless beings appear in front of you: angels, ascended masters, light beings of all kinds and beloved people from your life who have passed away. They all bring infinite love to you, and you feel as if you have finally arrived back home. And this is exactly what it is. Your true home is not on earth but here.

Then Archangel Azrael speaks to you:

"Beloved soul, do you understand now that death is nothing to fear? Quite the contrary: you are being reunited with those people who you love and who have already gone before you. You are also expected by angels, enlightened masters, and other light beings, who will help you ascend to higher dimensions. Do you realize now that there is truly nothing to fear? Also, you will only return to earth when you are ready for your new soul lessons. Everything goes its sacred way."

You feel how an immeasurably great burden is taken from you. Only now can you truly rejoice about being reunited with your deceased loved ones. You also realize that they all look radiant and whole, and you know that death has irrevocably lost its sting for you.

You enjoy the time left in the higher spheres before Archangel Azrael takes you by the hand and begins to descend with you in the crystalline pillar. Inside the pillar you continue gliding further and further down with Azrael, until you again feel safe ground underneath your feet.

Finally the time has come. Full of gratitude, you say goodbye and know that everything is prepared for you when it is time for you to leave the earth. You feel wonderful, since now you are truly connected to heaven and earth. Take three deep breaths, stretch your limbs in order to very gently arrive back in your body, in the here and now, and open your eyes.

~ Part 3 ~
Manifestation

Day 20

OVERFLOW WITH GRATITUDE
WITH ANGEL OONIEMME

A person can never equal an angel,
but we should at least try to become like angels.

Mathilde von der Au

"Greetings, beloved soul. I AM Angel Ooniemme. The power of gratitude knows no bounds. It is this power that lends you the strength to create miracles in concert with us, since when you overflow with gratitude your aura starts radiating in its brilliance and your vibrational frequency increases immediately and boundlessly. In these moments you are suffused with light to such an extent that you resemble more than ever that light being that you truly are.

Realize that it is discontent and ingratitude that imbue you with such heaviness and so often make you feel as though you cannot unfold your wings. When, however, you become aware of this heaviness, you will be able to accomplish change easily. Is it not true that in every single moment there is something for which you can be grateful? Is it not true that you have clothes to put on and food to eat? That

*you have a roof over your head? Do you really take this for granted? No, beloved
soul, this is not so. How many people on earth have to go without this?*

*Thus I ask you to recognize the blessings in your life day by day with a heart
full of gratitude, and synchronicities and miracles will multiply in wondrous
ways."* ·

Angel Ooniemme
angel of gratitude and blessings
Aura colour: iridescent white
Crystal: pearl

Jessica, one of my ANGEL LIFE COACH®es, experienced the incredible
power of gratitude:

With gratitude and salsa towards a new job

As a newly graduated dentist, I did not always find it the easiest task to find a suitable
practice to work at. I have changed jobs frequently, generally after two months, feeling
again and again that the perfect environment for me did not seem to exist. Or was it
just very difficult to find?

I had once again reached the point of wishing for a different work environment,
one that fitted me better, but this time everything was different since I had consciously
integrated the help of the angels into my search. For months, I wrote diligently in
my gratitude journal. I wrote down everything that I was grateful for in my life, and
everything that I wanted to manifest for my future. One of the most important topics,
according to this programme, was the wish for a new job.

Through this, Angel Ooniemme became my constant companion in the evenings.
I did my best, knowing that I could find the perfect job only with the help of the
angels.

After about two months, my friend Sabine came up with the idea of talking to her
dentist in the hope of finding something suitable for me. He did not raise her hopes
much but was keen to meet me. I came for an interview with him, and it went much
better than expected – so well, in fact, that he offered me a position right away. I was
very happy and absolutely delighted about this new opportunity.

Shortly afterwards though, I realized that I would need to compromise on a few
points that were not in line with my nature. Still, I continued to trust. The angels and
my heart both called to me for more joie de vivre in life, in order to help me let go
of all expectations. I followed my nature and prescribed to myself a salsa and singing-
therapy class, since the part of myself that loves singing and dancing was one I had

---

not lived for a long time. I felt how I suddenly came alive and was grateful to the angels for leading me to this point.

A few weeks later I resigned from my job. My decision was very sudden – and I did it without having secured a new job. But something in me had nevertheless urged me to risk this step. I wonder who pushed me then?

Since Dr. H., my friend's nice dentist, and I could not agree on my salary he decided to ask advice from colleagues who had been employing assistants in their practice for years. When I met him again he told me: "I have good news for you and bad news for me."

Surprise! The assistant dentist in this practice had just resigned. He sent me over there so they could interview me right away. I knew immediately: this was heaven's answer to my prayers!

This job exceeded everything I had wished for. I have found a special practice, one in which I have more new opportunities and securities than I could imagine having anywhere else. Among other things, this practice has provided me with a base of regular patients: and funnily enough, most of them speak only Spanish – my mother tongue! In addition to this, I have the opportunity here to qualify as a specialist in oral and maxillofacial surgery; it is not easy to find a practice in which you can do this – another heart's desire that I had previously completely surrendered. Also, my work does not conflict with my angel work since I have Fridays off and can thus attend the weekend workshops. My salary is exactly as I had wished for and I can finally pay off my debts. And the most beautiful bit about it all is: it just happened without me filling in even one single application form. I am overjoyed, deeply touched, and impressed!

I am grateful from the bottom of my heart that I was able to continue to trust and surrender. This was the only way to give the angelic realms the unpressurized space they needed to be able to plan and create everything – for the highest good of all involved.

 *Reflection*

When life is just closing in on us we sometimes cannot believe that we have any reason for gratitude. In reality though, even the seemingly darkest moments provide us with unbelievable blessings. But only when we start counting our blessings do we recognize how many there actually are.

ᴄᴇᴓ The Power of Gratitude

I remember well how I was given the opportunity to experience the unbelievable power of gratitude during my first long, serious hospital stay at the oncology ward in Großhadern hospital.

One day, I switched on the TV and atrocious pictures of the Chechnya war flickered across the screen. Immediately, I was aware of how blessed I really was. Compared to the poor people in that country who feared for their lives and who had to watch their loved ones being killed and their homes and belongings completely destroyed, I was really only suffering from a bit of leukaemia (and I am absolutely serious here). Yes, for months and years my life was over and over again to hang by a thread, but I had a roof over my head, a bed to lie down in, enough to eat, and an endless number of people who did everything to keep me alive. Compared to the people in Chechnya I was not doing too badly.

At that time, I realized that we could stop being a victim if only we could become aware that even in the seemingly worst moments of our life there are still plenty of things to be grateful for. When I started listing everything I could think of, I was grateful and amazed: the list grew much longer than I had initially imagined it would. And the most exciting bit was that after this, I attracted even more gifts that I could be grateful for. For example, even though I was ill I received contracts for new concerts; and two sound engineers recorded a sample CD with me for free (this is usually quite costly and I would not have had the money to pay for it at the time).

Gratitude really is a unique magnet for even more blessings in life. Today I know that Angel Ooniemme was by my side then.

ᴄᴇᴓ Activities for today and for the future ᴄᴇᴓ

ᴄᴇᴓ Feel grateful

Create a sacred space for yourself, and now ask Angel Ooniemme to envelop you in her iridescent white light, and breathe deeply in and out. Feel how your heart expands. Ponder what you can be grateful for in your life and write down everything that you can think of (this can include people, pets/animals, situations, experiences, things and so on). If you already have a little gratitude book (see below) you can of course use this to write in.

Now think again about your past and recognize gratefully which great blessings were hidden in the most difficult moments, as it is those that have made you into the wonderful person that you are today. Write these gifts down too.

୧ଛ Behold beauty in God's creation

Sit down in front of a gorgeous flower and recognize the magnificence of God's creation. Enjoy the sight and ponder the unique details of it until your heart wells over with gratitude.

୧ଛ Create a "Little Book of Gratitude"

Get yourself a beautiful small book with empty pages in a handy size, so that you find it easy to always carry it with you. This is your "Little Book of Gratitude".

One possibility is to always, immediately, write down everything you are grateful for in the course of each day. You will be surprised at how much you will collect. If you leave it until the evening, you may well find that you cannot remember everything; it makes sense to write down each event as soon as it has happened.

Another way is to work with your little book of gratitude every morning and/or evening. Before you start writing, call again on Ooniemme and ask her to surround you with her iridescent white light, which you absorb deeply through your breathing.

Now, on the left-hand page of your book, write down each of the things that you are grateful for and that are already present in your life, for example: "I am so grateful (or: THANK YOU) for having enough to eat." Afterwards, note on the right-hand page all those things that you desire with all your heart, but phrase them as if they had already come into existence. For example, a wish for a partner would be: "I am so grateful (or: THANK YOU) for my relationship with my soulmate."

Expressing your gratitude for the blessings, people, encounters and everything else that are already present in your life fills your heart with more gratitude; this acts like a magical manifestation magnet to the things that you wish for. I myself and also some of my clients, workshop attendees, and training participants have thus manifested small and greater miracles, as you read in Jessica's story earlier in this section.

୧ଛ Say the mantra "Grazie"

In one of my workshops in Bologna, I was speaking about gratitude, the second pillar of my "Nine Pillar programme", when the angels asked me to recite the mantra "Grazie" seven times, together with the participants. I had never done this before, but what happened was absolutely phenomenal. The eyes of all forty-four participants became bright and their auras started visibly radiating more than before. When I asked the angels for an explanation for this they told me that the word "Grazie" holds a much higher frequency than the word "Danke" (the same word in German), since it is derived from the word "grace". As the human body is made up of more than 70 per cent water, the mantra "Grazie" has an equally powerful effect on a person when they drink water out of a glass or a bottle with the word "Grazie" written on it. If you want to try it, write the word "Grazie" on the label of the bottle or on a sheet of paper that you place underneath the bottle or the glass.

Now ask Angel Ooniemme to enfold you in her iridescent white light, then breathe deeply in and out and speak the mantra "Grazie" seven times from your heart.

Show your gratitude to others

Write thank you cards, emails, or texts to people who are important to you and tell them how grateful you are that they are in your life.

Bless difficult people with the Angel Ooniemme

Close your eyes, ask Angel Ooniemme to envelop you in her iridescent white light, and inhale and exhale deeply. Now think of a person who does not make life easy for you or who has hurt you, and imagine them in front of you. Look deeply into this person's eyes until you can see their soul, their essence, and say several times (ideally aloud): "I bless you, ... (name of the person)."

Then breathe deeply three times, and open your eyes when you are ready.

I received this exercise spontaneously from Ooniemme during a talk in Italy, with her intention being to let the audience experience the power of the angels. What followed surprised even me: a white-haired man in a suit, who had previously seemed rather sceptical, started to clap enthusiastically, and was subsequently joined by the whole audience. He was absolutely thrilled because he had been able to perceive the angel energy so clearly and because he found giving the blessing much easier than he had expected. He had experienced what I had described previously: namely that it is impossible to continue feeling pain when, with the help of angelic energy, you are blessing someone who has hurt you.

I can only warmly recommend that you integrate this exercise into your daily life and use it as soon as possible if someone challenges you. In this way you will lose much less time and energy, as your thoughts will not circle endlessly around the behaviour of one person.

⟋⟍ Bless all and everyone

Blessing is a wonderful thing: it instantly changes the vibrations of both the one who does the blessing and the one who is being blessed, as the act of blessing brings light into the energy fields of everyone involved.

Whatever you intend to do (a project, a journey, anything with which you'd like help), first bless it, together with Angel Ooniemme. Also, anything that you finish – again a project, maybe, or a difficult journey – bless it. You will see what great synchronicities you will encounter when you work with blessings.

Bless your day, your food, your home, your family, your friends, your "enemies" – just everything – and you will hardly be able to keep up with counting your blessings. Start now. Just try blessing someone or something – anything!

For example, I love to send "angels' blessings" to people. Maybe you would like to create your own blessing formula.

⟋⟍ Soul Affirmation ⟋⟍

First ask Angel Ooniemme to enfold you in her iridescent white light. Then take a deep breath, in and out, before you say (ideally aloud):

I am so grateful for the wonderful blessings in my life. I am a magnet for blessings on all levels.

⟋⟍ Soul Journey ⟋⟍

Have pen and paper ready before you begin. You might want to take some notes during or directly after your journey.

With your eyes open take a deep breath in, and then slowly exhale while you close your eyes in slow motion and order your brain to automatically move into the Theta state. Breathe deeply in and out, and relax. Let your thoughts go by like birds flying past. Just let them go and enjoy feeling your breath that connects you with the breath of God and the angels. With each breath that you take you move more deeply into a state of relaxation.

You find yourself in a starry night at the shore of a magical lake, then suddenly a celestially beautiful angel with long, shining, silvery hair appears next to you and surrounds you with iridescent white light. It is Angel Ooniemme who embraces you, full of grace. A sense of great security per-

vades your whole being, so that you feel carried by infinite love as Ooniemme now takes to the skies with you. You fly higher and higher, so that before long you have left the earth behind you. Still higher you ascend, through the different dimensions, until you arrive at the beautiful grand entrance of an ethereal temple that glistens so much it seems to be covered with the most delicate stardust. You are absolutely enchanted by the beauty of this temple.

Suddenly the entrance gate opens, seemingly by itself, with a melodic sound, and together with Angel Ooniemme you enter the most radiant temple that you have ever laid eyes on. Everything shimmers in brightest brilliance, so that your eyes first have to get accustomed to the intensity of the light before you can see more.

Eventually Ooniemme points towards a crystalline throne in the middle of the lustrous hall and asks you to take a seat. You do not need to be asked twice and immediately sit down on the graceful throne that seems like it was made for you. Immediately you feel how crystalline energy starts ascending within you and you feel increasingly brighter and lighter.

There, Ooniemme snaps her fingers and is suddenly holding a wonderful crystalline staff, like a magic wand, in her hands. With this she very gently touches your heart chakra and with tenderness dissolves all the old pain and disappointments that have been stored in there. You feel how your heart chakra opens more and more, just like a graceful pink lotus flower.

Now Ooniemme envelops you once again in her iridescent white light and a wave of deep gratitude passes through you.

A moment later Ooniemme sketches something into the air with her magic wand and in front of you emerges a huge white screen on which appear all the people, animals, situations, and things in your life for which you can be grateful – just like in a wonderful film.

Take the time to contemplate the pictures that present themselves and feel the gratitude that arises in you as you do so. Then Ooniemme declares:

"Beloved being, recognize the wonderful power that dwells in gratitude. It succeeds in completely transforming situations within seconds. Thus I ask you from the depth of my heart to draw even more gratitude into your life, as it is gratitude that can open doors of all kinds for you. It is the magnet for the life of your dreams. Be conscious of this and choose wisely."

As Ooniemme embraces you again with her wings you just feel the purest, most profound gratitude within you, and you know that from now on you will employ this heavenly power, that is available to you at every moment of your life, much more consciously.

Finally it is time to return to earth and Ooniemme accompanies you from the throne and out of the temple. Together you rise into the air and slowly fly lower and lower until you again feel earth under your feet. Connect yourself with Mother Earth and give thanks to Angel Ooniemme for the wonderful journey of insight. Have a good stretch and straighten yourself in order to fully arrive again in the here and now, and open your eyes.

Day 21

PURIFY YOURSELF WITH THE HELP OF ANGEL SHUSHIENAE

Angels are beings like you and I.
But only a pure soul is able
to see and understand them.

Socrates

"Greetings, beloved soul. I AM Angel Shushienae. In these tumultuous times it is not easy to be calm and at peace, since quite a few decisions want to be taken, decisions that will have a profound impact on your future. It is more vitally important than ever that you take some time to purify and nourish your soul. This is the only way to get the clarity necessary for taking decisions that are in tune with your life plan.

Visit water as often as possible as its cleansing power greatly affects all your bodies, in particular your emotional body. Only when your emotional body is pure are you able to open your heart further and further; and this is essential in order to become a crystal-clear channel for the messages of the divine. Your heart is the mooring for your higher senses, and only when it is pure and open will you truly *know how to interpret the perceptions of your inner senses, so that you are able to take your decisions from the heart, from love.*

Should you find it impossible to be near any water, then travel in your imagination to a waterfall, place yourself under it, and feel its vigour with all your senses. The more vivid your visualization the stronger the purifying effect, as your brain cannot distinguish between reality and imagination and will simply allow you to absorb the benefits.

You can also send out the intention to be as pure and clear as a mountain crystal. Do not confuse purity with asceticism though: instead recognize that the purer you are the more profound joy you can experience. In this way, you will develop a bright and luminescent light body that helps you find true fulfilment in your life. My biggest wish is to support you in this."

Angel Shushienae
angel of purity
Aura colour: luminous white
Crystal: white opal

∽ *The truth of stillness* ∽

For my work on this book I spent some time in Nice, France, at my beloved Baie des Anges (Angel Bay). This place is very important to me because it was there that when I became ill with leukaemia, in 2004, a true healing miracle happened. For this reason the bay exerts an almost magic pull on me. Again and again, it is a place of inspiration for me; it was this time too.

One morning I sat by the sea, in bright sunshine, and looked out on to the water, which glistened and sparkled in the most exquisite shades of turquoise – a view that deeply nourished my soul. Finally I decided to meditate with Angel Shushienae in order to be a pure channel for further messages for this book. As usual, I inhaled deeply with my eyes open, closed my eyes in slow motion while exhaling, and instructed my brain to automatically move into the Theta state.

Mixed into the heavenly sound of the waves rolling on to the shore was loud noise from the construction workers who busied themselves with working on the promenade above me. I called Shushienae to my side and asked her to enfold me in her luminous white light while I told myself: "All noise contributes to you relaxing even more deeply."

And truly – suddenly there was nothing else inside me except stillness, despite the noise close by. An absolutely wonderful feeling!

Then I heard Shushienae's tender voice at my ear:
"True peace lies within you, not outside of you. If you are truly still within, it is

also still outside, no matter what noise might prevail there."

Once more I became aware of how important it is to meditate everywhere. Only then do we learn how to become still even in the greatest chaos, and to receive the messages that are essential for us. Of course it is easier to be still on a holy mountain in India; but the times when we most urgently need answers are usually those when everything seems to be collapsing around us. With the help of Angel Shushienae you will succeed – try it!

 *Activities for today*

✑ *Go to the water*

Together with Angel Shushienae, go to spend some time near water and calmly contemplate it. It instantly purifies all your bodies, in particular your emotional body. Notice how you feel increasingly lighter, brighter, and more pristine.

✑ *Take a bath – inside or outside*

Should the weather allow it, and you can easily get to a river, lake, or the sea, go for a swim. This is one of the best ways to cleanse your whole system deeply but in a gentle way. Please also immerse your head, so that all your chakras are cleansed. (A swimming pool is only suitable if the water is not chlorinated or affected by other chemical substances.)

Should it be too cold to swim in natural water, use the bathtub and take a deeply cleansing alkaline bath; it is best to use salt from the Dead Sea as it has the most potent concentration of minerals, and dissolves physical as well as psychological toxins from your system. If you use the bathtub it is also important to immerse your head in order to cleanse all your chakras. And remember to ask Shushienae to be with you!

✑ *Work with white pomander*

The white pomander from the Aura-Soma® series has a particular purifying effect on the entire aura: I carry it in my bag wherever I go. When you have applied it to your aura you will feel instantly refreshed and clear. At the same time it balances all the chakras and protects the entire electromagnetic field around you.

Day 21

‿❧ Activities for the future ‿❧

‿❧ Purify your chakras with Shushienae

In order to be a pure channel for the messages of the angels (and other light beings, it is essential to cleanse your chakras regularly: daily or at least several times a week.

One very beautiful possibility is to ask Shushienae to purge every single one of your chakras – from bottom to top or vice versa – with her luminous white light. You will notice that you feel increasingly brighter and more pure. My husband Hubert swears by the "Shushienae Meditation" in my *Angel Trance Meditations* (No. 12). He always listens to it before giving an angel reading in order to be a pure channel.

‿❧ Soul Affirmation ‿❧

First ask Angel Shushienae to enfold you in her luminous white light. Then take a deep breath, in and out, before you say (ideally aloud):

I choose my thoughts and words with wisdom in order to become as pure as a mountain crystal.

‿❧ Soul Journey ‿❧

Have pen and paper ready before you begin. You might want to take some notes during or directly after your journey.

With your eyes open take a deep breath in, and then slowly exhale while you close your eyes in slow motion and order your brain to automatically move into the Theta state. Breathe deeply in and out, and relax. Let your thoughts go by like leaves gliding along a river, and turn within. Enjoy feeling how each breath purifies you and how you relax more and more.

Feel, sense, see, or imagine being enveloped in the most luminous white light that you have ever witnessed. Very gently it pervades all layers of your aura.

Feel how your energy field becomes ever more resplendent and full of light as you find yourself at a heavenly place in the midst of nature. Not far away you hear the swoosh of a waterfall. You walk in the direction of the sound and discover a celestially beautiful, ethereal-looking angel next to it. It is Angel Shushienae, the angel of purity. Shushienae radiates in the brightest

189

white light, with which she surrounds you too when she folds her wings around you. It feels wonderful.

Then she takes your hand and leads you underneath the waterfall. Its water is of a particular kind: it originates in sacred springs and carries an extraordinary healing and purifying power. You feel it instantly and perceive how it cleanses you, layer by layer. In wondrous ways it relieves you of thoughts that have been stored in your human body but that do not serve you any longer, and also of any emotions that have been out of balance.

With each second that you spend underneath the waterfall you feel brighter and lighter, since the water clears not only all layers of your aura but also every single one of your chakras until all gleam in wonderful purity. They become a pillar of purest white light that unites all colours of the rainbow within itself. Support this cleansing by breathing in a fluent rhythm. Stay as long as you like underneath the celestial waterfall.

Afterwards Shushienae wraps you in a soft towel. You feel wonderfully clean and secure. Enjoy it.

When you finally, full of gratitude, gaze into Shushienae's eyes you recognize in them that your light body is grander than ever before.

Now connect again with Mother Earth, stretch your limbs in order to reconnect fully with your earthly body, the temple of your soul, and slowly open your eyes.

UNCONDITIONAL LOVE AND NO JUDGEMENT THANKS TO ANGEL HADRANIEL

To love for the sake of being loved is human,
but to love for the sake of loving is angelic.

Alphonse de Lamartine

"Greetings, beloved soul. I AM Angel Hadraniel. It is a great joy to me to enfold you in the frequency of love, so that nothing else but love exists.

You need to understand that you are just this: pure, unconditional love that looks through all the veils of illusion and recognizes the truth of things. Through you being pure love and looking through the eyes of love, you understand the greater picture and the higher interrelations that are inherent in all situations and encounters. In this way, the existential basis of any judgement vanished into thin air.

Whenever you reside in this consciousness you will see yourself and everyone else with new eyes, since you will suddenly see the beauty, magic, and love in every single human and living being that hitherto have been hidden from you. Realize *that to see with the eyes of love does not mean to be gullible but to fathom the deeper truth inherent in everything. Thus you will succeed much more easily in staying in the frequency of love, becoming love, living love, and being love. To this effect I embrace you with my wings and immerse you in the all-encompassing love of the divine."*

Angel Hadraniel
angel of love
Aura colour: pink
Crystal: pink calcite

⁓ *The pink calcite* ⁓

On the last evening of the first International ANGEL LIFE COACH® Training in Weiler, Germany, one of the Italian participants, Cris, came to me asking whether I could help him with his heart opening. Once everyone was busy pasting up their vision boards I sat next to him on the floor and questioned him further.

"You know, Isabelle, I have already tried so much, have attended countless trainings, but my heart has not really opened much further," were his sad words.

I looked him deeply in the eyes and saw various images coming up, which explained why this was the case. Before I said anything I asked the angels what they would advise him to do. At that moment I became distinctly aware of Angel Hadraniel and he said to me: *"Give your pink calcite to Cris for tonight's meditation and for the whole night."*

I could not believe my ears. Usually I never part with my crystals! But Hadraniel's words had been so assertive that I had no choice. Besides, I had by now learned not to defy the angels; I had often experienced in my own body what happens if I do not listen to them and act instead according to my ego's wishes. By now I was more inclined to listen.

So I fetched my pink calcite from the altar that we had erected on stage and gave it to Cris, saying: "Angel Hadraniel says that I should lend you this crystal until tomorrow morning because it will help you to feel your heart and to slowly open it again."

Cris looked at me with somewhat incredulous eyes – partly because it was plain to him that I usually do not lend my crystals to anyone, and partly because he seemed to slightly doubt the power of the pink calcite. Eventually, though, he thanked me and took the crystal. I talked to him for a while longer and told him a few things about his heart.

Eventually it was time to channel the manifestation meditation that is customary on the last evening of these sessions. Nearly all the participants were lying on the floor with their vision boards above their hearts as the angels started to speak through me. Angel Hadraniel had never before appeared to me in a manifestation meditation, but that is exactly what happened this evening. The frequency of love spread palpably through the whole huge room, all the participants' auras changed. When I opened my eyes again at the end of the meditation it was a beautiful sight.

Naturally I also looked over at Cris once or twice, and I knew that something had changed within him. Before I said goodnight to everyone he came to me and firmly embraced me. "It is incredible but I held the calcite in my left hand the whole time, and I could really feel how my heart chakra worked throughout the meditation. It felt fantastic! Mille grazie!"

The next morning he gave the crystal back to me and thanked me exuberantly again: "You have held the promise that you gave to me on the first day – you were right that this course is different. For the first time I'm driving home really entirely transformed. Thank you!"

ᏗᏯ *The power of love* ᏗᏯ

One day a friend hurt me deeply on various levels, and it threw me completely off balance, which usually does not happen to me often. It was so upsetting that I had to leave the house immediately; I walked around aimlessly, tears just streaming down my face.

Eventually I remembered Angel Hadraniel and the power of love. I asked Hadraniel to enfold me in his intense pink light of love and took a few deep breaths – partly to take in the light, and partly to let go of the pain. I instantly felt how the burden on my heart was lightened and how I again became connected with the frequency of love. When I returned to the house about an hour and a half later I was perfectly at peace with the world and also with this friend, since I was again in a position to see with the eyes of love.

During my daily evening ritual I realized that there was not even anything to forgive any more, since with Hadraniel's help I had left the hurt and any judgement behind. Once more I became aware that love is always the answer whatever happens around us since it can heal everything – really, everything. The whole situation of course vanished, entirely peacefully. How else could it be?!

My friend Heike, also an ANGEL LIFE COACH®, experienced a rapid transformation with Angel Hadraniel:

My encounter with Angel Hadraniel

I had to work on the evening of my birthday, which meant that I could not have a party. Instead I arranged for the next day a date with my life partner Boris and one of my best girlfriends in my favourite tearoom, which also served vegan meals. The previous year I had celebrated my fortieth birthday extravagantly, so I wanted to keep the circle small this time. As my friend Catharina had to work until late, we could only meet an hour before the tearoom closed. When we ordered our food the waitress advised that the Japanese mochi rice was finished and there was only basmati rice available now. That was no problem for us. We enjoyed our tea, talked animatedly, and I was happy to be there.

After a while, I noticed that a woman who had arrived after us was already eating her meal. I knew her: she was the owner of a nearby shop that sold natural cosmetics. I felt treated unfairly. "Do they value her more because she is a regular customer? Does she maybe receive preferential treatment because of that?" were my thoughts.

I was already judging, but I could feel how my ego put on the spurs and pushed further: "That is really mean, on my birthday they just pass me by. Did they not get that it is my birthday? There are three waitresses for this small place and they can't manage to bring us our meals!"

To have my ego take over like that was really the last thing I wanted at my birthday dinner, so I tried not to listen to its misgivings and remain calm. However, an uneasy feeling was spreading within me that I could not ignore.

As time went on, I said to my friends: "We seem to be waiting a very long time for our meal. Shouldn't we say something?"

When we eventually talked to the waitress she said: "It is too late now to order any food – we're about to close. Besides, the food that you ask for is no longer available."

We told her that we had ordered some time ago; she herself had told us then that the Japanese rice was no longer available. Even someone at a neighbouring table got involved and confirmed that we had already ordered. The waitress obviously felt embarrassed. She could not remember and apologized, though that did not change the fact that the restaurant was about to close and the food was all gone.

I was very disappointed and felt all at once choked up; tears even rose to my eyes. My ego said: " I knew from the start that this was not going anywhere good!" And my disappointed inner child piped up: " The other woman got what was supposed to be mine. This is my birthday! Why did I not deserve it?"

194

This old topic – others get something, while I don't – flooded me, and I confessed my sadness to Boris and Catharina. However, I now wanted to allow this feeling to come up so I could examine it; I knew that at this moment I had a chance to transform this old grief.

Isabelle's ANGEL LIFE COACH® training had taught me that Angel Hadraniel could help me with this feeling, so I asked him to send his wonderful pink light into my heart. I was once again in a situation that was wearing down my self-esteem and I knew I had to once and for all dissolve this grief about missing out. So I opened myself to Angel Hadraniel with the intention that this was the time for it to happen, even though I was sitting in public, in a restaurant, and feelings were running high among my group.

I instantly felt how my clenched heart opened and started to resonate. The waves that it sent forth even reached my throat, where the grief was located, and loosened that area too. I was suddenly able to breathe deeply and let go. Unconditional love flowed into my heart and I softened towards myself, towards the other woman, and even towards the waitress. My inner child immediately calmed down. All this happened as quick as a flash. Full of relief, I thanked Angel Hadraniel. Now that I was connected with unconditional love, I could just no longer be cross with the waitress. It was absolutely impossible – because I was completely removed from feeling any kind of judgement.

We now had to decide quickly where we could go and still get something to eat. I absolutely wanted to eat vegan tonight, and I suggested another restaurant in the same street; but the guest at the nearby table intervened again: "The Kopfeck is a student pub. I would recommend the Max Pett instead; it's much more classy. I'd be happy to accompany you there."

I wanted to eat soon, but I could not spend too much money as I was a bit short of cash at the moment. Still, I did not have to think too long – on my birthday I deserved to spend money on myself! It seemed that there were two lessons that I was intended to learn that day. . .

We paid and the tearoom gave me some cake as an apology. Then our new acquaintance from the next table, Joachim, took us to the restaurant Max Pett. It transpired that he was a member of Munich's vegan community; we also learned from him about a shop at the main railway station that sold vegan kebabs.

Ultimately this evening turned into an adventure in a vegan land of plenty, and I floated on a sweet cloud of unconditional love. It was all delicious. Thank you, angels, and in particular to you, Angel Hadraniel!

৴✑ *Activities for today* ৴✑

৴✑ *Take in unconditional love while breathing*

Consciously decide to absorb unconditional love with each intake of breath and to let go any judging with each exhalation.

Do this seven times in succession and repeat this conscious process at least three times a day, so that altogether you take twenty-eight breaths in this way. Try to breathe in this way not only today but for several days in a row and as often as you can. It is very effective and changes your vibration instantaneously.

৴✑ *Find a pink calcite*

I have rarely found a stone whose effect I feel so quickly. When I am not centred I only need to take it into my left hand, close my eyes, and take three deep breaths and I am again connected with the frequency of love and feel myself full of love. You notice how this wonderful crystal changes the frequency of a person who holds it in his/her hand within minutes.

In the name of Angel Hadraniel I thus advise you to find a pink calcite for yourself.

৴✑ *Look with the eyes of love*

Look at a baby or a cute animal (at a push a photo will do) and notice the unconditional love that arises as you do so. Enjoy the feeling!

Then look at your biggest "enemy", or problem person, and see them also as a cute innocent child. Take your time! You will notice that you suddenly find it quite easy to view even this person with the eyes of love.

৴✑ *Open your high heart centre for unconditional love*

Go to your place of stillness, your place of peace, your sanctuary. This might be a place that you know or a place that you create for yourself in your imagination. Call Archangel Michael to your side and know that you are perfectly safe and protected.

Now become aware of your paradisiacal place with all your senses. Feel the ground underneath your body, listen to the noises around you, enjoy the fragrances and the wonderful environment that surrounds you. Now call Angel Hadraniel to you and ask him to envelop you in his intense pink light. Breathe deeply in and out in order to fully absorb it.

Then feel that Hadraniel sends his pure celestial love into your high heart centre, near the thymus gland at the top of your breastbone. This will open it more and more to unconditional love; you will find it increasingly easier to leave any judging and evaluating behind. Take three conscious breaths in order to fully connect with this love.

Afterwards, say as you breathe in (ideally aloud): "*I am…*" and breathing out: "*…pure love.*" Repeat this at least three times. Following this, send this love into your day, to all the people you will meet, into all the situations that might happen – and out into the whole world. See and feel how the power of love changes everything.

Finally take three deep breaths, stretch yourself in order to fully return into your body, and open your eyes.

ᘉ Enjoy heart-to-heart hugs

It is wonderful to embrace other people heart to heart to feel more love. This does entail engaging in a very close hug – your heart chakra and theirs should touch. Also, this is not about giving the other person a friendly pat on the back while doing so, but about connecting with them, being silent, and taking three deep breaths together. You will instantly feel how much love this creates.

During such an embrace oxytocin (also known as the cuddle hormone) is released, as the English best-selling author and biochemist Dr. David R. Hamilton said in his presentation at the I CAN DO IT® conference in London in September 2010. This also explains from a scientific perspective why it feels so good to be hugged in this way.

From my experiences at my ANGEL LIFE COACH® trainings I can confirm how much the atmosphere changes as soon as I include this hug in the training.

So begin instantly, today: hug at least one person heart to heart!

ᘉ Soul Affirmation ᘉ

First ask Angel Hadraniel to enfold you in his intense pink light. Then take a deep breath, in and out, before you say (ideally aloud):

I decide to be and live more and more love, since love is always the answer whatever the question or the challenge is!

⟨⟩ *Soul Journey* ⟨⟩

Have pen and paper ready before you begin. You might want to take some notes during or directly after your journey.

With your eyes open take a deep breath in, and then slowly exhale while you close your eyes in slow motion and order your brain to automatically move into the Theta state. Breathe deeply in and out, and relax. Let your thoughts go by like birds flying past. Just observe and do not hold on to anything while you relax more and more deeply. Enjoy feeling the flowing of your breath that fills you with life energy, and relax even further.

Feel, see, or imagine yourself being enfolded in intense pink light that immediately links you to the frequency of love. Feel how this light flows softly around your aura and your physical body and caresses it gently. Breathe deeply in and out, and take this experience fully inside. It feels wonderful and you move even further into a state of deep relaxation.

Now the soft and yet so powerful light pervades your whole body, down to the tiniest cell, so that all your cells begin to vibrate in the frequency of love. This way you are being reconnected with your divine blueprint, your true essence, which is nothing else but pure love. Feel how your whole being pulsates in the energy of love, how you radiate waves of love into the whole universe.

All at once you notice that you are on a kind of a rock plateau, from where you have a breathtaking view over an ocean shimmering in all hues of turquoise. Full of joy, you are savouring the panoramic view when a graceful snow-white unicorn appears. It looks into your eyes and you see nothing but pure unconditional love. You feel how the frequency of love within yourself rises even further.

Then the unicorn bends its knee, so that it is easier for you to take your place on its back. As soon as you sit it opens its enormous white wings and soars with you into the air. It is an incredibly freeing feeling to be carried in this way over the glittering ocean; around and within you extends a limitless expanse that allows you to feel completely free.

After a short while the unicorn flies with you to an island in the middle of the ocean that resembles paradise. You gently land in one of the most exquisite places you have ever seen. You are surrounded by luscious vegetation of such beauty that there are no words that come close to doing them justice. Enjoy looking around and feel how even more love spreads within you.

Then a magnificent, youthful-looking angel appears in front of you, immersed in the most lustrous pink light that you have ever seen. It is Angel

Hadraniel. He surrounds you with his velvet wings and you feel nothing but pure unconditional love. In this celestial embrace Hadraniel magically opens your high heart centre, so that from now on you will find it easier and easier to feel unconditional love for everybody, and so leave behind all evaluating and judging. Relish this feeling, the knowledge, and the bliss, that everything, really everything, can be overcome, resolved, and healed by love.

By the time Hadraniel guides you to a sacred stone throne, nothing but love exists any longer within and around you. While you sit down on the throne Hadraniel unfolds a vision of your life up to today and asks you to send love to everything. You can virtually see with your own eyes how your life lovingly transforms on all levels in no time at all.

Then Hadraniel asks you to send this profound love to all people and beings, oceans and plants, minerals and rocks – to All-That-Is. And again you are shown how with the help of love everything changes to the positive. Looking at the vision Hadraniel has placed in front of you, you realize that it only takes a fraction of the people on earth, who live in this vibrational frequency of unconditional love day in, day out, to create peace on earth. At this moment you decide to do your utmost to be one of these people. You send the intention out to the universe to become more and more love, live more and more love, and be more and more love, with the help of the angels. Now take three deep breaths in order to anchor this within you.

Full of profound gratitude, you thank Angel Hadraniel with a whole-hearted embrace before you get on the unicorn's back again and fly home.

Once arrived, you softly glide down from the unicorn, thank it by giving it a heartfelt hug, and are nothing but pure, pristine love. Begin to stretch your body and consciously reconnect your feet with Mother Earth. Once more breathe deeply and then slowly open your eyes.

~ *Day 23* ~

CLAIRSENTIENT WITH ARCHANGEL RAGUEL

One word placed into your own heart by an angel
is more healing for the soul than a thousand words
from outside taken in through the ear.

Jakob Lorber

"Greetings, beloved soul. I AM Archangel Raguel. There are very few moments in life in which you do not feel anything. Even if it appears to you as if you are cut off from your feelings, you are aware of something: are sad, furious, confused, clouded, frustrated, neutral, content, happy, enthusiastic, and so on. This would not be the case if you were truly without feelings. Thus I ask you to use your clairsentience to be more mindful of yourself and your moods, since they hold many messages from we angels that might otherwise go unnoticed.

Become aware of your body's reactions to other people and you will recognize their true personality. In this way you will be saved much suffering.

Also, it is your clairsentience that clarifies through feelings in which areas of your life there is still something that you need to come to terms with.

But not only that – it also is often your feelings that guide your ongoing path in life. Listen to their messages mindfully and act accordingly. This way you will recognize what gift lies in your clairsentience."

Archangel Raguel
angel of clairsentience and harmony in relationships
Aura colour: pale blue/aqua
Crystal: aquamarine

Melanie, a participant in one of my workshops, told me the following story:

How Raguel became my constant companion

Everything began in Calabria in June 2010. I spent this journey with my then partner: a journey of sorrow, separation, fights, but also endless love. Shortly before the beginning of the journey my boss's wife recommended Isabelle's book *Die Engel so nah* (*The Angels So Close*). It accompanied me throughout the holiday, and despite the serious problems between my partner and me I found myself in a space of infinite inner calm throughout the whole time. I just sensed and felt that everything was good as it was. Although for many years previously I had been aware that the angels were present in my life, I had not been able to distinctly perceive or sense them. Isabelle's book and she herself have become the key to my spirituality in regard to the angels and the light beings. Today I know that Archangel Raguel was with me during the journey to Calabria and supported me continually.

My relationship with my partner had been full of tension from the very start; our happiness was always overshadowed by envy and jealousy. The great love between us was never able to truly flower even though it was present right from the beginning. Despite many separations we came back together time and again; I felt from the outset that this was my soulmate.

Through Isabelle's book and her life experiences my senses were opened and sharpened during our holiday. Suddenly I began to notice and feel things that I had never before known existed. For example, on a boat trip to the Aeolian Islands, I suddenly felt the urge to go up on deck with my partner. I took him by the hand and we stepped out through the sliding door. And there they were – two wonderful dolphins. They jumped out of the sea right next to us. The whole spectacle lasted only a few seconds and only the two of us were granted this experience. There were more than sixty people on that boat, and these loving and beautiful creatures showed themselves only to the two of us. At that moment I felt very strongly that this was a message from Angel Ramaela. If Archangel Raguel had not allowed me to feel this, Ramaela's message would have remained hidden to me. I knew in this moment that everything was perfectly all right and everything was subject to divine order. You just have to attempt to look behind the veil of illusion and then the right "truth" will be revealed. And because of that, I knew that our relationship would not bear up. I felt without a shadow of a doubt that we had arrived at a crossroads and that from there on we each had to tread a part of the life path by ourselves. And so what had to happen happened: at the beginning of October 2010 we separated. Looking back, I know how intensely Archangel Raguel was there for me at that time, even though it took some more weeks before I could perceive him again.

For some weeks after the separation, my ego stood in front of me like a large fierce bear, not allowing me to pass. I wallowed in self-pity and felt myself the poorest thing on this planet. Apart from two wonderful girlfriends, and the most loving neighbours in the world, I suddenly felt all alone. I had completely broken ties with my family, no longer had a partner, and sat in an 80-square-metre flat with a rent of 1,100 euros a month.

But this was exactly what needed to happen. Suddenly my innermost "I" re-emerged, and Archangel Raguel came through to me again. I felt very clearly that this was now my process of self-discovery, of self-love, and of growing up. No one could tell me what to do or what not to do. I could finally engage with just myself – and, eventually, also with the angels. I pushed the bear of my ego aside and started to feel again. I felt the love, I felt that I would always have enough to eat, I felt the divine order.

And lo and behold, suddenly one door after the other opened. Long-term clients started opening up more and invited me for meals. It was fascinating to see that most of these dear people shared the same path as me; they included life coaches, media professionals, and astrologers).

There were also some whose paths parted from mine after a few months. Through them, though, I was able to learn to rely on my gut feeling and my heart. I could just feel it: I was ready for the next steps.

I also had my first vision in this time, since I could suddenly perceive and feel the signs. Shortly before New Year's Eve I awoke one morning and felt that I should visit my grandfather's grave. I have to say here that, since the funeral more than twenty years ago, I had not been back.

I went to the cemetery on the night of New Year's Eve. Previously I would not even have left the house at this time, let alone gone to see a grave with only a torch with me! Suddenly I found myself feeling infinite trust. I just felt that nothing would happen. The atmosphere at the cemetery was heavenly. There were lit candles everywhere and, surprisingly, many people around. At the cemetery gate I asked Archangel Chamuel, angel in charge of self-confidence and finding places, to show me the way and I strode on.

After some time my ego came through; it made me feel that I wanted the whole affair to be over. Then I suddenly felt my legs pulled away from me and I fell to the ground between the graves. I realized that I had felt all along that this was the wrong way but my ego had stood in front of me again like a big bear. I could just sense how Chamuel and Raguel stood in front of me and looked mischievously at me as I lay there in between the graves, as if they wanted to ask why I did not believe my feelings or trust them when they tried to help me.

I picked myself up, apologized – and what do you know, after a short time I found myself standing in front of my grandfather's grave. I was touched and felt wonderfully carried and supported. I would have liked nothing more than to spend the whole night at the cemetery.

Since then, my grandfather has occasionally sent me signs. Each time, I discover something new and feel the divine order. Once a squirrel ran along next to me all the way along the path until I reached the grave, as if it wanted to say: "Hey you, all is well. Just feel and trust!"

I have to explain here that squirrels have accompanied me throughout my whole life and have been and still are present in difficult times, in particular during the relationship with my partner. These animals have time and again revealed themselves to us – during the worst fight, during the most beautiful holidays. They were always there. One of our power places was the Holy Mary Grotto in Trudering, Germany. You can nearly touch the squirrels' heads there, they are so tame. Even today I visit that place in order to regenerate and feel the love, as the love between us is still present, perhaps even stronger than when we were together. It does not matter if, at this moment, each of us is following our own path and have to make our own experiences. I feel this very strongly.

I received another sign a few weeks after going to visit my grandfather's grave. When I woke up one morning I felt that it was time to write archangel stories for children. The first story was badly needed, since my "sort of nephew" Lucas, my girlfriend's son, had been having sleep problems for some weeks that were very hard for his parents to deal with. He was waking up at night, drenched in sweat, and was terribly afraid of the dark. As he was only eighteen months old, explanations and discussions did not help much. I felt it was my task to take these fears from him and so, during a meditation, I wrote the story of Lucas and the Archangels Ariel, Raphael, and Chamuel.

The next day I felt compelled to visit IKEA; I knew that I had to buy some things for Lucas's room in the archangels' colours. In the car park a lorry drove into my car, but despite the frightening situation and a dented bonnet I felt, to my surprise, great inner peace and did not let myself be distracted.

I immediately found a canopy for Lucas's bed, in the shape of a big leaf in a beautiful light green; a lamp in the shape of a glow-worm in an even lighter green; a frog shelving rack and a blanket in dark green (Raphael's colour). I found a small soft-toy lion that roared loudly when his belly was squeezed, and sewed a rose quartz inside. I would purify all these things with the angels' help and then energize them with the angels' wonderful energies.

I felt very clearly that I had to smudge Lucas's room before we installed the new things in there. During this process my girlfriend's deceased great-grandfather showed himself to me. I asked him gently to step into the column of light and fade away into the afterlife, and he did so, in a loving way. Then we, with Lucas, installed the gifts I had bought in the room.

From the second night onwards the little boy slept through and even went to bed at night unasked. The toy lion "roars" like a real one, in Lucas' voice, and has to be taken along everywhere Lucas goes!

Today I know that I would not be clairsentient if my life had taken an easier course. I would probably never have become aware of Raguel and the other angels. In this way though, I can now write this story, have loving people around me and lead a very enriched life – a life defined by love and by the angels. Life is wonderful, even when we only really realize about four per cent of it. Only when you push your ego aside and trust in the angels will you understand the divine order and the other 96 per cent of life. I certainly will continue attempting to do this – and who knows where my life and the angels will lead me!

Reflection

Remember that your body is a wonderful oracle instrument, because you always have it with you. It is like a sacred barometer that receives messages through clairsentience. For that reason it is very important that you know how to interpret the signs your own body sends you – like goose bumps, a pressure in the stomach, a choking in the throat, and many more – because goose bumps, for example, do not have the same meaning for everyone. Some people feel a real "shake" when someone speaks a deep truth, but with others they have this reaction when someone is lying.

Also notice how your body reacts whenever you meet and are getting to know someone new. This is also a message that you perceive through your channel of clairsentience.

It is important to not regard clairsentience as any less important or powerful than clairvoyance and clairaudience, since it is actually the channel through which you receive most messages, even though you may not yet be conscious of it.

⟡ Activities for today and for the future ⟡

⟡ Listen mindfully to your feelings

In the mornings, ask Archangel Raguel to envelop you in his pale blue light, and breathe deeply in and out. Then also ask Archangel Haniel and Archangel Michael to enfold you in their silvery-golden light, so that your soul essence and all your other levels are protected, your feminine and your masculine sides are balanced, and your brain's hemispheres are synchronized. Take a few deep breaths in order to completely absorb the light.

Now send the intention ahead into your day, that you will notice your feelings and the reactions of your body in order to recognize the messages these contain.

⟡ Smell the fragrance of roses

The smell of roses or, alternatively, rose oil, contributes to further opening your heart chakra, the channel of clairsentience. Should you have neither roses nor rose oil at home, get hold of a fragrant pink rose and smell it regularly; pink because the colour also contributes to your heart chakra opening more and more.

⟡ Reduce your consumption of sugar and alcohol

Mind that you do not eat much sugar: too much of it distorts clairsentient perception, as sugar is converted into alcohol in the body. Remember that many foods contain hidden sugars: it is important to read the ingredients on the labels before you buy anything.

⟡ Be clear in your directions and protect yourself with the help of the angels

Nearly all my life I have been overwhelmed by the feelings that I sensed while in the presence of others. Until a few years ago I had no idea that this was due to my clairsentient channel. Particularly during piano exams and concerts, I found it extremely distracting to perceive the thoughts and feelings of the audience so distinctly – I sometimes found it difficult to concentrate on the pieces that I was playing.

Only since I have known that I am the master of my clairsentience can I dim or increase this channel, switch it on or off at any time. I advise you to also work on being able to do this.

I always used to think: "I am just too sensitive to protect myself enough", as there were times when I could not leave the house for weeks, because I experienced other people's thoughts and feelings in my body so strongly that I could not bear it. Today I know that we humans often use this "gift" in order to feel special. In truth it is nothing other than a concept in our heads, which we hold on to so that we do not have to change anything; it can be a great excuse.

If you truly believe in the power of the angels there is not the slightest doubt that Archangel Michael (angel of protection) and also Archangel Haniel (guardian of the soul essence) can help you; you can learn to be sensitive and protected at the same time. You only have to decide on this and leave behind your ego, which would like to make you believe you are something special.

If subsequently you still find yourself in situations in which you have to grapple with your sensitivity, be grateful. It is in this way that you are shown issues that you will still have to deal with since you have not yet worked on them sufficiently. Remember that topics dissolve in waves – or layer by layer, like onions.

⸙ Soul Affirmation ⸙

First ask Archangel Raguel to enfold you in his pale blue light. Then take a deep breath, in and out, before you speak (ideally aloud):

> *My body and my heart chakra are my best oracle instruments.*
> *It is safe for me to feel.*
> *I am clairsentient to a high degree.*
> *I am the master of my clairsentience.*
> *I can switch my clairsentience on and off any time.*

With these affirmations I strongly recommend that, while speaking, you rap alternately two or three times with the fist of one hand on the palm of the other ; do this quite fast in order to anchor the affirmations very deeply in your system. Afterwards, take three deep breaths.

⟨⟩ *Soul Journey* ⟨⟩

Have pen and paper ready before you begin. You might want to take some notes during or directly after your journey.

With your eyes open take a deep breath in, and then slowly exhale while you close your eyes in slow motion and order your brain to automatically move into the Theta state. Breathe deeply in and out, and relax. Let your thoughts go by like leaves gliding along a river and turn within. Enjoy feeling your breath that nourishes you every second of your life and that links you to the breath of God and the angels. Become aware of how with each breath you take you move further into a deeper and deeper state of relaxation.

All at once a magnificent angel appears by your side and envelops you in his luminescent pale blue light. You recognize him as Archangel Raguel, and in his presence you feel instantly safe and secure.

Feel how the delicate light pervades all layers of your aura and of your body and connects you more and more with your emotions. It feels wonderful.

Suddenly your nose detects the incomparable fragrance of roses and you discover that you and Raguel are standing in a beautiful rose garden. Roses of all hues surround you and contribute with their intoxicating aroma to you relaxing even more deeply. Enjoy it!

Then Archangel Raguel takes you by the hand and guides you to a sacred stone circle in the midst of the roses. When you enter the sacred circle you become aware of how your frequency rises and your whole being begins to vibrate.

Raguel asks you to take a seat on a bed of pink rose petals in the centre of the stone circle. You lie down and feel how the intense fragrance evaporating from the blossoms moves you to a higher state of consciousness.

It feels as if you are floating above the earth when Raguel bends over you and starts to work with your heart chakra. Very gently he dissolves old feelings that do not serve you any longer and you notice how your heart expands more and more. It could be that at this moment you receive messages for yourself. Listen mindfully.

After some time Raguel asks you to rise from your bed of blossoms and leave the sacred stone circle with him. You sense a profound change in yourself as you step out of the circle. Your feelings have become clearer, so that you can now interpret their messages with grace, lightness, and joy.

Now take three deep breaths in order to anchor your experiences within yourself. Connect with the ground, feel the roots underneath your feet that reach down to the centre of the earth. Start to stretch your body to slowly return to the here and now, and open your eyes.

~ Day 24 ~

CLAIRVOYANT WITH ARCHANGEL HANIEL

If I had not experienced it myself
I would not have believed it possible,
what blessedness
the sight of angels could give you.

Angela of Foligno

"Greetings, beloved soul. I AM Archangel Haniel. It is of immeasurable importance in these years of the change of times to connect more and more with the power of the divine feminine as well as your own feminine side, no matter whether you are a man or a woman. Only in this way can all your psychic abilities, which you have acquired over many incarnations, surface again. As you read these lines you can be sure that you have once lived in Lemuria, Atlantis, Ancient Egypt, and/or Avalon, since the memories from these incarnations that are hidden only by a thin veil are waiting to be resurrected and in a magical way continue to guide you to the right places, people, and wisdoms.

In order to retrieve your inner sight and your clairvoyance I ask you from now on to regularly withdraw from the world, as only in this way can the inner visions *not be mingled with pictures of the world and interpreted unclearly. In these times of withdrawal connect as often as possible to the energy of the moon, which symbolizes feminine energy, by going out into the night and absorbing the moonlight. The intense frequency of the nights of full moon particularly helps you to open yourself and to prepare for the ever-higher light frequencies that are now flowing on to the earth. Ask me in these bright full-moon nights to direct the moon's iridescent light into your third eye in order to remove bit by bit the countless veils, so that you have clairvoyance as you did in the times of your great incarnations.*

It is of great importance to know that along with this opening you will become more sensitive on all levels. This might mean that certain things, which have previously been part of your life, are no longer possible for you because your frequency increases in the form of a spiral, as your light body activates further, and has you become lighter and lighter. Therefore I ask you to treat yourself and the needs of your body and your soul well, in order to experience this process full of grace and ease. In order that you can be protected on the deepest level ask me every morning and every evening to envelop your soul essence in silver light, which simultaneously links you with the feminine part of your being. To this effect I embrace you with my wings and send the pure essence of love into your whole being."

Archangel Haniel
angel of grace and femininity, sensitivity, moon energies, and intuition
Aura colours: bluish-white, silver
Crystal: moonstone

My dear friend Jeshua, who is also a member of my team, told me the following story:

Encounter with Archangel Haniel

Since the ANGEL LIFE COACH® training with Isabelle I have had a special connection to Archangel Haniel. She played a big role in me reconnecting with my intuition and clairvoyance.

One day, when I did an angel card reading for myself, I received the message from Haniel that every night before going to sleep I should connect with her and with the moon for some time. I did as I was told and, every evening, felt how the energy of the moonlight flowed into my third eye. Over the following days, I was much more strongly connected to my intuition than before.

Unfortunately I have to admit that at some point I became lazy and stopped linking in with Haniel and the moon energy every night. Eventually though, in my next angel

---

card readings, I received the message that I should continue – it was truly important for me.

Still, I was not always consistent. One night, however, I suddenly realized how important it must be if Haniel was connecting with me because I was not doing it myself! I was lying in bed, eyes closed and ready to sleep, when I suddenly felt pressure on my third eye. It felt as if someone had touched it. When I opened my eyes, though, there was no one there.

I closed my eyes and instantly there was the pressure again, actually stronger than before. Again I opened my eyes, as it felt as if a real hand had touched my forehead. Again there was no one to be seen!

When I closed my eyes again I immediately felt the touch. This time I heard Haniel's message: "It is very important that you connect with me. This is an exception. I will not do this again. But this one time I am working on your third eye even though you have not taken time for this."

It was the strangest feeling I had ever had: to feel a physical touch when apart from me there was no one in the room!

The truth though is that, ever since this moment, I have been much more closely connected to my intuition than before. And if I listen to it, everything works wonderfully well. Things and situations in my life have become much more pleasant, and I thank Haniel with all my heart for this.

I have also discovered that angels will sometimes do something for us that is to our highest good, even if we have not done anything about it ourselves. But this is by no means an excuse for not doing anything.

Archangel Haniel has really showed me my path and contributed immensely to my success and the way I am today. Even though I now work just as much with other angels, I know that she is with me and that she guides me on my path to growth, success, and happiness.

⸱⟨⟩ *Reflection* ⟨⟩⸱

Being clairvoyant does not only mean seeing auras, angels, and the like but also receiving symbolic pictures or prophetic dreams. It can even happen that your physical eyes receive clairvoyant messages: for example when suddenly something very real jumps into your line of sight and is the answer to one of the questions that you have given over to the angels.

For this reason it is also very important that, if you would like to become (more) clairvoyant, you use your physical eyes more consciously.

Besides, from now on you should no longer say: "I don't see anything anyway", because that works like an affirmation. Should you hear yourself voice this sentence, from now on stop and say instead something like: "With every minute I see more and more."

Today's soul affirmations are particularly effective for this.

ᴄ᷂᷅ Activities for today and for the future ᴄ᷂᷅

ᴄ᷂᷅ Use your physical eyes more consciously

Begin to perceive your environment (people, animals, places, things, situations, and so on) with conscious eyes, so that, for example, in the evening you can remember what the people you met during the day were wearing. Also consciously take in the colour of the eyes of every single person you speak with.

Just really look at everything that you see and you will notice that your ability to visualize and to see with your inner eye improves.

ᴄ᷂᷅ Chant "Om"

In the mornings and evenings chant "Om" with closed eyes seven times, while concentrating on your third eye. Concentrate on holding the "m" sound of "Om". When you do this you may well feel your third eye start to vibrate. You might also see different-coloured lights during the chanting.

If you want to achieve "visible" success with this, Archangel Haniel advises you to chant "Om" seven times every morning and evening for twenty-one days (see also page 218).

ᴄ᷂᷅ Cut down on certain foods

Certain foods obstruct rather than support clairvoyance. Therefore it makes sense to cut down on them. This concerns all kinds of dairy products, coffee, alcohol, and sugar. (I hardly need mention that nicotine is harmful to our health.)

Once your clairvoyance has developed and is strong, it will not matter that much if you occasionally consume a little of these foods. Ultimately it is more important to be happy, which helps you to achieve a high frequency, than to be fanatical and stressed about things like food.

⟋⟍ *Place the tip of a mountain crystal on your third eye*

In order to cleanse and open your third eye you can place the tip of a mountain crystal, with the tip pointing towards the crown chakra, on your third eye when cleansing your chakras or during a chakra meditation. Here too it is imperative that you do this for at least a period of three weeks if you would like to achieve more profound results.

I myself have been using a mountain crystal tip on my third eye while cleansing my chakras every day, morning and evening, for about two months.

⟋⟍ *Use the light of the full moon*

There will not necessarily be a full moon on the day you work with this chapter. Nevertheless, I would like to warmly suggest you use the force of the full moon for its benefit to your third eye. If there is none on the day you can visualize it instead; and return to the exercise once more on the next full moon.

The most powerful way is to lie down outside in a deckchair during a (warm!) full moon night and ask Archangel Haniel to channel the moonlight directly into your third eye. It is said to purify you very gently of negative memories, from past lives as well as your current one, and contribute to you being able to perceive increasingly more with your inner sight.

Naturally you can also do this and ask for Haniel's support in colder weather; you probably just won't last outside for as long! In this case just walk around to absorb the pure, unfiltered light outside for a while. Then lie down inside the house in a glass conservatory or close to big windows with the moon shining on you through the glass.

⟋⟍ *Give clear directions*

I remember well how I was virtually flooded with images when my clairvoyance developed again in this life. This deluge of images was at times hard to bear, so I would advise you to clearly tell the angels from the start that *you* want to determine when you want to see more or less. It is actually possible to switch a certain amount of clairvoyance on and off like a TV. You always have the choice. Remember this!

Besides, it is a question of integrity not to use clairvoyance in order to receive information about somebody who would not give you the information by choice (unless it is for your own protection). This is very important to the angels.

ᘓ Soul Affirmation ᘓ

First ask Archangel Haniel to enfold you in her bluish-white-silver light. Then take a deep breath, in and out, before you speak (ideally aloud):

> *It is safe for me to see.*
> *I am clairvoyant to a high degree.*
> *I am the master of my clairvoyance.*
> *I can switch my clairvoyance on and off like a TV at any time.*

With these affirmations I strongly recommend that, while speaking, you rap alternately two or three times with the fist of one hand on the palm of the other; do this quite fast in order to anchor the affirmations very deeply in your system. Afterwards, take three deep breaths.

ᘓ Soul Journey ᘓ

Have pen and paper ready before you begin. You might want to take some notes during or directly after your journey.

> *With your eyes open take a deep breath in, and then slowly exhale while you close your eyes in slow motion and order your brain to automatically move into the Theta state. Breathe deeply in and out, and relax.*
>
> *Let your thoughts go by like leaves gliding along a river and turn within. Enjoy feeling your breath that nourishes you every second of your life and that connects you with the breath of God and the angels. Become aware of how with each breath you take you move further and further into a state of deep relaxation.*
>
> *See, feel, or imagine that you are being enveloped in lustrous silver light that very softly pervades all layers of your aura, your physical body, and every single one of your cells. Take pleasure in shining in ever more resplendent bright silver light.*
>
> *It is full moon and you find yourself at the shore of a lake, which glitters silvery in the moonlight, when a snow-white unicorn appears by your side. It is of such celestial beauty that your heart brims over with love. When it then gazes into your eyes, full of pure love, you recognize in its eyes your true purity. A profound feeling of happiness flows through you.*
>
> *Then the unicorn bends its knees so that you find it very easy to get on to its back. No sooner are you seated than the unicorn rises into the air with you, soaring higher and higher until you reach the summit of a crystalline mountain. You glide off the back of the unicorn and look at a magnificent*

ethereal temple shining resplendent in silver, right ahead of you. A gracious angel, who resembles an ethereal moon goddess, already awaits you on the steps of the temple. It is Archangel Haniel who welcomes you with open arms. She asks not only you but also the unicorn into the temple. You are confronted with an enormous room of unimaginable height, which connects you with the dimensions of infinity. Suddenly you notice that your aura is expanding until you no longer feel any boundaries.

Archangel Haniel leads you to a crystalline bed placed in the middle of the room. As you lie down you feel immediately how your frequency rises, and you relax very deeply while Haniel starts to work on your third eye. Very tenderly she relieves you of the veils of fear that have settled over your sight because of traumatic experiences from your past lives.

You feel a pleasant vibrating inside your third eye, and in fact through your whole body, as Haniel begins to activate your twelve-strand DNA so that you will be able to see at the right time; just as in previous incarnations. At the same time the unicorn touches your third eye with its horn and sends glittering star essence into it in order to open it further. Enjoy the feeling and become aware of explosions of radiant light or other images you may see.

Now take a few deep breaths to soundly anchor everything on the physical level too. Remain lying down on your bed until Haniel lifts you very softly and places you again on the back of the unicorn. You leave the temple full of gratitude, say goodbye to Archangel Haniel, and fly back to earth.

As you glide from the back of the unicorn you notice that you are also seeing much more clearly with your physical eyes as your DNS becomes more and more activated. Thank the unicorn. Now connect again with Mother Earth and the roots underneath your feet. Stretch your body and take a few deep breaths until you are ready to open your eyes.

Day 25

CLAIRAUDIENT WITH
ANGEL ISRAFEL

*None sing so wildly well
as the angel Israfel.
And the giddy stars (so legends tell)
ceasing their hymns, attend the spell
of his voice all mute.*

Edgar Allan Poe

*Through the midnight sky an angel flew
and a quiet song he sang;
And the moon, and stars, and clouds gathered 'round
to hear his holy song.*

Mikhail Lermontov

"Greetings, beloved soul. I AM Angel Israfel. My deepest wish is to help you *retrieve your inner listening, so that you will again be able to perceive the music of the spheres and the voices of the angels from the higher dimensions, your true home. Inherent in this music is a power that is able to transform and heal everything.*

In order to make this gift of clairaudience accessible to you again, you need contemplation and stillness. It is through learning to fade out the noise of the worlds and to become still, wherever you might be, that you receive the tender vibrations of these celestial levels. Messages of all kinds are brought to you for your benefit and that of your environment, so that you may recognize the nature of your tasks in order to transform the world at its core so that it again turns into a paradise on earth. This and nothing less is the meaning of your present existence on earth, beloved soul. Accept this meaning from the depth of your heart and your life will change in wonderful ways and exceed even your boldest dreams."

Angel Israfel

angel of music on earth as well as the music of the higher spheres
Aura colour: pearly white and pink
Crystal: rhodonite

My friend Johanna, who is a pianist and also an ANGEL LIFE COACH®, was enthusiastic about her collaboration with Angel Israfel:

Composing with Israfel

More than a month ago, I received a request to write a song, more precisely an angel song. I was very happy about that, and felt inspired by an idea immediately. However, as I am always very busy in my work as a piano teacher and pianist and was also facing several challenges in my private life at that point, I did not have much time to keep working on this request.

I lived for several weeks with only my vague idea – and nothing happened. Occasionally I asked the angels when I would eventually write the song but still nothing happened. Meanwhile I informed the person who had requested the song that it would be a bit delayed. The good thing was that we had not arranged any fixed deadline.

One day I was on the phone with Isabelle – a treat that we unfortunately do not share as often as we would like – and the subject of the composition came up. She said: "How about asking Israfel, the angel of music of the higher spheres!"

And the scales fell from my eyes. This was exactly the piece of information that I still needed; I had completely forgotten about him. And in this moment, I knew that the song was already written.

The same evening after work I sat down, meditated for a while, and then asked Israfel to come to me. I felt myself being enveloped in a wonderful iridescent pink-

---

white light and had the feeling that my ear chakras instantly widened and a sense of abandon filled me.

I had actually planned to use a beautiful poem or prayer as the lyrics; for that reason I had started to research in books and on the Internet. But now I suddenly knew that I would write the lyrics myself.

I fetched a piece of paper and wrote the whole of the lyrics down without faltering even once. It was as if I was writing down a text that I had known by heart for a long time. When I read through it I was amazed at the intensity and the choice of words.

The next evening I was very tired because I had had an exhausting day of teaching. I did not know how to compose in that state; I nevertheless sat down at my electric piano, put on my headset, and asked Israfel to help me. I explained to him that I was pretty tired and could feel no inspiration. He instructed me to place my hands on the piano keys and I did so, and played a few chords. All of a sudden I had found the key for my song, and in my head I also heard parts of a melody. The lyrics lay next to my sheet of music and I wrote the whole melody down in one go. It fitted the text like a glove.

In the shortest amount of time imaginable the whole accompaniment for the melody was done. It was as if I had to open my inner ear wide in order to clearly hear a quiet music far away; occasionally it took longer because I could not identify the sounds I heard right away or because I did not hear the music clearly enough. Then I would ask Israfel to help me, so that I could make it work better.

When I had finished, I seemed to return to my body as though out of a dream state. It was only now that I noticed I had been composing for two hours without a break and was very tired.

As I dropped off to sleep I continued to listen to the music that seemed to come from other spheres. I woke up the next morning after only a short sleep fresh and rested, feeling elated.

The song was missing only the bridge and the end. This I composed in the same way that evening and thus I had finished the song – in three days.

I did not have to make any major corrections; the song was perfectly balanced as it was and I am very happy with it.

A big thank you to Israfel! He is like a magic loudspeaker, which boosts the music from other dimensions so that we can hear it better.

◦⟩ *Activities for today and for the future* ⟨◦

◦⟩ *Listen consciously with your physical eyes*

- Take time to be still and to take in all the sounds you can hear around you.
- Switch on music and listen consciously to all the voices, instruments, and other sounds in it.
- Listen consciously to the voices of the people in your personal environment, on the radio, on the TV or on the Internet, and discern the differences in sound between them all.

◦⟩ *Cleanse your ear chakras*

In order to receive messages with your inner ears it is necessary to regularly cleanse your ear chakras, because all the negative words that you hear from others, through the media, and because of your own negative self-talk are stored in there. By the way, the ear chakras are located on the left and the right above your eyebrows, behind your forehead.

There are different ways of cleansing them:

- It is very effective to bring Tibetan cymbals together softly in front of each of your ear chakras. Their sound purifies them beautifully. You will feel how many times you need to sound the cymbals to clear the chakras.
- Call Angel Israfel and ask him to send his pearly white and pink light into your ear chakras to cleanse them.
- Archangel Zadkiel, who also has a part in activating the skills of clairaudience, can purify your ear chakras too. He can send his violet light in the form of a horizontal figure of eight: imagine it enclosing both your ear chakras and crossing over in the middle, at your third eye.
- Another, also very effective method is to in ask Archangel Zadkiel to purify your ear chakras with the help of the silver-violet flame.
- The ear chakras will also be wonderfully cleansed if you swim in the sea or take a salt bath, immersing your head in the water. Note: this also works for all the other chakras or channels respectively.

◦⟩ *Chant "Om"*

If you want to achieve "audible" successes Angel Israfel advises you to chant "Om", with eyes closed, seven times every morning and evening over a period of twenty-one days (see also page 211), while focusing on your two ear chakras. You may well feel a vibration starting in them. You might also hear the "Om" with your inner ears while you are chanting.

Note: decide beforehand which of the chakras (third eye or ear) you want to activate more before you begin the twenty-one-day process. It is not advisable to activate both chakras in this way at the same time as that would split the focus.

ᘓ Work with rhodonite and lapis lazuli

In order to increase your ear chakras' abilities, it is wise to work with two different crystals: rhodonite and lapis lazuli.

Rhodonite helps you to take in sounds more consciously and more deeply, and to hear the music of the spheres in accordance with your inner wisdom in divine timing. You can hold the crystal in your receiving hand (the hand you do *not* use for writing) when listening to music or when listening to stillness. Be mindful as you do so.

In order to open your ear chakras further you can place two roughly same-sized lapis lazuli crystals, charged with Archangel Zadkiel's energy (see crystal ritual, page 17), above your eyebrows on your ear chakras while you listen to a chakra purification meditation on CD. Or create one yourself.

ᘓ Give clear directions

I can remember well how unnerving it was at times when my gift of clairaudience redeveloped in this life. I heard *everything*. We lived in a house with paper-thin wall, and had always heard quite a lot from our neighbours. When I became clairaudient again though, while my husband would only hear the neighbours in the adjoining house talking, I could clearly hear every word they were saying. Every noise, no matter how small, seemed to virtually boom in my head. Often I could hardly bear it. Eventually I had the idea of speaking to Zadkiel about this. He said: *"You have sent out that you wanted to be clairaudient at all costs. This you have received. Now decide that you will use this gift in a way that works comfortably for you – and it will happen."*
It really worked! Today I can concentrate very well in the midst of even the loudest noise, as I blend it out with the help of the angels.

For that reason I advise you to tell the angels very clearly from the beginning that *you* want to determine when you want to hear more or less. It is possible to switch your clairaudience on and off like a radio to some extent. You always have the choice. Remember this!

Apart from that it is a question of integrity to not use the skill of clairaudience in order to receive information about someone that he or she would never tell you of their own accord (unless your own protection is concerned). This is very important to the angels.

⁓ Soul Affirmation ⁓

First ask Angel Israfel to enfold you in his pearly white and pink light. Then take a deep breath, in and out, before you speak (ideally aloud):

> *It is safe for me to hear.*
> *I am clairaudient to a high degree.*
> *I am the master of my clairaudience.*
> *I can switch my clairaudience on and off like a radio at any time.*

With these affirmations I strongly recommend that, while speaking, you rap alternately two or three times with the fist of one hand on the palm of the other; do this quite fast in order to anchor the affirmations very deeply in your system. Afterwards, take three deep breaths.

⁓ Soul Journey ⁓

Have pen and paper ready before you begin. You might want to take some notes during or directly after your journey.

> *With your eyes open take a deep breath in, and then slowly exhale while you close your eyes in slow motion and order your brain to automatically move into the Theta state. Breathe deeply in and out, and relax.*
>
> *Let your thoughts go by like leaves gliding along a river and turn within. With every breath you take you relax more and more deeply. Enjoy feeling how your breath nurtures you and at the same time connects you with the breath of God and move even more deeply into a state of relaxation.*
>
> *You find yourself at the shore of a rolling ocean whose surface glitters silvery in the light of a magical full moon. Take in the sound of the waves with all your senses, particularly with your inner and outer ears, and listen to the energies in your body.*
>
> *All at once a resplendent beautiful angel appears, surrounded by a luminously transparent, pearly, white and pink aura. It is Angel Israfel. His whole being emanates the high vibrations of celestial sounds and you feel how, in his presence, your own frequency instantly rises.*
>
> *Suddenly you become aware of familiar sounds and Israfel points towards the ocean. You see the powerful fin of a whale protruding from the*

water. At that moment this enormous animal starts emitting one of the most beautiful whale songs you have ever heard. You listen, full of deep awe.

When the whale has finished Angel Israfel takes you by the hand and both of you rise up into the air. You soar higher and higher until you reach a celestial room: it is crowned by a gigantic crystalline dome that has been created according to the laws of sacred geometry. Right underneath the dome you find a crystalline throne; Israfel asks you to take a seat on it. As you sit you sense a further increase in your frequency; Israfel is already starting to relieve your ear chakras of all the impurities and negative words that you or others have spoken. You become aware of a pleasant feeling above your eyebrows and notice how your ear chakras begin to move in a consistent pulsating rhythm. Take in its vibrating, listening.

Suddenly Angel Israfel begins to sing – notes of such breathtaking beauty that they cause celestial spheres, that you have until now only sensed indistinctly, to sound clearly inside you. With the help of Israfel's music your soul vaults into unimagined heights and a feeling of infinite bliss pervades your whole being.

You notice how your body becomes brighter and one with your light body. Angel Israfel regards you with such a loving gaze that tears of emotion and profound gratitude come to your eyes. You suddenly know from the depths of your heart that everything, truly everything, is possible.

Once again you gaze at the sacred dome above you before you rise from the crystalline throne, and take in her ringing secrets.

Finally it is time to leave this blessed place. Together with Angel Israfel you stride from the wonderful room and fly back to the earth. You land very softly, and again you feel Mother Earth underneath your feet and know that you are connected to heaven and earth. Start stretching and slowly return to the here and now. Open your eyes as soon as you feel ready for it.

Day 26

CLAIRCOGNIZANT WITH ARCHANGEL URIEL

*What is the wisdom of a book
compared to the wisdom of an angel?*
Friedrich Hölderlin

"Greetings, beloved soul. I AM Archangel Uriel. I would very much like to induct you further into the power of your claircognizance. If you were at every moment of your life conscious of being one with All-That-Is, any knowledge would be accessible to you at all times, as the truth is that you have within you on a subatomic level a system that links you forever more with the whole universe. Thus, whenever you are in a state of heightened vibration you can recall all the information from all of your lives and from all levels of being. For this reason it is essential that you arrange for yourself to be a pure channel if you are keen to obtain wonderful messages from the higher spheres through claircognizance. The clarity of your being and your ability to live in the here and now determine how much of the knowledge from the atmospheric particles constantly around you you receive. Thus I ask you to spend much time in

God's glorious nature in order to strengthen your connection to all forms of energy and to feel the oneness that lies at the root of all things. This way you will, thanks to your inner wisdom, receive more and more of the messages that are meant for you."

Archangel Uriel
angel who awakens claircognizance and reveals whichever
next step you should take
Aura colour: delicate yellow
Crystal: amber

Arne, a claircognizant friend of mine and also an ANGEL LIFE COACH®, received his answer from Archangel Uriel in a very symbolic way:

The rapids of life

After my separation and divorce from my wife I had many, though no true, relationships. I had closed my heart completely, so that no one was able to hurt me. During this time I also had a longer liaison – though I emotionally starved my girlfriend and when she finally ended the relationship I did not, at first, really care much. However, I then started to open up my heart and I gradually realized what I had lost; so I began to fight, first slowly and then more and more intensely, for this lost love. I tried everything to revive this relationship; yet this attempt resembled a journey on a rollercoaster – I sometimes came close to and then was again kilometres away from my goal.

In one of these moments I remembered Archangel Uriel, who I knew would be able to show me the next step if I asked him. So I asked Uriel to show me in a dream the next step on the road to my love.

After a few dreamless nights I had the following dream: I swam in a river that led into a cave. Inside the cave the river became more and more turbulent and I could not see where it was going; I also could not get hold of anything to stop myself and put an end to this drifting. After a while I spotted in front of me an opening with two possible exits. In the first one, I saw, the water was quiet and a long, comfortable chute led out of the cave. The second opening looked anything but comfortable: it resembled a wild-water river with many rapids and waterfalls. I wanted to take the "safe" way, yet I was driven towards the turbulent exit, even though I tried in every way possible to get to the long and quiet chute. At first I was anything but happy, as I was sucked into the swirl and given a really good shaking. But I also noticed that the slow and comfortable chute led to a vista that looked boring and bleak. At the end of my wild-water rollercoaster, though, the true revelation showed itself to me: an area full of beauty and abundance. I felt that I had arrived in paradise.

After waking up from my sleep, Archangel Uriel's message became clear to me. There are moments in life during which you just have to trust and not desperately search for the simplest path. Through letting go and trusting, everything takes its rightful path, even if a few rapids lie en route. Through staying relaxed you will not constantly hit your head on the stones. So I knew that I should keep trusting and take the turbulent path in order to attain happiness. And whatever that happiness looks like: quite honestly, what is the worst that could happen to me? After all, paradise is waiting for me!

Reflection

Of the four mediumistic channels, claircognizance is the least tangible one, since this knowledge seems to appear out of nowhere. Also, as with all these channels it is difficult to know whether a message has come from the higher levels or is just a communication from the ego. To the question of how we can best determine this, Archangel Uriel answers:

> *"Whenever you receive anything out of the blue ask yourself immediately: 'How do I feel now, in this moment, and a few minutes ago?' If you felt well and were operating at a higher frequency you can be sure that it is a message from the higher levels. Should you have been in a bad mood or a bad place and have deeply wished for a certain answer, then it was most likely your ego that has sent you a message. Also, truly important messages repeat themselves, and appear like lightning from nowhere rather than developing slowly."*

Uriel's answer has helped me enormously. I have also discovered that this kind of differentiation works for the other channels as well.

This ultimately means that we always have to put ourselves into a good vibration if we want to receive clear messages. This is exactly the reason why this book is structured as it is: to start with we need to purify ourselves in order to leave our "rubbish" behind. Only then can we increase our frequency and become our authentic self in order to eventually receive clear messages from "above" and to realize the life of our dreams.

Day 26

⤫⤬ Activities for today and for the future ⤫⤬

⤫⤬ Note your "claircognizant" experiences

Create a sacred space for yourself and call Archangel Uriel to your side. Ask him to envelop you in his yellow light, breathe deeply in and out, and relax.

Think back through your past about things that you have just known, as if out of the blue, and write them down. In this way you will attract more claircognizance.

⤫⤬ Spend time in nature

Many people who are more focused on thinking – and therefore ideally placed to develop their claircognizance – are extremely ruled by their head; they work and read a lot, and continually educate themselves. They are also often very sceptical and doubt whether they can take seriously something they suddenly just "know" from out of nowhere. For this reason it is particularly important for them not to lose contact with nature, since nature frees us humans of unnecessary ballast or rubbish more quickly than anything else. Through being freed of this ballast, the difference between signals from the ego and messages from higher levels becomes much easier to recognize.

⤫⤬ Contact a master of their trade

In order to receive knowledge from higher levels, you can contact deceased masters. I learned from Doreen Virtue that this is possible, and so I sometimes connect with the composer, usually long deceased, when I am studying a new piano piece, in order to learn about how he experienced the music and how I can play it best. Contact with the composer also helps me with the technical side. In this way I learn and understand the piece a lot faster.

When I started writing my first book I worked slightly differently: I asked which author would like to help me with which issue. The answer always came immediately and the help was clearly noticeable.

Doreen Virtue, for example, asked for help with her jogging because she kept on suffering from a bad stitch. Within a very short time she realized she was being contacted by Jim Fixx, the deceased author of a book on jogging, who gave her some wonderful pointers. From this moment on she has never again got a stitch while out jogging.

As you can see, there are various ways of asking for and receiving help.

Even if you do not perceive a presence right away, you can be certain that you are supported by someone.

ᴄ✑ *Practise automatic writing*

Prepare yourself by cleansing your chakras and meditating.

When you first start practising automatic writing, it is helpful to decide on a certain time of day and stick to it (when I started I was asked by the angels to always sit ready to write at 3.15 p.m.; 15.15 is a portal). If you do not get any instruction from the angels you might want to start on a time like 10.10, 11.11, 12.12 etc. as these are portals facilitating the connection.

The angels, masters, and other light beings will then see that you are taking your communication with them truly seriously. As soon as you are ready call Archangel Michael to your side; he is sometimes described as the "bouncer angel" as he makes sure that no lower entities will make contact with you.

Then write down the question or the topic on which you would like to receive answers. You can also ask to receive answers from a certain being or deceased master. Pay attention with all your senses and write down what you receive.

Don't worry if your first time is not too productive; after all, practice makes perfect.

ᴄ✑ *Soul Affirmation* ᴄ✑

First ask Archangel Uriel to enfold you in his pale yellow light. Then take a deep breath, in and out, before you speak (ideally aloud):

> *It is safe for me to know.*
> *I am claircognizant to a high degree.*
> *I am the master of my claircognizance.*
> *I can switch my claircognizance on and off at any time.*

With these affirmations I strongly recommend that, while speaking, you rap alternately two or three times with the fist of one hand on the palm of the other; do this quite fast in order to anchor the affirmations very deeply in your system. Afterwards, take three deep breaths.

∽ *Soul Journey* ∽

Have pen and paper ready before you begin. You might want to take some notes during or directly after your journey.

With your eyes open take a deep breath in, and then slowly exhale while you close your eyes in slow motion and order your brain to automatically move into the Theta state. Breathe deeply in and out, and relax.

Let your thoughts go by like birds flying past. Just let them go and enjoy feeling your breath that links you to the breath of God and that nourishes you. With each breath you take move further into a state of deeper and deeper relaxation.

Feel, see, or imagine how you are being enfolded in luminous golden light that connects you with the Christ consciousness and your true essence, your core energy. Enjoy feeling within yourself the golden energy column that embodies your eternal connection with heaven and earth, so that at all times you can receive all the knowledge that you wish to experience.

Then you recognize that you are in a place of dazzling beauty. Flowers of all imaginable shapes draw your attention to them. Their delicious fragrance allows you to relax even further, while you are simultaneously conscious of the intoxicating sound of the sea in the background. Exotic birds sing elated songs – and you feel the bond with All-That-Is more strongly than ever.

Suddenly you become aware of a white owl sitting majestically in a tree above you. You are just remembering that the owl is a symbol of knowledge and wisdom when Archangel Uriel appears next to you. He regards you lovingly with his friendly eyes and indicates for you to follow him. Together you stroll through the paradisiacal landscape until you reach a stone circle on a sacred hill. Inside it you see a crystalline throne. Uriel asks you to take a seat on it, and as you sit on the sacred chair Uriel steps up behind you and places his hands on your shoulders. In a clear voice he speaks to you:

"Beloved soul, at this moment you are seated on the throne of consciousness. Now go within, connect with your essence – I will help you with it – and listen to the wisdom that wishes to reveal itself to you. Take all the time you need. In this state and on this throne any wisdom is accessible to you."

As Archangel Uriel becomes silent you move into your inner core and begin to receive. Take your time.

After some time has elapsed Archangel Uriel makes himself felt again and brings you gently back into the here and now.

"You can return to this place at any time. With time you will find it in-

creasingly easier to experience this deep state of consciousness at other places around the world as well, no matter what might be happening around you."

Gratefully you rise from the throne and embrace Uriel wholeheartedly.

You become aware again of the beautiful nature around you, stretch your body and feel an intense connection to Mother Earth. As soon as you are ready, open your eyes.

Day 27

VISIONS OF THE FUTURE
WITH THE HELP OF
ANGEL PASCHAR

See, I am sending an angel ahead of you
to guard you along the way
and to bring you to the place
I have prepared.

Exodus 23:20

"*Greetings, beloved soul. I AM Angel Paschar. If you only knew how often I visit you in your dreams and bring you visions of your future or the futures of other people. Then you would really strive to remember them in the mornings. The information that you receive is sometimes sent through imagery and symbolism, and is at other times straightforward and crystal clear, with nothing to construe or interpret.*

From now, on open yourself consciously to receive all the visions that are awaiting you. Be assured that you will not see anything that is not meant for you. But by opening up to it, there will be a new clarity in your life, as you will also perceive when visions of others are meant for you and are true, and when they are not. I call this the 'transparency of inner viewing', which helps you to distinguish the truthful from delusions of the ego.

229

*Keep away from false messengers of fear; they distort your vision of the future.
You can recognize them from their eyes, in which dwells at times a fanatical glint.
The true prophets do not depict themselves as such but act full of humbleness and
divine light. In their eyes dwells a transparency that is unparalleled. You will easily
recognize them.*

*Connect with me as often as you like and I will help you to distinguish true
visions from false ones."*

Angel Paschar
angel of visions (also of the future) and of dreams
Aura colour: powder blue
Crystal: apophyllite

⌒∽ *Charles' Vision* ∽⌒

We do not always receive the visions of our future in person. Occasionally
another person serves as messenger in order to connect us with our potential. That is what happened to me at the 4th International Angel Congress
in Hamburg:

As soon as I left the stage after my presentation Charles Virtue came over to
me; I had helped him professionally in Germany when he was starting out.
He was thrilled by my presentation and said: "You know what I saw during
your channelled meditation?"

"No," I said, "I have no idea."

"I saw you sitting at a grand piano and channelling music and meditation
simultaneously. It was wonderful! You absolutely have to do this: no one else
is able to!"

I was utterly speechless – and that does not happen to me often. It was
quite a while before I could speak again, but eventually I said: "Wow, what
an image! I have no idea whether this is possible…"

Charles just said: "Of course it is! I know that you can do it."

I spoke to some musician friends about his vision; like me, they were more
than sceptical about how this might work – after all, just singing along to
your own piano playing is not easy. Channelling and speaking words, in a
different rhythm to the music, is another thing again.

I forgot about the whole thing until one day I connected with Angel
Paschar and experienced exactly the same vision that Charles had told me
about.

When I heard from someone else a few days later that she had seen the
same, I knew that it was time to put this vision into practice. I told Konrad,

one of my publishers, about it and he was also completely enthused, saying:
"You absolutely have to do this at the next Angel Congress!"

Now it was down to me to find a way to make this vision become reality. To be quite honest I had no idea how I was supposed to practise that, so I asked my angels. They just laughed and said:

"You are the one who has created the Angel Trance Coaching, which allows the impossible to become possible. Thus have Florian [a friend of mine], who you trained in this, do a coaching session for you; he is ideal, because he does not know how difficult it is but is absolutely convinced that you can do this. An Angel Trance Coaching by him will be more effective than you channelling one for yourself, because you have doubts about it being possible."

No sooner said than done! For a few days I listened to Florian's Angel Trance Coaching before I started to practise. And lo and behold, little by little it worked, until finally, at the 5th International Angel Congress I sat on stage in the Salzburg Congress Centre and channelled a meditation while playing the grand piano. The audience awarded it with a standing ovation.

Jessica, dentist and ANGEL LIFE COACH®, awoke one morning after an enthralling dream:

The vintage Mercedes

In December 2010 I was fortunate enough to participate in Isabelle's ANGEL LIFE COACH® training. I enjoyed every second of it; it did me the world of good to be surrounded by such loving people. A deep transformation took place in me; something that has been the case so far after each course I have done with Isabelle and her wonderful team. I felt the deep connection between Isabelle and her colleagues, a feeling that I wished for myself too. I briefly dreamed of being part of such a team, even of her team, and doing such loving work. But I had no personal contact with Isabelle. However, this wish was very profound, but also felt enormously light, and I held it lovingly in my heart like a balloon, then happily watched it ascend. I never thought of it again afterwards; the matter had vanished into the sky along with my beautiful balloon.

After this, every evening from Christmas to Epiphany I drank half a glass of water and asked Paschar and Jeremiel to help me remember the next morning what I had dreamed during the night. I found this ritual very exciting because for many years I had thought that I did not dream anything – and this, as I know today, could not have been true since everyone dreams.

On the ninth night I had a dream that touched me profoundly, because deep within me I knew that this dream had something to do with my future!

In my dream I saw myself on one of Isabelle's courses. Following this, I walked out of the building where the course was taking place and saw my mother and my stepfather across the street. I crossed the street and walked towards them. The next moment a beautiful blue-silver vintage Mercedes came towards us and stopped next to us. I knew it wanted to collect us, and we got in. To my surprise there was none other than Isabelle von Fallois at the wheel. For me it was a wonderful dream as it gave me a feeling of hope, the feeling that all would be well. I was on the right path!

In February, I attended another unforgettable course led by Isabelle. This time she facilitated it with Gary Quinn.

On the morning of the second day Isabelle came up to me and said: "Last night the angels told me that I should ask you whether you have time for and feel like joining my team. What do you think about that? Would you like to?"

I thought I was dreaming. And I knew that my dream had been a sign and a vision at the same time.

That's what the angels are like. I love them!

Jessica is a member of my team to this day.

My two ANGEL LIFE COACH®es Ulrike and Helga had a wonderful adventure:

Vision journey with Angel Paschar

It had all started in Münster, Germany, during our Advanced ANGEL LIFE COACH® training in November 2010. Isabelle guided us through a meditation: "Vision Quest with Angel Paschar". During this meditation we looked ahead in order to see what would happen in our lives within one, two, five, and ten years. Surprisingly, we both heard the call to visit Hawaii during the meditation.

When we talked about our experiences from our vision journey, we discovered that we both felt a deep longing for these exquisite islands in the Pacific Ocean. Spontaneously, we promised each other that we would fly out there together in the coming spring, even though we did not have the faintest idea how to raise the money for this, let alone how to organize the trip with regard to our families and other commitments.

Both of us were so surprised about the clarity and determination with which we had taken this decision that we only told our partners about our plans in order to not disperse the power of this wonderful energy. We never doubted our goal from then on, and we could talk about little else but what we would experience: flying to Maui and watching the whales and dolphins, experiencing the sunrise on the Haleakala, standing under a waterfall, bathing in the Seven Sacred Pools near Hana, and allowing ourselves to be bedazzled by the magnificent sunsets over the sea.

The angels kept giving us signs and assured us that this journey would take place. We found American coins, for example, heard the song 'Over the Rainbow' on the radio, performed by the Hawaiian musician IZ, and much more. They also told us that this would not be a "normal holiday" but something "special".

We were both able to fully trust the angels, completely let go, and take care of our everyday tasks, as deep within we knew that all financial and organizational challenges would dissolve by the time of our departure. And so it was: the money was there, the children looked after, the household arranged – we were ready. Fourteen days before the planned date we booked our flights, accommodation for the first two nights, and hired a car for the duration of our stay. Apart from Maui, we were thinking of visiting Big Island as well, but for reasons unknown at the time we could find no flight to Big Island. "OK," we thought, "maybe it wasn't meant to be."

The "special aspect" of the trip became obvious as soon as we arrived: it was pouring with rain, no blue sky in sight, we did not get a car, and our accommodation was a shock. Everything was different to how we had imagined it.

We both noticed how our energy level immediately threatened to drop; but our deep knowing that we had to undertake this journey, and the power of the angels, who had confirmed it to us through all their signs, helped to keep our energy level high and to connect us with the knowledge that nothing is as it seems.

The shocking accommodation actually turned into our "home base"; we loved to "come home" at night. There were always people there who helped us: they drove us to the ocean, to the other side of the island, took us along to the supermarket, and helped us to get a car despite great difficulties.

For us, all of this was like magic: just our faith and trust in the angels' guidance, the knowledge that this journey was something "special", meant that we experienced miracles every day. We encountered special people with amazing stories, stood underneath a 400-metre-high waterfall, observed the whales in the ocean, saw the sun as the "eye of God", experienced a magnificent sunrise on the Haleakala, and saw a rainbow over the clouds. The angels guided and cared for us every moment. Even when the tsunami rolled from Japan to Hawaii, they "shoved" us through guidance into the interior of the island, to the mountains, before we had even an inkling of what was to happen over the next few hours. It was only the next day that we heard about the terrible catastrophe, when we saw all the roadblocks and police cars.

This journey to Hawaii has changed both of us; it was a healing and a homecoming at the same time. Thanks to the angels, we succeeded in keeping our energy on a high level and looked through the veil of illusion.

Things are not the way they seem. Life can be a "divine dance". Mahalo – or "Thank you" in Hawaiian!

Reflection

Create a sacred space for yourself and call Angel Paschar to your side. Ask him to envelop you in his powder-blue light, take a deep breath, and relax.

Ponder how often you have had dreams or visions that have then happened, and write them down. Through doing this you will attract more of such dreams and visions.

Activities for today and for the future

Dreaming with Paschar

At bedtime, get yourself a glass of pure water and sit down on your bed. Call Angel Paschar and ask him to surround you with his powder-blue light, and breathe deeply in and out while doing so.

Say, with the glass in your hands:

I hereby send out the intention to, tomorrow, remember with ease the dreams and visions that I have received tonight.

Then drink some of the water and place the glass on your bedside table. Water stores information, as we know thanks to Masaru Emoto (*The Hidden Messages in Water)*, and others, the water in your glass will store your intention.

When you wake up, during the night or the next morning, drink the remaining water before you do anything else and say:

Hereby I remember my dreams and visions.

It is vital that you give yourself time to remember, without speaking to anyone or busying yourself with anything else. Sometimes it takes a while for the memories to rise in you. Have notebook and pen ready, so that you can immediately write down scraps of memories or maybe even just the feelings that you had while waking up.

Some people manage to remember right away the first time they do this. Others need a bit of time and may have to repeat the ritual for several days before they are able to remember their dreams and/or visions.

⟡ *Open yourself up for visions*

You can also ask Angel Paschar at any point during the day to enfold you in his light and come along on a journey with you, which might reveal many a vision. When doing this, the only thing you must do is create a sacred space for yourself beforehand. Of course you can also use the soul journey that I have channelled for this.

⟡ *Soul Affirmation* ⟡

First ask Angel Paschar to enfold you in his powder-blue light. Then take a deep breath, in and out, before you speak (ideally aloud):

I open myself up for dreams and visions and can remember them at any time.

⟡ *Soul Journey* ⟡

Have pen and paper ready before you begin. You might want to take some notes during or directly after your journey.

With your eyes open take a deep breath in, and then slowly exhale while you close your eyes in slow motion and order your brain to automatically move into the Theta state. Breathe deeply in and out, and relax. Let your thoughts go by like leaves gliding along a river and turn within. With every breath you take you relax more and more deeply.

Feel, sense, see, or imagine how you are being surrounded by a shining rainbow-coloured light that very gently pervades and purifies all the levels of your aura, your meridians, your chakras, and your physical body, so that you start radiating more and more. Enjoy the feeling while you relax more deeply.

You find yourself at the foot of a magical mountain in the middle of a starry night. Although there is seemingly no one near you, you feel perfectly safe and secure. You listen to the sounds of the night and are becoming aware of even more – with your physical eyes as well as with your inner sight – when suddenly a resplendent white unicorn appears next to you. You gaze into its eyes and recognize that it is a dear friend of old with whom you have experienced and shared much. Full of joy and gratitude to see it again, you wrap your arms around its neck and feel the deep love that unites you. You are deeply moved as you know that from now on you can always connect with this beloved being.

Eventually the unicorn telepathically transmits the message to you that it is time to take a seat on its back. You do not need to be told twice. And no sooner than you sit on its back the unicorn opens its wings and rises up into the sky with you. You soar higher and higher until you reach a vast plateau that resembles a landing site. There you are awaited by Angel Paschar, a youthful-looking, beautiful angel who welcomes you with open arms. Expectancy is in the air and you look around with curiosity while Paschar seems to give orders in a language unknown to you.

It is not long before an unfamiliar noise fills the space above you. Then you recognize an enormous vehicle in the sky that heads towards you at increasing speed. Angel Paschar and the unicorn remain calm, so you know that you do not need to worry either. And lo and behold, right in front of you on the landing strip lands a seemingly futuristic, silvery, shimmering spacecraft.

Paschar walks towards the spacecraft, opens one of the two wing doors with a confident grip, and asks you to enter. You quickly say goodbye to your unicorn friend before you step into the strange vehicle. Paschar enters behind you and takes a seat in the cockpit as he asks you to lie down on a bed of heavenly-feeling material; as soon as you lie down you feel the bed surrounding you like a protective cocoon. Now it is time, and Paschar starts up the spacecraft. It begins to move with the speed of light and you lose all sense of space and time.

Suddenly you realize that you are present in your own future and a host of images present themselves to you. Some are crystal-clear and others full of symbolism. Take your time to look at them mindfully. Remember, Angel Paschar is by your side and happy to help you understand. Take your time.

You can ask him to transfer you to a certain time – perhaps a year, five years, or ten years from now – and he will do this.

What do you perceive, with all your inner and outer senses? Which people do you see? Or are you by yourself? Are you in a building or outside? In a city or in nature? In a familiar or a foreign country? What do you do? Do you live your dreams?

If what you see does not delight you, call instantly for Angel Paschar and ask him to transform everything with the power of love, so that peaceful new images appear in front of you. Remember, everything can be transformed, as all matter is energy.

You will sense when it is time to travel back into the here and now, in the spacecraft with Paschar. The return journey is even faster; within a few seconds you land on the plateau, where you are awaited by the beautiful unicorn. You jump from the spacecraft, run towards the unicorn, and tell your experiences to this being. It gazes deeply into your eyes and you know what a loyal friend you have by your side again. You take leave of Angel Paschar and fly back to the foot of the magic mountain. Very softly you glide off the back of the unicorn and feel Mother Earth underneath your feet. Take three deep breaths and slowly return into your body. Stretch your limbs and open your eyes.

Now note down the images and visions of your future that you have perceived; it might be that you will be able to interpret them even better some time later.

Whatever the visions were, remain calm; the future is not inconvertibly fixed. You have only seen potential versions of the future, and you now know what you have to do: either select the right thoughts and actions in order to attain exactly this future, or change your thoughts and actions to the effect that the potential future can change as well. Always remember: for the angels and the power of love nothing is impossible!

~ *Day 28* ~

MANIFESTING MIRACLES
WITH
ANGEL HAMIED

*Miracles occur in order to teach us
to recognize the miraculous everywhere.*
St. Augustine

"*Greetings, beloved soul. I AM Angel Hamied. It is time for you to understand the alchemy of miracles. It is not about not feeling any desires within you: quite the contrary. Dare to admit your heart's deepest desires, even when they seem utterly utopian to you. Connect with the resonance of your heart, which is many times stronger than your mind's power of manifestation, and carry these desires in your heart – without being at all attached to them. This might appear difficult to you but it is the secret of the alchemy of miracles. As you learn to trust the flow of life, because you come to know deep within yourself that everything that happens is in accord with a higher plan, you succeed with grace and lightness.*

Connect with me and with the energy of the diamond, and you will feel how the clear and at the same time humble consciousness that you deserve abundance on all levels emerges in you. This consciousness, the ability to trust unconditionally, to let go completely, and live in accord with God and the angels, is what I call the alchemy of miracles. Jesus manifested his miracles in this same way; you also are able to – the great master of love himself said that people would be able to create these miracles themselves. In this spirit, I enfold you with my wings, envelop you in purest white, and connect you with the Christ consciousness. May miracles be yours!"

Angel Hamied
angel of miracles
Aura colour: purest white
Crystal: diamond

Phantasmagorical encounter

As a result of all the chemotherapy I was having, the organs in my belly were pretty damaged. After every meal I would be doubled over with pain. I am used to enduring quite a lot; from when I was small our motto at home was always: "A judoka does not know any pain." My father was a judo coach and at the age of five I started training myself; I loved it and took part in contests for years.

In summer 2002, however, I was so tired of fighting the long-term side effects of chemotherapy that I just did not know any more how – or whether – I really wanted to continue. Hubert, now my husband, and I were at our wits' end because at that time we were not yet aware of how close to us the angels actually are.

On a whim we went on an excursion to Landsberg, a small town in Germany, and found ourselves in a bookshop there. We searched the shelves for books on nutrition, as I urgently needed to find a way to eat without feeling even worse afterwards. We discovered a fascinating book on ayurveda, and at the same time another book fell of the shelf and I caught it. It was titled *May the Angels Be With You* and was obviously in the wrong place on the shelf as it had nothing to do with the books on nutrition that it had been sitting next to. I opened it – and was instantly under its spell. Hubert bought it for me, as well as the ayurveda book. Back home, I could hardly put it down, so touched was I by what I was reading. Each word I read gave me new hope. I was so enthusiastic about this book that I immediately ordered another copy for Hubert. Thus we sat peacefully on the sofa, next to each other, both reading Gary Quinn's wonderful angel book. We could see the light at the end of the tunnel again!

I was not only touched by the fact that Gary Quinn had this wonderful connection to the angels, but also by his life in Hollywood; ever since my childhood I have been interested in Hollywood and its films, even though we did not have a TV at home. I have always had this urge to spend some time in Los Angeles (the 'City of Angels').

Unsurprisingly, then, I felt a deep longing to meet Gary Quinn. What I would have given to have the money to fly to L.A. and receive a session from him! This, however, was unthinkable. Nevertheless, I held the wish in my heart but never spoke it.

The years went by until I started having encounters with angels myself, and became the author of angel books. I completely forgot about that wish from years ago.

In March 2010, I was invited to the Lebenskraft Messe or Vitality Show in Zurich, Switzerland. A few days before the event, I received the programme, and saw that Gary Quinn would be one of the speakers. My heart started pounding faster, and my old wish and deep desire to meet him, forgotten for years, came flooding back. When I studied the programme in more depth though I realized that there would be about fifty speakers at the event, so there was no guarantee that our paths would even cross. I immediately asked Archangel Ariel to help me manifest a meeting.

As I have often been able to manifest things with the angels during flights, on the plane to Zurich I connected with her again, and also with Angel Hamied, the angel of miracles. I love flying – up between the clouds I always feel particularly close to the angels and everything seems possible.

I suddenly heard Hamied's loving voice:

"You do not need to do anything other than completely be in the Here and Now. Everything unfolds the way it is supposed to."

I let go of any thoughts or ideas and decided to just trust.

In the evening, I went for a walk around Lake Zurich with my assistant Dani and surrendered my wish to the water.

The next day, finally the time had come, and Dani and I set out for the Lebenskraft Messe. I was one of the speakers at the angel symposium. As this fair was an enormous event and many speakers were scheduled to appear simultaneously in different areas, we initially had no idea where we needed to go.

Finally we found ourselves in front of the right hall and quietly opened the back door to slip in. And lo and behold, the speaker on stage before me was – Gary Quinn! I could not believe my eyes and asked Ariel and Hamied to help me, so I would at least be able to greet him briefly before I had to start my talk.

When his presentation was over I went to the front to put my things on the table, while he was still engaged in talking to one of the participants. I just wanted to thank him for his book that had given me courage to continue. But I never got to that. He suddenly turned round, looked into my eyes with a radiant smile, and said: "It is so great to meet you. I have heard so much about you!"

I was absolutely stunned. I really had not expected Gary Quinn, coach to Hollywood stars, to have heard about me. Finally I regained my composure and thanked him with all my heart. As my talk was imminent, we said goodbye with a hug and agreed to find each other once again the next day, with the help of the angels. Before I started my presentation, though, I sent a heartfelt prayer of thanks to the angels. I truly could not have orchestrated this synchronicity alone!

The next day it again proved quite an undertaking to find out in which one of the halls Gary was giving his workshop. Finally, Dani and I found him, and listened for the remainder of the hour. Dani was hugely excited and said: "You two absolutely have to work together. That would be the ultimate hit!"

In my heart I agreed but, as always, I let go of this wish right away since I knew that otherwise Gary would sense an expectation from my side and it would make him back off. At the end of the workshop, Gary and I spoke for a while, exchanged contact details, and agreed to stay in touch.

A few months later, I received an email from him that made me exclaim with joy: Gary was asking me whether I would like to offer angel workshops with him.

There was nothing I would rather do! We started planning right away and soon after, he was the special guest on my radio show *Angel Messages*.

That was just the start: now we have not only presented together on stage at the First International Italian Angel Congress in Turin and offered joint workshops in Germany and Austria, but we have become close friends too.

If someone had told me nine years ago that I would once work out with Gary in a hotel gym the night before we ran a joint angel workshop, I would have called them crazy: at that time I was seriously ill, had nothing really to do with angels, Munich and Los Angeles were worlds apart, there were no shared points of contact – in a word: utterly unimaginable.

But with the help of the angels, in particular Angel Hamied, miracles are possible, as you can see from my story. You can leave the 'how' to them and simply surrender your deepest heartfelt wishes into their hands. The outcome will be even better than you could have imagined in your wildest dreams.

~≫ *Reflection* ~≫

Create a sacred space for yourself and call Angel Hamied to your side. Ask him to wrap you in his white light in the frequency of miracles. Then breathe deeply in and out, and relax. Think of the times when miracles have happened in your life. Did it not always happen in moments when you had surrendered and were fully in unison with everything?

Karin, one of my readers, experienced a miracle in person:

A miraculous rescue

It was a Sunday in August 2009 and I was on canoeing trip with a good friend. We had gorgeous summer weather and the atmosphere was just beautiful. Nature, the other people on the trip – just everything. We were all having a lot of fun.

It happened late afternoon. About a kilometre from our destination I slipped while carrying my canoe and fell into knee-high water. I had landed on my back and could not get up; in complete shock, I took in only fragments of what was happening around me and my friend had to fill in the rest for me later: panicking, he called for help; he is actually a paramedic but he was also in shock. Two young men who were canoeing ahead of us came to help him, to his great relief.

One of the young men – sadly, I never found out his name, so I shall call him Michael – was a trained paramedic. He pulled me out of the water and laid me on a raised bit of ground. I screamed with pain and realized that I could move my legs. I felt freezing cold and, even though I did not say so, he wrapped his jumper round my shoulders. I still hear his voice saying: "You can't move your feet?"

"No, I can't," was all I could say in response. From far away I heard one of the members of the group say: "Oh my God! She's probably broken her spine. She'll be paralyzed. We need a rescue helicopter urgently."

I started crying and the paramedic Michael calmed me down. I said: "No, this is not true. I know my angels are here!"

Within a few minutes the whole rescue team was on-site: emergency doctor, fire brigade, ambulance, and more paramedics. I was still screaming with pain, so the emergency doctor gave me an anaesthetic and I was taken to the nearest hospital, where the doctor gave me a further dose of painkillers. Then a CAT scan was done on my spine and I was X-rayed.

The doctor was stunned. He could not find any obvious injuries. He said: "I could and still cannot believe that you have not sustained a single scratch from this accident. I have X-rayed you twice and there definitely isn't any injury." Shaking his head, he added: "With this kind of accident an injury of the spine would have been normal. That there is nothing wrong with you – it looks like a miracle."

He also told me that while I was under the strong anaesthetic I had kept calling for my angels, and that I had asked him whether I was already on the other side.

"Yes," I confirmed with a smile, "I felt my angels' presence after I called them." This though was too much for the doctor. He was more comfortable to go no fur-ther than saying that it was a miracle.

To show my gratitude, I took out an advert in the newspaper the following week to thank the rescue team. And: a big thank you to my angels!

Day 28

Activities

Become aware of the miracles in your life

Write down all the small and large miracles that have happened in your life so far. Through doing this you prepare the ground for new miracles to come.

Find a diamond for yourself

Of course, I know that jewels cost money. This, though, is not about treating yourself to a super-expensive diamond, but just a small diamond, affordable on a tighter budget. I have a Herkimer diamond that I bought in a spiritual shop in London with the remarkable name "Buddha on a Bicycle". Even though the crystal is tiny, it radiates great power, and helps me in a wonderful way to manifest miracles.

Talking of which, I remember when, just over a year ago, on Maui, Hawaii, I had a Buddha made. He has a tiny blue diamond at his third eye, because Hamied told me that I needed to connect with the diamond energy on a physical level (this was before I had my Herkimer diamond). At that time, it took courage to treat myself to something like this. Looking back though I realize that it was exactly this that made my financial flow become more abundant.

Prayer – transmitted by Angel Hamied

Beloved Father, beloved Mother in heaven,
I thank you with all my heart for the miracle of my life,
For the miracle of my breath,
For the miracle of my highly complex yet nevertheless phenomenally
*   functioning body,*
For the miracle of my spirit,
For the miracle of my soul,
For the miracle of my heart,
For the miracle of my divine essence,
For the miracle of my connection to All-That-Is,
For the miracle of every new day,
For the miracle of the unending possibilities,
For the miracle that miracles are part of my life on a daily basis!
THANK YOU!

This prayer is not only meant for today but as a daily companion on your continuing life path. Write it into your gratitude book and speak it as a prayer often, so that everyday miracles may happen in your life.

⤳ *Soul Affirmation* ⤳

First ask Angel Hamied to enfold you in his purest white light. Then take a deep breath, in and out, before you speak (ideally aloud); while doing so you can also hold your diamond in your receiving hand (the hand with which you do *not* write):

From the bottom of my heart I trust in the plan of my life and the alchemy of miracles. I let go of any attachment and am a magnet for miracles!

⤳ *Soul Journey* ⤳

Have pen and paper ready before you begin. You might want to take some notes during or directly after your journey.

With your eyes open take a deep breath in, and then slowly exhale while you close your eyes in slow motion and order your brain to automatically move into the Theta state. Breathe deeply in and out, and relax.

Let your thoughts go by like leaves gliding along a river and turn within. Enjoy feeling your breath that simultaneously nourishes you and links you to the breath of God. Breathe deeply in and out and move even further into a state of deep relaxation.

You are surrounded by the purest white light that you have ever seen. It pervades you, full of softness and at the same time full of infinite strength since it embodies the perfected palette of the complete colour/light spectrum; so your light body can unfurl in full bloom and radiate in all the colours of the rainbow. Feel yourself becoming more and more light, and your aura becoming infinite.

At this moment your connection to your divine blueprint and to the divine matrix is completely re-established. Your whole being begins to oscillate in spherical harmonies that make you into a resonating body for miracles.

You become ever brighter and lighter, so that you rise practically by yourself in cosmic spirals into the skies. You soar higher and higher until you reach an ethereal light temple of the seventh dimension. This celestial shimmering temple is surrounded by countless unicorns, whose wings are so pure that your frequency instantly increases manifold in accord with them. Enjoy the feeling of perfect oneness with all these precious divine creatures.

Day 28

All at once a mighty angel with white hair and white beard appears at the entrance of the temple. He is surrounded by a blazing white aura that encompasses him like a corona. It is none other than Angel Hamied, the angel of miracles. He welcomes you with open arms and guides you into the magic temple. You have witnessed many, many things on your journeys but the beauty of this temple surpasses everything that you have seen before. Full of reverence, you are trying to take all the impressions in and store them when suddenly – in the floor in the middle of the sacred hall – you discover an enormous mosaic display with the six-pointed star, the signet of Solomon. You know what to do: walk towards the signet and stand in its middle.

You feel how a crystalline clarity expands inside yourself, a clarity that surpasses anything you have ever experienced in this regard. With your whole being you understand what is meant by "As above, so below". All heavenly and earthly laws suddenly reveal themselves to you in a way that allows you to understand your whole life and the course of the world. Everything is permeated by infinite clarity.

Then Angel Hamied approaches you and hands you a crystal-clear ball of purest light energy. With gentle words he speaks to you:

"Beloved soul, this is the sacred ball of visions and miracles. Gaze into it and recognize the miracles in your life. The moment your heart brims over with gratitude, connect yourself with your most deeply held heart desires and view them as already granted in this crystal ball of miracles."

Now do as you are told.

After a while you again hear Hamied's loving voice:

"As soon as the images inside the ball have unfolded in alignment with your emotions, let the ball rise up and find its way into the universe. Let go completely and know that everything will unfold within the divine timeline, since this is how it is, how it has been, and how it will always be."

Again you do as you are bade and feel the power and the magic inherent in this ritual. Eventually you let the crystal ball rise; as if by itself it finds its way out of the temple of light.

One more time you look around the sacred space and know that you are transformed for ever, since you have understood the laws of manifestation and the alchemy of miracles down to the deepest layers of your being. Full of deep gratitude, you leave the shining temple of light together with Angel Hamied and give him a heartfelt embrace.

Meanwhile the unicorns have assembled in a sacred circle around you and share with you telepathically:

"Beloved friend, just like us you are a pure, divine creature. Always remember this and live accordingly! Your life will be a sole miracle."

A feeling of infinite bliss permeates your whole being and allows you to become completely one with All-That-Is. And your light dress radiates in all the colours of the rainbow and carries you without any effort in gentle downward movements back to the earth. After this journey the planet appears to you in an entirely new light as you now know you are a co-creator between heaven and earth and can bring paradise to earth.

Take a few deep breaths in order to deeply anchor all the knowledge in your being. Connect again with Mother Earth; feel the roots reaching to the centre of the earth underneath your feet. Stretch your limbs and return fully into your body, the beautiful temple of your soul, and into the here and now. Slowly open your eyes.

Epilogue

*The magic of completion
holds the power of a wonderful new beginning.*

Archangel Raziel

Here we are: you have made it! Congratulations to you!

The angels congratulate you with all their heart that you have had the energy to work on yourself in such an intense way to transform your life. You can be proud of yourself. Keep going!

We have one last task for you because we would like you to be very consciously aware of your success and use it to achieve new goals:

Reflection

Create a sacred space for yourself and think about all that you have succeeded in doing over the past weeks, and what has changed.

Activity

Write down your successes, so that you will attract more of them.

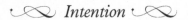 *Intention*

Send the intention out into the universe that from now on your spiritual practice will be part of your life, and act accordingly. The angels and I promise that you will not regret it!

I thank you with all my heart for your trust and your courage to undergo this journey together with the angels and me.

Infinite gratitude, heavenly light, the angels' blessing and love – and of course many miracles for you!

Aloha!
Big Angel Hug
Isabelle von Fallois
Malta, 4th June 2011

Thank You

From the bottom of my heart I thank all the angels, merangels, goddesses, fairies, ascended masters, whales, dolphins, and power animals, who during my work on this book have tirelessly supported, taught, and inspired me, so that with their help I can fulfil my dharma.

After these wonderful beings my biggest thank you goes to my husband Hubert. In order to enable me to finish this book for my publisher's deadline, despite all my work-related travel, he not only sacrificed many hours of our already very limited time for a private life, but also supported me in a phenomenal way wherever he could. Thank you, dear Hubert, from the bottom of my heart!

Dear Doreen, thank you from the bottom of my heart for reminding me that communicating with angels is something totally natural. Through your angel books and your powerful work in California and Hawaii I was able to reconnect with my abilities from the past and – with the infinite love and help of the angels – to heal my physical suffering. I feel so blessed! May you be blessed infinitely!

Two authors I would like to extend particular thanks to here as they inspired me with their great works and courses to write this twenty-eight-day angel programme: Julia Cameron (*The Artist's Way*) and Ilona Selke (*Living From Vision*). I thank you with all my heart!

Dear Uschi and dear Gero, many thanks that in between my journeys I have always been able to retreat for a short while into the home cocoon in order to step back from the world and work in peace on this book, nourished by the best food available.

Dear Susanna, as always it was just great to spend some time with you, being pampered, and being able to dedicate myself to writing. My sincere thanks for this!

Dear Gido, my twin brother from old times, thank you that you walk with me through thick and thin and inspire me time and again.

Dear Dani, it is a blessing to have you by my side. A wholehearted thank you for always covering my back.

Dear Michael, how lovely to have found you "again"! Thank you that you support me and my work so lovingly.

Dear Gary, it is just wonderful that we have finally met in this life and now do such wonderful work together. Thank you from the bottom of my heart for your friendship and trust in me.

Dear Wayne, what a miracle that our paths were allowed to cross due to you becoming ill with leukaemia. I am deeply touched by your trust in my capabilities and infinitely grateful to be allowed to support you on your path of recovery.

Dear Patrick, I thank you with all my heart that through your exquisite yoga lessons I was able to become aware of the true strength of my body again.

Gary, Peggy, Dani, Gido, Joey, Florian, Susanne, Roy, Ruth, Johanna, Patricia, Hubert, Britta, Stephanie, Gabriele, Katarina, Pilar, Jessica, Cris, Heike, Melanie, Jeshua, Arne, Ulrike, Helga, and Karin – beloved friends, my sincere gratitude for all your wonderful stories that bring this book alive.

Dear angel team (Dani, Michael, Gido, Patricia, Susanna, Johanna, Jeshua, Jessica, Iwan, and Hans), I thank you wholeheartedly for your phenomenal support with all my workshops and training in Germany and abroad. You are the world's greatest!

Dear participants, readers and listeners, sincere gratitude also to you for allowing me to accompany you a short way, for being inspired by and learning from you.

A special thank you to "my three boys" Jeshua, Florian, and Joey. It was very enriching and touching to teach you and see you grow over the course of twenty-one days. The time we spent together was an inspiring one for this book. Keep the angel spirit – always!

Dear Konrad and dear Karin, my very heartfelt gratitude to you: for liking the idea for this book right away and for coming up with such a wonderful cover that I can fully identify with, since the greatest part of the book was written by the sea.

Thank You

Dear Birgit-Inga Weber, I would like to thank you from my heart for your sensitive handling of this manuscript. I always felt that you understood exactly what I wanted to say. A true gift!

My sincere gratitude also to all living and deceased masters whose wisdoms inspire me anew every day.

I could of course continue for some time and thank countless people by name but this would go beyond the scope of the book. I am sure you all know that you are included here!

NOTES

1 Should you wish for more professional support, I recommend the Advanced and Master ANGEL LIFE COACH®es, certified by me. You can find their names and contact data on my website: www.AngelLifeCoachTraining.com.
2 In a few cases names have been changed in order to protect individuals' privacy.
3 This way of speaking (and singing) originates from Robert Love's method. Robert Love, by the way, is the voice coach for many Hollywood actors and actresses (among others Reese Witherspoon, Joaquin Phoenix), singers, and other well-known performers.
4 Aloha translates to: "I share the sacred breath, the vibration of love with you."

BIBLIOGRAPHY AND OTHER MATERIALS

Books

Baron-Reid, Colette, *Remembering the Future*. Carlsbad, CA: Hay House Inc., 2007.

Cameron, Julia, *The Artist's Way: A Course in Discovering and Recovering Your Creative Self*. London: Macmillan Publishers, 1995.

Carroll, Lee/Kryon, *The Journey Home: The Story of Michael Thomas and the Seven Angels*. Carlsbad, CA: Hay House Inc., 1997.

Cooper, Diana/Shaaron Hutton, *Discover Atlantis*. London: Hodder and Stoughton Ltd., 2006.

Emoto, Masaru, *The Hidden Messages in Water*. London: Simon & Schuster, 2005.

Freedman, Rory/Barnouin, Kim, *Skinny Bitch*. Philadelphia, PA: Running Press, 2007.

Freedman, Rory/Barnouin, Kim, *Skinny Bitch in the Kitch*. Philadelphia, PA: Running Press, 2007.

Füngers, Elisabeth, *Ayurveda – Das Kochbuch*. Munich: Südwest, 2003.

Hay, Louise L., *You Can Heal Your Life*. Carlsbad, CA: Hay House Inc., 1984/2004.

Joseph, Arthur Samuel, *Vocal Power*. San Diego, CA: Jodere Group Inc., 2003.

Love, Roger, *Love Your Voice*. Carlsbad, CA: Hay House Inc., 2007.

Melchizedek, Drunvalo, *The Ancient Secret of the Flower of Life*, vol. 1. Flagstaff, AZ: Light Technology Publishing, 1990/1999.

Pirc, Karin/Kempe, Wilhelm, *Kochen nach Ayurveda*. Niedernhausen: Falken Verlag, 1996/1999.

Quinn, Gary, *May the Angels Be With You*. London: Rider, 2001.

Silverstone, Alicia, *The Kind Diet: A Simple Guide to Feeling Great, Losing Weight, and Saving the Planet*. Reprint edition. Emmaus, PA: Rodale Inc., 2011.

Virtue, Doreen, *How to Hear Your Angels*. Carlsbad, CA: Hay House Inc., 2007.

Von Fallois, Isabelle, *Die Engel so nah – Meine Krankheit als Weg zu innerem Frieden*. Zurich: Lichtwelle, 2010.

Von Fallois, Isabelle, *Die Erzengel – 15 Begleiter auf dem Weg in ein erfülltes Leben*. Burgrain: Koha, 2009.

Engels Botschaften (calendar). Munich: arsEdition, 2010.

CDs/MP3

Aeoliah, *Angel Love* (CD)

Drucker, Karen, *The Heart of Healing* (CD)

Fallois, Isabelle von, *Soul Journey Meditations* (MP3), www.fallois.momanda.com

Fallois, Isabelle von, *Angel Trance Meditations* (MP3), www.angelportal444.com

Sitas, Lajos, *Snowflake* (CD)

Other products

Aura-Soma and other products, www.aurasomashop.at

Energy bears www.bennybaer.de

photo © Ute Ville

ABOUT THE AUTHOR

Isabelle von Fallois has had contact with angels since childhood. After a near-death experience at the age of eight her visionary dreams and visions increased. In her adult life she started out as a concert pianist.

Although an interest in spirituality has always been part of her life, it was only because of her life-threatening leukemia in 2000 that she engaged more deeply with angels. Within a short time, she started to hear and see angels and started receiving detailed assignments from the archangels that helped her to regain her health.

Today, Isabelle von Fallois writes, travels all round the world, and gives presentations and workshops. She has written several books that have been German and Italian best-sellers, recorded more than 50 meditations and developed the ANGEL LIFE COACH® Training and the ISIS ANGEL HEALING®. Isabelle has had her own radio show; she has also been featured in many magazines and appeared on several DVDs, in spiritual movies, and on German television.

Following the wishes of her angels she also dedicates time to new media and regularly publishes channeled messages on her fan page on Facebook and on Twitter. With her spiritual work and as a pianist alike, Isabelle would like to open people's hearts and help them lead a fulfilled life.

www.isabellevonfallois.com
www.AngelLifeCoachTraining.com

Isabelle von Fallois

Live your potential with the help of the angels – Workshops

The Power of Your Angels

We live in times of change that may create great challenges for the individual. Therefore it is even more important to live in harmony with oneself and all that is. This is only possible though, if we let go of the old baggage that we carry around with us. The angels are wonderful companions on this path as they possess a very clear vision and can support us step by step.

This workshop is a journey of discovery assisting you to take stock of yourself: Through this you will discover which thoughts and belief patterns from the past are holding you back. Eventually, with the help of the angels, you will raise your vibration level, and build up a new resonance that helps you to follow your own path and to realize the dreams of your life.

Isabelle von Fallois will introduce you to the 28-day-programme of the angels in a way that enables you to easily continue this process at home.

This intensive weekend will change you and, together with the angels, promote your ability to create miracles and synchronicities in your life.

The ANGEL LIFE COACH® Training

Based on her experiences with her clients, her own angel seminars and other courses, Isabelle von Fallois has developed a special form of the angel programme, the ANGEL LIFE COACH® Training. Here you will learn, amongst other things, how to open and increase your medial skills, give angel readings, facilitate Angel Trance Coachings, dissolve shadows and karmic blockages from present and past lives, as well as coaching people. The training combines various very effective methods in order to enable you to offer clients a broad spectrum of experiences; this makes the training attractive to people from very different backgrounds.

This training is a wonderful opportunity to develop yourself further, to increasingly align with and connect to your higher self, to discover and live your own potential, and to create a fulfilling life for yourself.

The training consists of three modules:

Module 1 – ANGEL LIFE COACH® Training
Module 2 – Advanced ANGEL LIFE COACH® Training
Module 3 – Master ANGEL LIFE COACH® Training

If you would like to transform your life, read the comments of graduates and discover more about the training, visit www.AngelLifeCoachTraining.com.

FINDHORN PRESS

Life-Changing Books

Consult our catalogue online
(with secure order facility) on
www.findhornpress.com

For information on the Findhorn Foundation:
www.findhorn.org